THE
CALL TO
FREEDOM

ISBN: 978-1-7389071-0-6 (paperback)

ISBN: 978-1-7389071-1-3 (ebook)

ISBN: 978-1-7389071-2-0 (audio book)

THE
CALL TO
FREEDOM

HEAL YOUR PAIN

AWAKEN YOUR LOVING PRESENCE

DIANA LOCKETT

Dedication

I lovingly dedicate this book to my greatest teachers, my children. To Julia for being my first experience of unconditional love. To Ben for being the embodiment of acceptance and forgiveness. You both inspire me every day. I love you. And, to my 3rd 'child,' Ian, for your courage and curiosity. You have become my teacher of truth.

Thank you to all the spiritual gurus who had to do what they did so that I could learn what I learned and the ones who showed me the way back to love. And finally, thank you to the generous and benevolent Universe for always having my back.

In loving memory of my book designer, Dania Zafar. Your light, beauty and creativity is sprinkled in these pages. May your soul rest in love.

Testimonials

Diana Lockett really understands people. In this powerful book she shares openly her own raw and painful evolution from a baby so acutely aware of her abandonment to a young girl who was silenced by daily fear and neglect, to a woman disassociated from her body and feelings, to a recovering people pleaser and eventually into a woman who is fully responsible for how her heart shows up in her life daily.

There is so much life experience and self-awareness that unfolds throughout 'The Call to Freedom'. If your heart needs healing, this book offers the gentle reassuring comfort of a cashmere blanket with a cup of cocoa on a chilly day and the soothing whisper of wisdom, fortitude and bravery which will stir from deep within you, building the healing acceptance that your life, though full of trials and tribulations, is a gift.

Diana skilfully and gently guides the reader to the liberating knowledge that how we experience our life is very much a result of how we choose to experience it. This is a powerful reminder of our right, responsibility and gift of choice and the powerful impact that has on our life journey.

Thought provoking 'Re-Alignment Steps' in every chapter transform this beautiful, emotional and connecting book into a compelling and highly individual blueprint for each reader's personal Call to Freedom. This will be the gift you will want to give everyone you know who needs a self-esteem injection.

Tracy Stone, Cl.Hyp, CPPD, ARTT, GHR (Reg.).
Transformational coach, clinical hypnotherapist,
international bestselling author, inspirational speaker
and founder of Limitless Potential UK

This book is a phenomenal read that will encourage you to embark on a journey of self-discovery, healing, and transformation. Author Diana Lockett holds your hand and guides you via an array of relatable personal moments in her life that serve as a reminder that we are all *one of the same*, and we all *feel* in the same way. Her actionable advice, filled with pearls of wisdom at the end of each chapter, will be the catalyst that lights the way for you through this remarkable journey of finding courage, strength, understanding, and happiness in your life. I recommend this book to everyone searching for enlightenment and inner peace.

Mimi Safiyah - Editor

I am in love with this book! Diana takes us on a journey in which we are asked to consider the beliefs we made up in our childhood to keep us safe. She illustrates through her own journey how our subconscious beliefs, when we're not aware of them, orchestrate our adult lives. Her journey is inspiring, poignant, adventurous, and often painful, yet she chooses to open her heart, listen to her spirit and embrace her divine presence.

Alex Blake - Editor, Heart Coach

Contents

Introduction

*When we awaken in our lives, we allow our
hearts to remember the gift of how it feels to
be connected to everything and everyone
and that we truly are the Universe
embodied.*

The Universe (or the God of your understanding) went to so
much trouble to create YOU. Not a version of you—YOU
as you are today. And, because of that, my wish is that you
take this information and use it to awaken your freedom, heal
your pain, and live from a place of loving presence.

As you journey through this book, I trust that you will find
your path back to the remembrance of who you are at your
authentic core and in your heart. The YOU before others hurt
you, rubbed their tension and stress into your being, or began
to tell you who you should be. The YOU that is ready to go
out into the world unapologetically and with an open heart.
The YOU that remembers that you are truly a gift, and so is
everyone else. This remembrance is the revelation that will
result in transforming your life. This revelation takes you back
to your purpose. And, if you are not able to see, feel, and be
your purpose just yet—that is why you are here, reading this
book, saying yes to reclaiming your purpose.

This book is the sum of my 25 years of personal and spiritual development work and practices, 35 years of communication coaching, 12 years of research, certification, and teachings on these topics. Plus, a lifetime of the perfect combination of sweet and bitter ingredients, some I am still digesting, to drive me to want to 'awaken' and claim freedom in my life. It draws upon teachings from eastern philosophy, ancient spiritual Tantrik teachings, life and mindset coaching, neuropsychology, somatic/embodiment practices, positive psychology, and other life-affirming teachings and practices. This is MY journey of turning my pain into love and choosing to serve that into the world.

These pages are written with the understanding that we are a product of all of our relationships, and they shape everything we know about our world, our thoughts, our beliefs, our energy, and our emotions.

Personal growth is about self-awareness and goal focused change to function better in the context of life. Spiritual growth is about your understanding that you are here for something bigger, beyond your limited self, and that *something* is a common thread that we all share. It is called Love, Freedom, Connection, Grace. It needs no goals and nothing to be done. In fact, it can be accessed anytime. With Spiritual growth, there is nothing that needs to change to be who you are because you are already THAT which you seek. When we focus on both of these paths, we see how our conditioned beliefs, thoughts, feelings, and actions can shield our truest 'Self.' When we undo all the conditioning that has prevented us from being the light that we are, we can see a path to greater interconnection and interdependence with others. Through these relationship awakenings, we have the opportunity to create the deepest transformations in our lives, families, communities, and the world. When you commit to this journey, which some call "the work," you will have the opportunity to unwind your nervous system, reorganize and create new neural connections, bring yourself into wholeness, and reassign meaning to your life that feels more digestible, free, gentle, and joyful. This is how YOU can become the CHANGE. This is the path to awakening.

As you begin this book, please know that there is nothing wrong with you. Let me repeat that... *There is nothing wrong with you.* You are not broken. You do not need to be fixed. You have simply had experiences that led you to forget who you are and took you out of alignment with your true nature, purpose, and joy.

Throughout this book, I wish that you remember that life isn't just about what happens; it's about who we choose to be in the midst of what happens. There's an intimate connection between what we experience in life and how we live that experience. We cannot change what we have already experienced in the past and some of it is incomprehensible—I know. Yet, we can always change our *relationship* to the *lived* experience, creating a knowing that allows us to be better nourished in the present moment and alter the way we engage with our future. It comes through a willingness to forge your path back to your authentic self, awaken your heart, and cultivate an intimate connection to life. This is the pathway to freedom.

As you savour these chapters, you will have opportunities to wake up to your life in a way that will invite you to step into your personal responsibility, self-love, and a deep appreciation for all life. It is a pathway to becoming, and we are always becoming... The question remains, *what are you becoming?* When you step into your heart through these stories and strategies, your 'work' will be to remain present to the resistances that show up—and they will. Know that these resistances are simply there because you are ready to challenge everything you know about yourself and your relationship to the world. Be willing to acknowledge, be curious, and let go of these resistances with love and gratitude. Know that they might have been helpful protective strategies when you needed them at a younger age and embrace that now, they are no longer needed; when you remove them, you can step fully into your life's light.

Each chapter of this book will be a memoir of my lived experience blended with tools and strategies I have used on my awakening journey. At the end of each chapter are *Re-Alignment Steps* to guide you to your own self-study and self-practice to reawaken your heart and life with freedom. These are lifelong practices, and I encourage you to come back to them repeatedly and make them daily invitations. Just like going to the gym, it takes regular commitment to create the strength that you desire. Here, too, your level of commitment will be directly correlated to the level of shifts that you experience in life.

My greatest desire, dear reader, is that you will GET to remember that life is truly a loving playground in which you can always choose how to respond. No matter what has happened to you in your life and what you have done, you can heal your pain, live from a state of loving presence, and become free. When this happens, you awaken to the truth that you are not your thoughts (you have 70,000 thoughts daily, and as silly humans, we *believe* them). You are not your body. You are *not* your trauma. You are *not* your stories. You are *not* your pain. You are *not* your joys.

As we go through these chapters, you will begin to deconstruct all that you were once told about yourself that you hold true, and discover your path back to your true essence of loving presence. In that space, there are infinite possibilities for forgiveness, for 'non-attaching' to stories (the stories happened, yes, but how you engage with them can shift), and for, most importantly, love.

Here, you will find your worthiness as your birthright. You do not have to accomplish anything to be worthy. You are *already* worthy because you exist. With all the infinite possibilities that could have been created, the Universe created you and offered you the unique set of experiences you call your life. Throughout this book, I encourage you to reflect, pause, and breathe.

This story offers my personal experiences that led me to forget all of the above and the strategies that I have used as an offering for you to consider tasting and digesting life with a different perspective. It is a 13-chapter spiritual and life mentoring experience disguised as my story. If you commit with a full YES, know that this will require work. You cannot read this book and expect change *unless you create change*. Just like you cannot read a recipe and describe what the final product will taste like *without tasting it*. It is sometimes uncomfortable and confronting, which is a normal part of healing. If you commit to the *Re-Alignment Steps* inside this book, you will begin to see how you have the capacity to heal and awaken to the love that is always inside you. This awakening is *The Call To FREEDOM*.

This is not a therapeutic manual, nor is it intended to replace the need for professional help. Please be self-responsible, and at any time, if this is too much, find professionals to support you.

Before you begin, please read the message below and insert your name as you read it aloud. It is an affirmation that you, truly, are a Miracle:

> "I, (your name), am a Miracle. A perfect child of the Universe. I am life's prayer of becoming and its answer. I am here to love without limit, awaken each time I fall asleep, and dream despite fear. Everything I have experienced has been a stepping stone for this day, and I am proud to be here, to reflect on my life with grace, and to step forward with the courageous wisdom of the adventurer that I am and always have been. My life has forever altered the course of history. I am the Universe embodied."

Chapter 1

I'm not FINE. But I am a Miracle.

You are more than FINE. You are a forgotten miracle.

You are a miracle, just like me. You do not have to prove anything for that to be true. You do not need to prove your worth, fight for belonging or seek love. Your birthright is worthiness, and you not only deserve love, *you are* love. Over your lifetime, you may have forgotten this truth. Allow me to remind you of what, somewhere deep inside you, is already felt and known. Imagine feeling the most incredible love for yourself. Place your hand on your heart and repeat several times: *I am Love.*

We are all miracles. Depending on the research, there is a one in 400 billion chance that you would be here today, right now, reading this book. The odds of you being here are as great as throwing a dart to a bullseye that is thousands of miles away with millions of obstacles in the way. The odds of you being here today are statistically zero, and yet you are here not in spite of what happened in your generational lineage but *because* of those events. Your parents, whether they remained together, in love, or not, met and created you. That, of the millions to billion of sperm cells available in a single ejaculation, somehow one chose an egg, and that egg grew to a fetus, and the fetus grew to a baby. You survived all these years, through your joys, grief, pain, and celebrations, to today. I bow to you... you are nothing short of a miracle.. just like me. You are the outcome of generations and generations and generations multiplied hundreds of times, of miracles and, no matter what has happened in your life, you are still here. If we are all miracles, how do we conclude that life, our experiences, and our sense of self is a problem? Let's begin with this story about a clay Buddha.

In the 1950s, there was a clay Buddha that was being transported. It was housed in a quiet monastery outside the city for almost 250 years, forgotten, and ignored. In 1955, it was moved to a new temple, and in the process, it began to crack. Beneath the clay was a $250 million gold Buddha. In 1781, the statue had been covered with clay to protect it from a Burmese invasion. The true identity of this statue was left concealed for almost 2 centuries.

The Golden Buddha now sits in a new temple and is one of the most prominent attractions in Bangkok today. I had the privilege of seeing it in 2017. In its presence, I felt my own golden essence.

The significance of this golden Buddha, covered in clay, is a beautiful reminder to us that we are all made of golden stardust. We are all born essentially golden, and when we were born our parents thanked God and began teaching us their version of divinity and thus we forgot the divinity that we were born with. With time, we were taught to wear masks to fit in, layers of clay to hide our golden essence. Behind those masks resides our truth, radiance, and beautiful *Self*. Our job in this lifetime, should we accept the challenge, is to chip away at the clay until our Golden heart is revealed to ourselves. Only then can we recognize the golden essence of everyone around us, and realize that we have all simply been dropped into this movie of our lives. The script that was written for us by generations past and our current conditions with beliefs, imprints, and trauma is what is playing out. But, there comes a time when we realize that we have choices: To follow the script or to uncover the genius hoax that we've been living and reveal our Golden Buddha.

Throughout the words of these chapters, I reveal to you my journey to uncovering my golden heart, and I champion you to uncover your own golden heart so that we can recognize the hidden value residing in each of us. However, in order to awaken, we must go to sleep. I do not judge the times I slept because I didn't know any better. I slept for the first 32 years of my life. My sleep was required for my survival. And, when I began to awaken, I still went to sleep at times; my slumber just happened to be a little shorter and my awakenings a little longer. And, as we go into this story together, I want you to take a deep inhale, exhale, and realize that,

you always did the best you could given your circumstances, your conditioning, your capacity,
and your resources… just like everyone else.

Here's how my story began:
I was born on April 26, 1965, as a twin to parents who

had many stressors in their lives, including financial, lack of support, and 2 toddlers, my older sisters, waiting at home. My parents were not expecting twins. Ultrasounds were not part of the prenatal care those days and my mother, who was anesthetized for our birth, remembered birthing only one child. When she woke up, she imagined the other child in her room was from a previous delivery and simply had not yet joined its mother. Once the surprise (and I imagine fear) wore off, my mother's family scrambled to supply all of the duplicate baby supplies she would need. We were born premature (by about 3 weeks), and were required to stay in the hospital, in separate incubators, for a few weeks. My father had to return to work. My mother had to care for her toddlers at home, so my twin and I were left in the hospital, alone, separated, with a distant second uncle who visited us every few days to make sure we were still alive.

As a newborn baby, this would have been the first of many traumas. Trauma is anytime the nervous system is overwhelmed beyond its capacity to deal with the event, and when one is preverbal and does not have language to process the event, or a repair is not done by the adults in the child's life, the event gets undigested and shoved deep down into the body. I imagine that my cries were not responded to, I was not held, and I learned to shut down my tears as they would not elicit a response in my environment. I learned early on to disconnect from my needs, body and longings. As a new-born baby, I would have learned to silence my unmet cries, freeze my nervous system, armour my heart, and essentially numb my body. This would have been my first experience of disconnecting from my body, also known as dissociation. On the first day of my life, I learned to shut down my nervous system, my life force, and my heart to protect myself from feeling the abandonment of being alone, separated from my twin and my mother, and lacking in basic touch and love.

Research shows us that our nervous systems are all interconnected. If you are stressed, I am stressed. People are not often aware of their stresses and how they are projecting these into the world, the workplace, and the home. When parents are stressed, they are also very freely sharing these stresses. Without blame, they teach these little ones in their care to be stressed because the adults don't know how to manage their stresses. They do not have tools to self-regulate, so how could they co-regulate or teach their little ones how to manage stress? It is not a wonder that we have a society of, now adults, that are unable to self-regulate and instead numbly react with hostility, anger, and project all the tension in their bodies as blame to others. Wow... *that's a lot.*

As my nervous system was attached to the unprocessed and unhealthy nervous systems of my mother (who was quick to shut down) and my father (who was quick to react and flip out), I was left on my own to figure out how to regulate my own system (without the adequate tools), and as a result, my world felt unsafe and the only way to navigate an unsafe world was to shut down my own nervous system. My disconnection from my stress, tension, and trauma led me to live outside of my body for 32 years because it was not safe to be in my body. I didn't have an imprint of how to manage the big feelings and stress. In today's fast-paced and often disconnected world, the numbing strategies we use to avoid feeling include gaming, weed, alcohol, sex, binging shows, and overworking.

As a result, our society is losing capacity for resilience, to feel, and recover from those feelings in a healthy way.

While my nervous system was receiving unhealthy imprints and shutting down, my unconscious mind was open to receiving whatever was implanted in it by the world around me. This included all the unhealthy relationship dynamics and stress responses from my parents, the competition from school, and the need to achieve at all costs by society. In the first 7 years of life, many of our beliefs get installed as programmed software to the hardware of our minds. It is through this programming and the perspective from which it is modeled to us that we learn about the world and the way it functions. Many of these beliefs remain bubbling below the surface of awareness—our subconscious, and define much of how we move through the world, what we do, say, and act. I became a "good little girl" who was "seen and not heard" and took the dutiful role of the student of my parents and my society. I sat up straight. I kept my elbows off the table (for fear of a jab of a knife by my father). I didn't protest..anything. And, like all good little girls and boys are supposed to, I let the lessons of my parents, school, society, partners, and media instruct me on who I should be, how I should feel, and what my life should consist of (notice the SHOULDS). That is when I started to be FINE:

FINE = f*cked up, insecure, needy, and empty.

I was FINE throughout most of my childhood and early adulthood.

I was FINE when my mom was passed out on the couch from having to take Valium to disconnect from her FINE every day when I came home from school. It was her survival strategy.

I was FINE while I waited, sometimes for hours, after the threat "wait until your father gets home" that was always followed by a belt to my bare bottom or a hand across my face taking FINE from his day out on my immobilized little body.

I was FINE when my parents had full-out yelling matches on the lawn, and my mom got in the car and drove away, leaving me and my 3 sisters in terror alone with my father.

I was FINE when my voice was shut down, and I learned that what I had to say didn't matter.

I was FINE when I found my sister after a suicide attempt, and my parent's response to her cry was to brush it under the carpet.

I was FINE when I was sexually abused as a teenager and ran away in shame, believing I had done something wrong and it was MY fault.

I was FINE through betrayal, heartbreak, and loss.

I was FINE through my early years of therapy, in fear that if I touched what was beneath the FINE, I might fall like Humpty Dumpty and never get put back together again.

My survival strategy through most of my life was to be FINE. It was served with a smile and often a cool hug, a mask, and a closed heart that prevented me from letting others in.

As a result of being raised in a FINE home, I learned very early on how, when, and what masks to wear in my home and how playing the roles that were expected of me became important to my survival.

I believed that my upbringing was normal. Everyone *had their dark secrets that came with dread, abuse, neglect, and loneliness.*

I grew up in a home with 3 siblings and felt alone most of my childhood. I had few friends and was always surprised when someone saw me and recognized me, something I carry to this day. I felt invisible and unimportant most of my life.

It would take many years for me to realize that I had the ability and the responsibility to explore my values, beliefs, and longings. Until then, everything I lived, breathed, and believed was downloaded as a program from others, and I believed it as my truth.

YOUR MENU

Imagine, on the day you were born, you were assigned a blank menu with your name on it. From that first day, your parents began filling the menu with the ingredients they valued. Soon, other family members, teachers, society, and friends added their items to the menu. Every day, you order your life from the items on your menu, not knowing that you can begin to tweak your menu, delete items that no longer taste good, and add new items, new ingredients, and new specials. Some items on the menu are very helpful; you may choose to keep them, and the key words here are YOU CHOOSE.

As a young girl and adult, I did not even consider that I had the right or the responsibility to alter my menu. I simply continued to repurpose the menu that was written for me. Some of the options were wonderful and allowed me to be very successful in my life: how to cook, drive, do laundry, make appointments, pay bills, study, help others, achieve, go to work, be responsible, care for others. It also includes all the parts on the menu that are often unspoken: judgments, stresses, limiting beliefs, ridiculous values that I don't necessarily believe, and all the other items from my menu that are unconscious. They are unconscious because I was not aware of them. I was not aware of how they impacted all aspects of my life, my relationships, and my purpose. Part of the reason I could not read these parts of the menu is that they were essentially written with invisible ink. In that invisible ink were the parts of me that I was told were unworthy, that were denied, shamed, and made wrong. Because they were invisible, I was incapable of recognizing them. So, I went on with my life. Choosing off the limiting menu pages that were evident and easy to interpret. The items that I was told were the most welcomed in the world were: looking good, staying quiet, wearing a makeup mask to go out to the store, going to school, finding a job, getting married, having children, retiring, traveling, and dying. That was essentially the order of my menu. It took little effort to follow those menu pages. It was reinforced by society, my family, and my belief systems. And, through most of my life, I lived from the conditioned menu that was written for me——as most people do, to define love, relationships, work, politics, religion, and media.

It is only when you decide to pay attention and try to read the invisible ink on your menu with a willingness to upgrade it with a more mature palate that you bring the unconscious into the conscious. It is not a matter of deleting off the menu all the items but simply recognizing which ones are obsolete and which are more likely to remain in service of helping you to evolve into the human that you were created to become. The truth is, unless you have chosen in your lifetime to upgrade your menu list, most of those items on your menu are not yours. And, they're probably not even your parents. They are items placed there generations ago by your grandparents and their parents and their parents and so on. This is not because they woke up one day and said, "let's create a messed up menu for this beautiful child." Menus have been created for thousands of years, and we have all accepted the menu for part of our lives. Some people accept the menu for all of their life because they never get to shine a light on their menu to read the darker pages thoroughly and to read between the lines of what's unwritten. Perhaps that would be too painful, perhaps it would feel like a parental betrayal, perhaps it would uproot their life in a way that would be too uncomfortable. One of the techniques to read invisible ink is to wave the paper over a hot stove and wait until the paper distorts to read it. This heat is uncomfortable, and the discomfort is part of the essential journey of being willing and able to read the unconscious invisible messages.

Through this book, I invite you to be willing to shine the light on your unique menu, even in the corners that are dark and uncomfortable. Be willing to touch the heat of the moment as it challenges you beyond expectations. Only by deeply inspecting all of its ingredients, even the smallest ones that seem meaningless, can you begin to see what needs to come off the menu: toxic thoughts, sour values, acidic behaviors, bitter language, and fiery reactions.

Be willing to explore with curiosity and non-judgment. When you cast a mindful, conscious light and are willing to reform and customize your menu, you get to create a menu that is zesty, tangy, sweet, earthy, full-bodied, juicy, rich, and fresh. A menu that is authentically YOURS. As you shine the light on your menu, check in regularly to ensure that you are exploring with understanding and love. It does not serve to hold onto denial or judgment of what is on your menu. The truth is judgments were written on the pages of your menu by others, so meeting them with judgments only continues to add judgment to your life.

Change can only happen in your life when you accept the ingredients and choose to change them, day by day, every day. Some days, you may want to pick up the old menu because it's comforting, and its familiar ingredients are easier to digest on that day. Give yourself permission to order from that old menu and start again the next day. There is no failure when you do this work. There are simply opportunities to wake up again, and again.

All of our conditioning, stress, life experiences, and traumas result in the cumulative design of our personalized menu. Our menu is what determines how we experience the world, how we show up in the world, the meaning that we assign to every experience in our lives, and how we view ourselves and others. Until we can do this work and until we can assign meaning to our experiences, we will continue to pass on this menu to our future generations, our children, their children. Today is the day that you get to stand up and declare,

"I am exploring and looking to understand my menu for me, my children, their children, and future generations."

When we become intimate with all parts of our menu, we

can understand how we created the narratives in our lives, and how we view ourselves and others. The meaning we assign about everything we have experienced. Until we realize there is an option to alter our menu, deeply explore it, experience it, and alter it; we are asleep. We are unconscious. It is not enough to simply proclaim, "I will erase my menu and create a new one because I want to feel better and successful." That is what we call the "Spiritual Bypass" and all you are doing is temporarily closing the pages, but the words remain powerfully inside the unspoken and unopened invisible pages. Rather, to truly alter a menu, it must be digested and honored, sprinkled with a heavy dose of compassion and forgiveness, and fully explored.

This is "the work," and most people will choose to stay "asleep" or unaware of their menu because "waking up" means having to confront the items on the menu, where they come from, and how they have controlled us and limited us. It requires a deep exploration into the caves of the psyche and all its beliefs, of the heart and all its greatest joys and deepest pain, of the parts of the body holding the tension or shut down and numbed because the pain was too great. It would reveal to us all the times that we have lived in duality or separated from our true *Self* and resisted life including the highs and the lows, ups and the downs, hatred and love, fear and courage. This is a gentle and slow process. It does not happen in one day, one book, or one year. Without the tools to navigate this awakening process, most people would feel too disturbed and confronted. Their nervous system would essentially close the menu pages as it shuts down the willingness to explore the options. Most people go back to sleep and return to being simply and utterly FINE. And, for most people on the planet, that is ok. Still, it comes at a significant cost to life itself because, when we are asleep, it is difficult to acknowledge our divinity, feel our golden essence, connect to our goodness, and live life with the purpose that we were created to design and live. Upgrading the menu of our life is remembering that we are, and always have been miracles.

Throughout this book, take the time to reflect on your life experience and your menu, and use this question to bring consciousness and compassion to each chapter:

"What would I love to place on my menu today?"

That question will never take you astray and always lead to creating a powerful menu that begins to realign more closely to your life purpose, truth, and heart.

I remained fully asleep and ordered my life choices from my conditioned menu for the first 32 years. Once I had my first child, something in me began to rumble, longing to be explored, felt, reviewed, rewritten, and awakened. In order to understand more deeply why I needed to remain asleep and how I came to be 'woke,' I will share in more depth the highlights of my conditionings, stress, and traumas leading up to the day that one statement became the biggest *soul slap* and the catalyst for my awakening.

Re-alignment Steps:

1. As you did in the beginning, begin this Re-Alignment step with your hand on your heart and whisper to yourself "I am a miracle" over and over until you feel your heart softening to receive this truth.

2. Where have you been living from a state of FINE? How often do you respond to "How are you?" with "FINE" as a mask to hide what you truly feel? Can you notice when you say "FINE" and see if it is my definition of FINE? No need to change it yet. Simply notice the power of your words.

3. If you were to reflect on your childhood essence, how would you describe yourself before your menu was filled up? What are a few words to describe what you either imagine or know your authentic state to be if you were to peel back the shame, the stress, and the trauma? What do you know to be real about yourself from the day you were born? Imagine looking at yourself as a newborn baby. As you look at that baby, how would you describe him/her? Journal the qualities you know were true about you from that first day. Recognize that those qualities remain in you today; they have simply been covered by the menu of others.

4. Reflect on the menu of your life. What ingredients (values, judgments, beliefs, and rules) remain on your menu today?

5. Do not judge these items today; simply observe them, and become curious about them. We call this mindfulness, observing with loving attention, kindness, curiosity, and non-judgment (do not make them wrong). At this point, there is nothing to change. *You cannot change what you cannot see* so do a deep check-in with your programming and feel into each of these values or beliefs to see how they feel.

6. Next, decide IF you want an upgrade to your menu. Yes? No? Maybe?

7. If you were to rewrite your menu today, which ingredients would you want to add? What are your core values, and how are you living daily from these values? (when I work with leaders, they often state that family and downtime is a core value, but their calendars reflect otherwise, so be honest here). What are your needs in a relationship, and what are your deal breakers? What do you you long to touch, create, and believe in your lifetime about yourself, your relationships, your work, and the world? *What are you yearning to call into your life?* As we move through these chapters, I will offer you tools and practices to call in your magnificent self. From that place, *anything is possible*.

Chapter 2

The powerlessness of silence

The quality of your life is determined by
the quality of the issues in your tissues.

My authentic nature was to be a social, joyful, loving, trusting, and chatty little girl. My mother, who did not have much capacity to care for me with 4 children under the age of 3 and no support, would let my sisters and I play alone most days.

As a little girl, I loved talking, singing, and making up stories. I spoke so much that my twin sister didn't need to speak until she was almost four years old, as I spoke for myself and her. That's how vocal I was. I don't recall the specifics of it, but I grew up hearing that narrative… a lot.

My family used to call me 'Chatterbox.' I'm sure it was meant to be funny, but I received the message that my voice was "too much" with each passing joke, "Diana is the chatterbox of the family," and "We can never get a word in when Diana is around." This didn't feel like a badge of honor to me. As a little girl, I received the message that I was too much and that my voice was not welcomed. I felt ridiculed and shamed.

I would come home excited to tell my mom about my school day to find her, once again, on the couch, asleep and medicated. I would retreat quietly to my room, my excitement crushed and my words swallowed. In time, I learned that, as a good little girl, it was best to be seen and not heard.

As my words were silenced, I dimmed my inner light and became shy, withdrawn, and unable to express my needs or boundaries. I carried an invisibility cloak that kept me hidden and feeling unseen for the first 3 decades of my life. This cloak became part of my identity and a core ingredient that formed my identity, dictated my thoughts and feelings, and drove my behaviors and habits. That was my initiation into the journey of the powerlessness of silence.

I kept quiet during childhood physical abuse with silent tears as my Dad expressed his fury with his belt to my bottom or his swift hand to my cheek. I kept silent during a teenage sexual assault, where I didn't dare make a sound, not even a tear. I silenced my voice during moments of betrayal. I kept quiet when I was 'encouraged' to have an abortion. I kept silent through an acrimonious divorce. I kept to myself when my 'friends' started a public slaughter on Facebook, questioning my worthiness in opening a new business after previous failures. I lost all words when everything I owned was taken away, and I had to declare bankruptcy. Each of these experiences in my life led me to swallow my voice, dismiss my pride, and relinquish my power a little more. I put a lid on all my feelings, and instead of expressing myself, I held them in as shame. I showed up with a smile and the familiar words, "I'm FINE."

Hiding behind closed doors, under tables, and in my silence, I grew up with few friends and felt invisible in the presence of others. I rarely expressed my opinion as I didn't feel it would be received. I shut down all 'negative' feelings: anger, grief, fear, and disappointment. There was no place for these 'big' feelings in my home or life. The problem is when we silence one feeling, we silence all feelings, so not only did I not feel anger, grief, and disappointment, I rarely felt joy, excitement, and love.

I embodied the narrative that my presence was only welcomed if it came with a dose of sweetness and mostly silence. Anything else was met with punishment. As a child, I was shamefully made to kneel in the corner of the kitchen facing the wall if I spoke out of turn during dinner. My silence was wrapped in shame, and shame became the default emotion that commanded my entire childhood. Shame for my body, shame for my emotions, shame for my conflicting beliefs, and shame for my voice.

On the outside, we were viewed to be a good Catholic home. I went to church twice a week and, like a good Catholic Girl, I sang in the choir and folk group. I dressed up on all special occasions with the coordinating outfits my mom made us. We were very cute and played the beautiful role of being the perfect family. Behind closed doors, however, the tension was thick and heavy. My parents fought a lot, each argument landing in my own body as my inability to take a deep breath. In the midst of their quarrels, my little mind and body studied their every movement and words looking for any sign that my mom might leave, abandon us and leave us with my raging father. At a young age, I learned how to feel his emotional state before talking and even moving in my childhood home. If he had a bad day, I kept my distance. My survival depended on my being able to read him and respond in a way that would minimize conflict in our home. I learned to read others' emotional energy and shut down my emotions and needs in their presence. Feeling others became more critical to my survival than feeling myself, and I became overly empathic to the point where I felt others more than I felt myself and became fused with their needs more than my own. When feeling others became too much for me to carry in my little immature system, I would stop feeling completely. When it was often too painful to feel my mother's loneliness, my father's anger, my sister's fears, I became very good at leaving my body and would turn to an imaginary world through my play.

This severance with my body served me when I would return home to find my mother curled up, asleep on the couch, with a sweet upward curl of her lips. This was her happy place.

"Mommy?" I would whisper.

There was no reply. I quietly walked away to play in my bedroom.

She was in her own survival state and unable to be present for me, nor could she protect me from my father's wrath.

Although my father's coping method was bigger, louder, and scarier, my mother set us up for abuse with her "Wait until your father gets home," a phrase that I often heard as she felt powerless in navigating parenting four girls. Those six words, "*wait until your father gets home,*" would haunt me well into the evening as I tried to fall asleep before he returned, hoping that he would not wake me. As I heard him walk through the front door, I would tightly clutch my blanket around my neck, hold my breath, and pray that my mother would forget to remind him of my wrongdoings. Some days the pills she took helped her forget. On other days, she would recount my misdeeds, and he would swing open the door to my bedroom, remove his belt, rip the blankets off my little, quivering body, and begin to whip the unforgiving leather onto my tiny bare bottom. I would silently plead, "Daddy, please stop," but somehow, the words didn't leave my mouth.

My waking hours were no safer, as a wrong word or action could be met with a swift strike from the back of his hand across my cheek, sometimes knocking me to the floor. My father, who was raised by an abusive mother, was a workaholic. He used alcohol to relax; however, to me, it seemed only to amplify the fury and speed of his backhand.

When relatives visited, I was always dressed properly and remained quiet. I was forced to hug and kiss them as an obedient little girl and sit on unsafe laps. I was also forced to kiss my father goodnight every night, even when doing so, repulsed me as he puffed out his inflamed cheek to receive a kiss. It became clear that listening to my body was not my option or choice, and I was not safe in my physical body or my home.

Even though I was young, my survival instincts were sharp, and I learned how to be the best 'good little girl' I could be as a way to avoid pain. My nervous system, however, remained in an active state of anxiety that tightened my chest and left me gasping for breath. I was in a constant state of alertness, and I did not know how to relax or feel safe in the world. As I matured, I realized my childhood traumas, neglect, confusion, and fear impacted my developing nervous system and my ability to navigate intimate relationships.

I craved attention from my mother. I feared and avoided

my father. My joyful moments came as sighs of relief when I played with my sisters. We would play hand games like rock-paper-scissors, run around our familiar neighborhood, bask in the heat of the summer sun reading books or comics outside, or create imaginative and more joyful realities with our dolls. My most joyful memories are rooted in those times with my sisters. My most painful one as well.

When I was 11 years old, I came face to face with the potential fragility of life and the truth of how much stress and trauma was hidden in the narrative of my family. It was a beautiful sunny Saturday. The birds were singing, and the sun was bright and warm. My parents were at a wedding. My sisters and I were alone at home. I went to see if one of my sisters wanted to play cards and carefully opened the door to her bedroom to find her in bed, asleep. I shook her playfully. She did not wake up. On her nightside table, I saw a note that simply said, "I'm sorry, I didn't mean it." The "It" was a broken chair. Next to the note was a bottle of pills—the medicine for her pain. She was unconscious. I panicked; I tried to shake her frantically "Wake up" I yelled with a pleading cry; my hands shook as my tears slipped to her shoulder. I felt overcome with a sense of fear and powerlessness. I remember asking myself *what should I do?* Already, at that age, my first instinct was not to call 911 as I was so used to living in secrecy. If I had called 911 they would have known what my sister had done. The shame of the experience overrode my 11-year-old's common sense. I didn't know what to do and panicked.

Lost in my disheveled thoughts of what to do, I was startled by the phone ringing. It was my parents checking in. I told them what had happened. I begged them to tell me what to do. They assured me by telling me that they would return home immediately. I remember feeling relief, knowing that they would take care of things and that my sister, who had awoken, would be FINE.

I kept my sister awake, and by the time my parents arrived, she was able to stand up. They took over, and I sighed with relief for her and myself as I no longer had to carry the responsibility for her life. My parents would make it FINE. And, they did. They made her wash her face, get dressed, brush her hair, and return to the wedding with them. To this day, that event is one of our family's secrets, remaining unspoken, an unmentioned reality that was FINE.

What became a key ingredient on my menu on that day would shape my life for the next 21 years: What other people think of me is more important than anything else, even my physical health and wellness. My heart armor grew thick that day. My mask pasted firmly on my exterior self. It would be another 45 years before anyone, in this case, a coach, heard about this story and asked me how I was nurtured, held, or supported after that day. It would be 45 years before anyone asked me, "how were you, and how are you today because of that?" It would be 45 years until I talked about this experience, felt the grief and the shame for my sister and my inner little girl, and burst into tears.

As I grew into my teens, I found myself navigating a menu with a shame-filled body and no boundaries. I had a few relationships and lost myself in those relationships. When I was in a relationship, I picked up my partner's menu, borrowed some of their ingredients, and molded myself to their beliefs and needs. This usually led to betrayal, abandonment, and an inner confirmation that I was not enough. I was insecure about my body and spent hours trying to look different. More makeup. Bigger hair (it was the 80s). Tighter jeans. I was doing all I could to mask my perceived imperfections to be accepted. The good little girl now had become a shiny attention-seeking young woman who delighted in attention with a well of fear and insecurity attached to that exterior persona.

I wanted to have some photos done for my then-boyfriend and won a free portrait session. I dressed in a very short white skirt and a small white tank top. I was dressed to 'impress' my boyfriend. I was barely 18 years old. I walked in with false confidence and said I wanted something "sexy." After a few moments, the photographer began to physically adjust my positioning from the back. Tilt my head this way, lean this hip to the right, relax my shoulders. With each command, I felt his breath on the back of my neck, and tension grew. Everything inside me yelled danger, run, run, and yet I was paralyzed. I had learned early to freeze in the presence of fear. Without access to my voice or boundaries, I stood silent, not even a tear, until he finished using my body for his pleasure. I turned around, walked out of there, and I'm pretty sure I even thanked him for his time because, after all, I was "a good little girl." As soon as I was out of the building, I ran as fast as possible. I ran home, took a shower to scrub the memory off my body, and quickly put it out of my mind. I didn't tell anyone about that incident for 25 years. I felt responsible because of how I was dressed. I felt immense shame. I didn't do something bad; I was bad. Any residual amount of voice that I had going into that photo session would soon be permanently swallowed up by the heaviness of my shame.

That shame continued into my adulthood and was expressed as a lack of boundaries and poor communication. I went to University and received an undergraduate degree in Psychology and a Master's Degree in Communication Sciences and Disorders; I began a fulfilling, exciting, and successful career as a Speech-Language Pathologist. I married the man that I met at the age of 17. We spent 20 fun, cordial and friendly years together. They were not affectionate or loving. The greatest outcome of our relationship was our beautiful daughter.

Parenting was fun and effortless for me. I loved this little girl who was very easy going and adventurous at the same time. 6 months after her birth, I was pregnant again and was excited to have another child so close in age. My children would be best friends. My husband did not share my enthusiasm. So, without my voice and boundaries, I allowed myself to be talked into an abortion (and I take responsibility for that decision today). I remember going that day, sitting in the clinic like a zombie, deprived of sensations and only moving when following the commands of my then-husband, the nurse, and the doctor. I left without ever talking about it. Without feeling the pain of it. It became another secret experience to tuck away and try to forget. More shame on the invisible ink of my menu. I put it out of my mind and tucked it deep in my body, another issue in my tissue. We eventually divorced with a very acrimonious separation filled with anger; I was locked out of my home. Still, I showed up at work and put on my smile; after all, I was "FINE."

With my history of abuse, stress, and trauma, my menu was filled with shame that I could not process. As a result, I learned to shut down my voice, deny my feelings, forget my truth, and live in a state of being "FINE," but it came with a dangerous price tag. The cost was:

Not having clear boundaries.

Not speaking my truth.

Not being authentically who I was.

Denying my happiness for the sake of others.

Protecting my pain, my joy, and my love with fierce and impenetrable walls.

Being unable to feel myself.

I was living my life with a stone wall for my heart, a thorn in my solar plexus, a heaviness on my shoulders, and a darkness in my thoughts. I lived an anesthetized life that looked amazing on the outside with the perfect job, home, clothes, makeup, hair, and family. My biggest fear was the possibility that others would see my real menu, which would horrifyingly become a sudden death and the end of my existence as I knew it. That is exactly what happened when I was 32 years old.

It was a crisp fall day. I was picking up my daughter from my friend's house. Yes, I had a friend. This was a big deal for me as I had grown up with very few friends and didn't know how to be a friend. When I met this woman, who would later become my daughter's first care provider, we instantly hit it off. We did many activities together as new moms and supported each other. As much as I wanted to be a good friend, I could not share my own life and heart with her. I didn't talk about my relationship concerns, childhood fears, and shame, and how much pain I carried in my life. I had learned to keep all that inside and protected. On this fall day, we were chatting, standing on her front porch. We were talking about the weather, her plans for the weekend, and how big the kids were getting. All the surface conversations that shielded me from the vulnerability of speaking the truth and revealing my pain. Then, she shared a conversation she had with her husband that would change my life forever. In this conversation, her husband stated, "Diana is so accomplished, kind, and professional—but she is an ice queen." I felt the stinging truth of these words. That was the day my previously unaware self was destroyed, and I moved toward learning more about myself, my beliefs, my behaviors, and my heart. I spent the next 25 years processing my undigested experiences to gently disarm the "Ice Queen," investigating my old menu and giving birth to a more mature, conscious, and authentic menu.

Re-alignment Steps:

1. Reflect on your life. What are some of the key events that you recall that might be considered big Traumas (abuse, neglect, divorce, bankruptcy, loss of life) and which might be little traumas (parents fighting, heartbreak, your own divorce, loss of jobs)? Imagine yourself at the ages of each of these experiences and imagine holding your younger self's hand, looking her/him/them in the eye and letting her know that you are here with then, and offering the nurturance that you needed them but did not receive. This is called "reparenting" and is an essential tool to support your inner child that did not receive the love/attention/support as a younger self. You can re-parent yourself at any age. Ask your younger self *what do you need right now?* and give THAT to yourself NOW. When you find yourself triggered in a situation, instead of blaming the other, ask yourself, *what do I need at this moment?* and give that to yourself (we will explore trigger tracking in later chapters). This is how you begin to take responsibility for your life from the wonderful mature person you are today. This is how you can begin to alter the menu/conditioning/brain patterns and belief systems from your traumas. This is how you can begin to rewrite the narrative of your life and create meaning that will allow you to show up with a softer heart. You are not your

traumas or the experiences that happened to you. Begin to separate your self-identity from these experiences to see how you are truly made up of many different parts, and each of these parts has had different experiences. Some are more painful than one can imagine.

2. Note how you carry stress in your body. My stress always showed up as bronchial asthma. When the body is holding stress, current or past, it still responds with the same sympathetic nervous system response: Your sympathetic nervous system is best known for its role in responding to dangerous or stressful situations. Its job is to get you into fight/flight/freeze as a response to the danger. The problem is not the stress activation, which is a normal response to stimuli in life; the problem is we no longer have tools to put down the stress, so we become busier and even more stressed without a break. Further, the brain does not know the difference between real stress, like a dog running in front of your car that requires a quick response, and a memory or a thought of stress. However, in both cases, it will flood your body with a cascade of stress chemicals that, over time, create havoc in your mind, body, and nervous system. Therefore, commit to practices that will allow you to put down the stress response and activate your parasympathetic (calming regulated nervous system) response by using yoga or other

movements, meditation, and breathwork. Nothing changes until something changes. Choose 1
self-loving practice to start daily and remind yourself that you are worth it.

3. Honestly, reflect on the ways that you cover up
   feeling stress (or any other feeling) to numb yourself. What are your habits and numbing choices?
   Examples of numbing: seeking perfection, working
   excessively, needing to be in the spotlight, drinking, drugs, work, porn, shopping, sex, and TV. As
   you engage in these activities (and none of these
   are judged as wrong when done in moderation and
   for the right reasons), ask yourself, "am I avoiding
   feeling something by doing this activity?" Journal
   about these habits that may have been your survival
   strategies when you didn't know better or when
   you needed them most (like my Ice Queen was
   needed for my survival). Thank them now and
   let them know you might choose a new way of
   engaging with your life, feelings, and stress. Be
   willing to find equanimity in your feelings. Hold
   space for them (which simply means be present
   and feel) without making them wrong.

Chapter 3

Wake up Loved One

*When you are willing to pull back the
curtain on the hidden parts of your life, life
will reveal itself to you, and you will see it
with a new set of lenses, forever changed*

Even though my relationship with my own voice was weak
and guided by my shame, as a Speech Language Pathologist I helped children who were minimally verbal or nonverbal
access their voice. I didn't realize that in doing so, little by
little, I was finding my own. I still lived in the realm of FINE
and achieved immense success. I became one of the leaders in
my field and a board-level consultant. I trained others, supported families and schools, and had a small private practice
on the side. I took 2-3 trips a year and had a beautiful home
in a nice neighborhood. I got up every morning eager to greet
my daughter and the day ahead. I was grateful for my successful life.

However, I didn't trust most people, and I didn't trust
my own body. Despite my success, I remained feeling like

an imposter in my life. I was fully guarded in my personal and professional relationships with a mask of "having it all together" and being "FINE."

I see now how all of my experiences have not only shaped my life but also how I identified in my life. I began to connect the dots of my life. I began to see how I learned to respond to a menu filled with stress, avoidance, disconnect, and anger as my primary ingredients, with complete shutdown and masks to 'look' successful in life.

When my friend's husband called out my armor, calling me an "ice queen," I paused. I realized some truths I had ignored. I had few friends throughout my life, a distant relationship with my husband, and could not tell anyone how I felt because I could not truly identify and connect with my feelings or my body. My history of abandonment, abuse, disconnect, and inability to trust people was now evident, and I was living essentially disassociated from my body (unable to feel fully), which was a defensive strategy that served me well as a child and teenager but, as an adult, left me cold and untouchable. That was the day I realized what it meant for me to be FINE:

- I was f*cked up - beyond my previous imagination
- I was Insecure- about my career, my body, my relationship, and my life
- I was Needy (in a sneaky way where I wouldn't ask for what I wanted but expected others to guess)
- I was empty - emotionally empty

I didn't know how to thaw my frozen heart and fix the issues in my life that were so deeply bound in my tissues and my subconscious. I was still sleepwalking and hoping that no one noticed, but inside, my soul was screaming and fighting to come alive. The "Ice Queen" comment sent me to the edge of a critical choice: do I strengthen my mask, or do I fully surrender to this healing journey?

I began to ask deep questions about my life:

How did I get here?

How can I create a new menu when I wasn't fully aware of my old menu or how to read invisible ink?

How can I be more loving if I didn't know how to love?

How can I be more forgiving if I didn't know what to forgive?

How can I release my masks?

I read a quote from the Buddha:

"Show me the face you had before you were born."

I became curious about that face's shape, quality, and essence. Of my face, of my heart, my desires, my longing, my life. As my curiosity expanded, so did my inner fire to learn more about myself, my life, my pain, and my love. Slowly, my menu began to reveal itself to me, and I didn't like everything that I saw on my menu. Still, I came to compassionately understand how those ingredients were placed and that my concealment for 32 years was required for me to feel safe and move towards this place of expansion and revelation that would fuel the next 25 years of my life.

I heard Dr. Wayne Dyer say,

"When you change the way you look at things, the things you look at change."

I had a choice at that time to continue to feed my life from my unconscious shame-filled menu or to listen to the dark, achy emptiness inside me that was begging me to draw closer to it and be willing to look beyond what was on the surface of my menu. I knew that something else was waiting to be revealed and revered; it would take decades to uncover it fully. I began to take a closer look at the invisible writing on my menu. I knew that going there would require that I be daring enough to pick away the old ingredients and stand naked in my menu, totally stripped of my known identity until my new menu could be created from a place of a conscious, awakened, mature perspective. I started to follow the bread-crumbs of my life and became curious and excited about a potential new menu and life experience. My enthusiasm was also met with urgency.

I needed to heal as quickly as possible as if there was a timeline for healing itself. I sourced many different healing modalities and therapies. I read all the books on childhood trauma, inner child healing work, and shadows (the parts of ourselves that we have disowned and are written in invisible ink).

I went to therapy but ran away, never to return, when the therapist told me that our time together would last about 10 years because my wounds were so complex, deep, and dark. I felt I did not have 10 years to work on myself. My cause was radically urgent, and I had to attend to it with the same urgency and speed that I had learned to bring to my life. As an FYI, urgency and speed are other ways of numbing and masking pain. If I go fast, I don't have to feel as much. I was eventually introduced to spiritual practices. Practices that required me to slow down, to find breath in the pause, to be willing to feel. I went kicking and screaming until I noticed that there was a pause between the kicking and screaming. This was when life began to reveal itself to me.

I began to meditate and felt every nauseous response to my attempt to witness my thoughts and my body. I studied energy work and became certified as a Reiki practitioner. I found a new therapist who blended modalities, including somatic (embodiment) work, and I began to work intensively with an energy healer, my now friend, Darrin.

In June, 2003 I walked into Darrin's office and announced that I was giving him the privilege of "fixing me," and he had to do it in 3 months, as I was returning to work in September, and I wanted all this healing shit to be done and the new me to be revealed. Today, I can laugh about my demands because today I know:

All healing has its time.

When I worked with Darrin, he would tell me, "Diana, you just need to be present."

Presence… *What did that mean? What was the secret to being present?* I googled it, and there was not one definition that helped me to understand this mysterious word.

I, painfully, read The Power of Now by E. Tolle. Today I am in full awe and admiration of his work, but the slowness of his voice triggered me those days because of my accelerated need to heal quickly and resistance to slowing down to feel life. Tolle's definition of presence is:

"Presence is when you are no longer waiting for the next moment,

believing that the next moment will be more fulfilling than this one."

I returned to Darrin's office the next week and said, "I have no idea what that means." "Teach me to be present."

In our treatments, I would feel a gentle stir in my body and sit curious about the sensations.

I began to stop and smell the flowers.

I lay on the grass and watched the clouds.

I listened to song lyrics on the radio and noticed how they made me feel and spoke right to my soul.

I felt my breath.

I looked at the person I was speaking with.

I slowed down enough to savor moments.

I realized that I knew how to do this presence thing. I had been present for many moments of my life. I experienced it when my daughter was born, and I would get lost in the beauty and curiosity of her eyes or the smell of her newborn skin, and I would find myself laughing uncontrollably when she and I made up silly songs. I would watch her dancing in the rain, catching snowflakes on her tongue, and hugging me for no reason; I knew this feeling of presence. It was not unfamiliar, but it was infrequent. I felt it when I experienced deep nausea every time I sat to meditate in the early years of meditation. Now that I knew what presence was, I was being called to a deeper relationship with presence as part of my awakening journey. It came with dragonflies, sun, and a river on a beautiful day, the day my heart began to melt, I connected to a greater presence and purpose in my life.

I woke up early. It was July 1, 2003. Canada Day. A time when everything is closed, and most people celebrate together with parties, BBQs, and fireworks. My previous Canada Days had also been filled with festivities. But, on this day, I craved solitude. On this day, I knew I needed something gentle as I had begun to deeply investigate my life menu, recalling my childhood wounds and traumas and connecting with my inner little girl who needed so much reparenting and gentleness. This was all happening, of course, while walking through a vulnerable, inevitable end of a 20-year relationship with my husband that also involved a beautiful little girl. On this day, I craved peace. I drove to Ottawa with my daughter, who spent the day with my sister, allowing me the quiet space I needed. I packed up a water bottle, a towel and headed outside without any agenda for the day.

The air was densely hot (I love the heat) with a blanket of humidity. I walked to the nearest riverbank and sat on the dewy grass for what felt like hours. I stared at the vast ceiling above me, admiring and studying the occasional cloud that dared to shadow the sun. An elephant, a duck, a wheel. Each new shape morphing in and out of its existence. Am I like that? I thought… *do I morph in and out of who I am to show myself as others wish to see me?* I was so good at complying with the expectations of others. That was primary on my life menu. I spent my life being who everyone else wanted me to be. But who was I without all those masks, expectations, labels, and roles?

A hawk flew overhead, a few grasshoppers serenaded each other, and only the odd couple or family walked on the trail behind me, some quietly, some laughing or talking. I heard a couple arguing and thought, "it's Canada Day, a day to celebrate, not to fight." I had left my own husband at home, 6 hours away, to ensure that there would be no arguments that day and weekend.

I began to meditate, a regular practice that I devoured, equally for the promise of being able to "wake up" and escape my life. I also meditated as a desperate measure to change something in me that I felt was tremendously broken. I meditated to avoid dealing with the decline of my marriage. I was in pain, I felt confused and unable to make life decisions those days, and I prayed that meditation would give me clarity. On this day, I could not have been more clear.

As I sat on the solid river bank, eyes closed, breathing in the warm air, listening to the whispering flow of the river, something encouraged me to open my eyes and I felt the need to comply despite my begrudged feeling that opening my eyes was taking me out of my meditation. I fluttered my eyes open. I was blinded for a moment by the brightness that met my gaze. It was like I was seeing the world for the first time. I saw the immense shimmering of the sun, each of it's rays stretching beyond view. I saw the infinite stillness of the water, the courage of each leaf tenderly being held by the trees, and a tingling on my skin that I had never quite felt before. My senses became alive, and the world was born to me. Without question, I knew I was being given sight to see the world from a new and present perspective.

My gaze was then drawn to a dragonfly, not an unusual vision by a riverbank. Then a second dragonfly joined the first, and they began to dance, rhythmically swaying back and forth. Soon another joined, and another. Dozens and dozens of dragonflies surrounded me. They were beautiful, fluttering their wings gracefully around me, willing to delight me with their dance. I heard and felt a clear and loving voice whisper to me at that moment: "Life is a gift to be celebrated, not a struggle to be overcome." They were here to help me to know the truth of who I am to myself and others. To recognize that

This moment, this very present precious moment,
IS MY LIFE.

And, if this moment is my life, so is each and every present moment that I get to inhabit in this body that is simply rented for this lifetime. Now the question became: What do I want to do with this precious life? A question that became a moment-by-moment inquiry. What do I want to do at each unfolding moment? Could I follow those impulses? I knew I was here to awaken to touch my purpose, potential, compassion, love, wisdom, and light. This moment was here to help me know at my core that there was nothing wrong with me. I was not broken. My menu was not a bad menu. Simply an outdated one that required a very gentle and compassionate acknowledgment of its previous purpose (to protect me) and the realization that I get to start, today, at this moment, to re-write my menu. The message continued to caress my ears softly:

"Wake up, loved one, you are here for a reason,
I am with you, and I always have been."

What happened next filled my body with an ecstatic state of being that was unfamiliar, exciting and exhilarating. I felt like I was awoken from a very long sleep. I felt fully ALIVE. All of my senses simultaneously activated. My sensations in my body, skin, hair, and cavities in my body, tingling with aliveness. My mind was calm and clear, and I was witnessing myself as if I had eyes that stepped outside my body and watched playfully from the sidelines. I had heard the term "taking the witness stance," and had no concept of it until that moment. I was OUT of my body and watching myself. And, when thoughts like *Am I going crazy?* came up, I witnessed them instead of attaching myself to their seductive and conditioned magnetic pull as I had in my past. I observed my body and its many releases, from tears, to laughter, to movement. I felt joyful waves of emotions penetrate me and a deep feeling of gratitude. I felt these all as individual expressions of that present moment, simultaneously flooding my body with an ecstatic cocktail of sensations. It was all welcomed. I felt years of containment breach my heart and then release just as quickly. I felt FREE; I felt released, I felt whole. I felt complete. I felt perfection. I felt safe. I felt LOVE. I felt ME. I knew with certainty this was presence. This was the first moment of belonging that I experienced in my life. I was 38 years old. And, it came when I remembered I was a miracle... just like you.

Now here is where it gets interesting... if I am a miracle... and you are a miracle... then everyone is a miracle... and... my work is to remember this truth.

I began, at this moment in my life, to rewrite my menu. The first ingredient was Presence.

Re-alignment Steps:

1. If you don't already have one, begin a daily meditation practice. In my resources you will find my heart-centered meditation to practice. You can also find your choice app or any Youtube™ meditation. I cannot stress this enough. Meditation is a wonderful tool to begin to witness (not necessarily quiet but slow down) your mind, reprogram your brain, and relax your nervous system.

2. Practice presence throughout your day. The best way to do this is to set a reminder on your watch or phone at every hour. When it goes off, take 30 seconds to stop and observe your surroundings, notice your feelings, smell the air, feel your lungs expand with your breath, taste your food slowly, feel the raindrops on your face, notice your thoughts, etc. When I practice presence, I attend primarily to my sensations. Sensations are the language of the body and include words like prickly, warm, smooth, tingly, spacious, tight, open, cool, etc. This is the beautiful way that your body communicates with you what is happening in your life in each and every moment with the remembrance that this moment is your life. We will review this in future chapters.

3. Place one hand on your energetic heart space in the center of your sternum. Take deep breaths and bring in a feeling of appreciation for something or

someone in your life. Take 5 deep breaths, gently allowing your belly to expand with each inhale. With each exhale, let your heart space soften. This is the medicine for the Ice Queen that may be residing in your heart space.

Chapter 4

Loving Boundaries

Loving boundaries are the brave
heart's way to open the door to
your authentic freedom.

As excited as I was in my waking up by the riverbank experience, I quickly learned that the risk of falling back asleep was almost guaranteed. Just because I had a moment of awakening by the river bank didn't mean I was a "woke" being who would remain there. In the 18 years following that experience, my life became my practice of "woke" versus "sleeping." Every day, my practice would be to notice when life would whisper to me, *do you want to be conscious today?* And, sometimes, my response would be "absolutely," and others, it would be a clear and firm "no" expressed as a triggered reaction, an unkind gesture, a fear, a shutdown of my life force. As I continued on this journey of waking up, some things would be very painful to face and would result in my need to shut down and go to sleep for a while, but once I had that hit of waking up, I knew that I had the tools to re-awaken when I chose to or when I found myself asleep. And, being asleep rarely felt good since I knew better, but it had its purpose, to delight in the re-awakening.

Being awake is what we call consciousness. The opposite is living from the unconscious space. As Carl Jung said,

> *"Until we make the unconscious conscious, it will direct your life, and you will call it fate."*

In order to make the unconscious conscious, we have to understand how we become unconscious.

Up to the age of 32, I lived out my conditioned perceived reality, and life was FINE. I was choosing my beliefs, values, and actions from the menu created for me.

That menu included ALL of my conditioning and unexpressed tension, stress, and traumas—Including those of my parents, their parents, and generations past. Not to mention all that society, school, religion, and the media had added to my menu.

Dr. Wayne Dyer said, "On the day you were born, your parents looked at the Heavens above and said, *Thank you, God, I'll take it from here.*" Our parents, then, begin the long and arduous road of creating our menu and (unknowingly) teaching us to forget our wonderment. Our core values are based on what others placed on our menu, and our beliefs about the world and who we are in the world gets defined for us. Soon, our identity is formed by what others believe us to be, and the most incredible thing happens; we begin to believe it ourselves. This is our unconscious programming written in seemingly permanent markers on the menu or blueprint of our life. Most of it is written by the time we are 7 years old.

Most parents have little awareness of how they are projecting their pain, imprints, stress, and menu onto their children.
Their Ego looks at their children as extensions of themselves,
and they project their fears, their longings, and their conditioning onto their children. Then, when adolescence hits,
which it will, the children begin to see their parents less as a
savior, and more as a nuisance. These poor parents wonder,
*what went wrong? Where did they fail? How could they be so quickly
and painfully discarded by this little one? Don't they realize how much
I have sacrificed for them? I gave up my life for them? How could they?*
Now, the Ego starts to dominate that conversation as it becomes
about the panicked parent. "How did I lose control of my little
angels?" Let me make it clear. You didn't lose anything. You
have raised a strong little human who needs you now more
than ever, but their own ego won't let them admit that. The
best thing you can do at this point is to take your new role
proudly and patiently: cook, driver, and occasionally consultant. When my daughter was a teenager, she would call me at
10 pm at night on her way home from hockey practice. "I'm
starving." I would start an entire meal for her at what would
be my bedtime. Then I would sit with her while she ate. That
was the way she could welcome me into her world at that time,
and, to this day, she remains grateful for those late-night meals.

As conscious parents, we have an incredible opportunity
to elevate consciousness on the planet by being aware of our
own triggers, teachings, and expectations of our children. I
am not suggesting that, as a culture and in our parenting, we
should not teach our children how to be responsible, functioning global citizens; what I am suggesting is to bring a level of
consciousness into our parenting that allows us to reflect on

who we are, what we are, what we believe, how we interact and encourage a dialogue with our children that allows them to be fully who they are, not little versions of us but the best version of themselves as a whole and complete loving human being, even when they disagree with us.

Because of the pain I endured as a child, I knew I never wanted to be physically abusive with my children, and I brought that consciousness into my parenting. That was relatively easy, and I never felt the impulse to physically harm my children. I had taken a vow of Ahimsa (a Sanskrit word for non-harming) for all creatures, especially my children.

My imprint of neglect by my mother was a more slippery slope to climb. I spent hours a day focusing on my own healing while recognizing that the end of my marriage was imminent (by the way of a preview: this happened not once but twice), and could also easily become consumed with work. I had to remind myself daily to be present for my daughter despite the distractions of my life, and I would repeat this years later with my son. I was not perfect, but I did my best in those moments, given what I was processing. My childhood trauma was coming back fiercely into my consciousness, and the pain of those undigested and unprocessed years made it difficult to be fully present some days. I recognized how my deep healing process at that time had the potential of distracting me from being present for my daughter, it also informed me how I was fiercely committed to showing up consciously as a parent who was committed to ending the cycle of abuse and neglect.

Instead of trying to control and make my daughter wrong, I listened to what she said and what she didn't say. I observed her playing out her own unconscious world through the play of her ceramic teddy bears, projecting her own emotional experiences in the play. I noticed how she projected her inner world through her interactions with our dog, which allowed me to be aware of what she needed. In age-appropriate language, I encouraged her to define her own values to place on the menu of her life, and I gave her a "no, thank you" exit as often as possible so she could practice her boundaries. Today, my daughter is one of the clearest and most conscious beings I know, and she can say "no" without guilt, doubt, or fear.

As a Speech-Language Pathologist, I always encouraged parents to celebrate their child's first "NO". That is the child communicating, establishing boundaries, and sharing their truth. Unfortunately, most parents cannot hear "no" because it triggers in them an old response that usually has to do with their inability to say no or have boundaries. Instead, when a child says no, here's what I suggest: Change the question. Do not make it a yes/no question; give them options (e.g., do you want me to stay with you for 5 minutes for bed or would you like to go to sleep on your own tonight?" not "do you want to go to bed now?").

Even with this skillful communication reframe, when a child says "no" what is a parent to do? Acknowledge the "no." Silently celebrate that your child is asserting their boundaries and put on your negotiation hat. If you are thinking "wait, my child is supposed to do what I tell them to do" (Ego) then it's time to look at where that conditioning comes from and reflect on your own triggers and your dictator imprint (ouch). Boundaries are a way of telling the world how to treat you. Boundaries are your way of letting others know what you will accept and not accept in your life. And:

NO is a complete sentence.

It does not require an explanation. It does not need to be defended. If you are clear about a "NO" in your life, own it. And say it with kindness and firmness. Boundaries have nothing to do with controlling another's behavior and everything to do with how you will allow yourself to self-honor, self-respect, and self-love. Reread that sentence, please. If your boundaries are about controlling another, they will never stick. NEVER. Because you cannot control another. But you can consciously recognize and communicate what is important for you to feel seen, heard, safe, and loved.

As you begin to practice setting boundaries yourself, you will become more skillful at using boundaries with your children and better equipped to support them in understanding and expressing their boundaries. Now, that means that you might have to   eady to hear a whole lot more "nos" for a while than you are comfortable with, but this journey is not about comfort. Then, as everyone has the freedom to feel their "no" and express t as a clear channel from their heart, they also have the freedom to be clear with their "yes". Doing this creates a relationship dynamic and communication imprint that allows everyone to be honored and respected.

Unfortunately, that is not what typically happens, and as the 2-year-old saying "no" starts butting up against a parent who cannot hear "no," the triggers are pulled because, as children get older, they are harder to control (yes I did say control which is what many unconscious parents try to do with their children). Your "no" might be totally valid. Soon, your child is now having a full-on temper tantrum in front of your mom. Shit. You know this will come with the familiar "you never did that as a child" or worse, in front of your Mother in Law who says, "My boys never had tantrums." (Of course, we/they didn't; we were too afraid to be disrupters and became people pleasers).

Typically, parents lose all sense of consciousness in these moments and grasp to make the tantrum stop or at least to get it away from those that are witnessing it. Often parents will negotiate, bribe, yell, hit (Which is NEVER OK, but I know it still happens) or tell a child to take a "time out" away from the parents ("go to your room until you can be quiet," "go sit on the stairs by yourself and think about this" or, in my case "go and kneel facing the wall in the corner" or I received a swat across my face). What the child now receives as an imprint is:

1. Communicating how they feel is not safe or welcomed.
2. Saying no is not an option; therefore, they will not learn how to establish boundaries
3. The risk of authentic expression might come with pain, withdrawal of love, or connection with those that matter the most to them.

Any child will choose connection over self-expression because that is a survival need. Therefore, they begin to suppress or hide the parts of themselves that seem to lead to disconnection, danger, or punishment and, unconsciously, carefully curate and bring out the "sweet" parts of them that are met with love and connection. These hidden parts get tucked far away until no one can see them, even the child themselves, often well into adulthood. These undesirable parts of us then become unconscious and make way for the birth of the People Pleaser.

Soon, we have a culture of people walking around unable to communicate their boundaries, feel their authentic selves, and feel whole and complete. They have become people pleasers, all because, at an age where they could learn their own values and self-expression as an honor of their divine voice and being, they were told that wasn't welcomed. They were told (unconsciously) that love is available only when:

They are compliant

They are helpful

They are cute

They are quiet

They are less (or un) loved when showing anything but those qualities.

People pleasers have immense difficulties with boundaries because boundaries are not welcomed. Further, people pleasers will almost always lead to co-dependent relationships whereby they look for others to fulfill a need to be loved. Doing so reinforces their people-pleasing value, which leads to them doing even *more* for others, to the point of denying what *they* need. People pleasers often give away their power and allow others to define them. When I ask them, "what do you need?" They have no idea.

Deep Breath.

Me Too.

I am a recovering People Pleaser. And it was served with a side of the Ice Queen. As a people pleaser, I went along with others' opinions, choices, and beliefs. I became burnt out hosting events, parties, and dinners that no one else wanted to host. I volunteered for all the school activities and work functions. I organized all the play dates, the trips, and the holiday shopping. I stayed in an unloving relationship for 20 years. I allowed myself to be coerced into having an unwanted abortion. I became paralyzed when I was sexually abused rather than run away. I lived my life ordering from the offered menu and had no clue what my values were, what I wanted for my life, and how to say "NO."

Another big breath.

My first marriage, already on shaky grounds, needed to crumble for me to seriously rattle my life, face my people-pleaser tendencies and explore the immense discomfort that lay ahead. It was time for my system, my life, my beliefs, my heart, and my soul to receive an upgrade to my operating system and turn on my authentic voice through my boundaries. This would require embracing my brave heart to open the door to access my freedom. It was not easy, and it was essential.

To my menu, I now added the word "NO."

Re-alignment Steps:

1. Reflect on the values that were written for you on your menu. List these. Which ones are still important to you? Which ones no longer serve the evolution of your life as you are consciously waking up to experience it? Circle the ones that no longer are to be served from your menu and notice how easily they can still sneak up as judgments or decisions/behaviors. Then, look at the ones that you really want to honor and make present in your life. Reflect on your schedule, actions, and thoughts daily, and ask, did I align with my deepest core values today?

2. What gifts do you wish to bring into the world? What brings you joy? How can you serve from a place of joy? Can you begin to say "yes" to experiences that light you up and allow those that are life and energy-sucking or do not light you up to be a clear "no"? (P.S. you still have to change the diaper, clean the kitchen and go to work but recognize that, in between those daily tasks, there are many opportunities to practice your "no" to bring more balance into your life and onto your menu).

3. Begin to notice what you say YES to in your life when you want to say NO and how that feels in your body. Usually, the gut will strongly react to a false "yes". What if you considered that "NO" is in service of a yes? When you say "no" to others,

you are saying yes to yourself, your well-being, your time, and your life.

4. Practice saying "NO" to others at least 3 times a day. At first, choose easier opportunities, saying "no" to a second serving of food, an upgrade to a sale, or "no" to letting someone in front of you in line. This isn't about what you say no to; it is simply about flexing the "no" muscle. Then, try saying no to people closer to you: your mother, your siblings, your partner, and your children (note: when I said no to my children, they would often persist as children do when given the freedom to express themselves. I would calmly say, "Let me think about it for an hour. However, if you continue to persist because you want me to give you an answer right now, the answer will be "no.")

5. Practice saying "no" to yourself concerning the habits that keep you feeling unhealthy, sluggish. No to the 6th episode of that binge-worthy show. "No" to the 2cd bowl of chips. "No" to going out drinking every night. "No" to unhealthy habitual relationships. Every time you say no to self-sabotaging behaviors, you are saying YES to your health, to your vitality, and your life.

6. As a parent, celebrate your child's "no" and help them to communicate their boundaries in loving ways. If you really don't want to hear a "no," reframe the questions. Instead of making it a Yes/No question, ask, "do you want to do it

now or later?" or "do you want me to help or do
it yourself?"

7. Notice if you are setting a boundary to control
another or to ask for what you want/need in a
relationship. If your boundary is about controlling
another, it will almost always fail because you can
NOT control others. If your boundary is drawing
a line in the sand about what you need/want to
feel healthy, cared for, safe, and loved, and you can
express that as "I need..." with love and clarity,
the chances of it being received and successful is
greater.

Chapter 5

Divine Courage

It takes courage to live life on your terms.

I didn't know how I would have the courage to find my boundaries. I had one foot in the door and one foot out of the door of my relationship with my husband. My daughter was 6 years old, and I carried so much fear about what a potential separation might do to her that I could not clearly define my boundaries.

I realized how much of my life I lived in "shoulds" and by the menus created for me. My people pleaser had been well curated, and I had done all the right things, but my unease with life was undeniable. I found myself in the deep judgment of a decision I feared to make: Should I choose to leave my marriage and risk being alone and 'break up my family'? I turned to my meditation for guidance, night after night, day after day, waiting for answers. I looked for guidance. I prayed for clarity. I was riddled with uncertainty. A part of me was fearfully ready to leave my relationship, and rationalized and eventually conceded that I could stay for another 12 years until my daughter was 18. I was stuck in the middle, incapable of finding the strength to confront that decision until one stormy February evening, sitting on my meditation stool, I was gifted with a moment of divine courage that would change the course of my life and became a courage that I would continue to access for the rest of my life.

I sat (a term for sitting in meditation) as I did every night. The guided meditation took me deep into my peace for that moment while the candlelight flickered behind my eyelids. The guided meditation ended, and I heard a voice say, "stay." It was a familiar voice that often came during my meditations when I felt the need to "cut and run" from the discomfort of sitting. I obediently stayed. What happened next almost knocked me off my stool.

My eyes flew open, and in front of me appeared a life-size version of Jesus. In that moment, he appeared real, in the flesh. I shook my head several times to erase what I perceived as my imagination running wild. He remained. He appeared to me in the exact image that I had studied all those years in church and Catholic education. Having avoided church for 2 decades, Jesus and I had not been in a relationship for many years which compounded my shock. I caught my breath, and I looked into his eyes.

I asked him, "Why are you here?"

His response "To remind you that you have courage."

I began to cry. "I cannot feel it or find it; where is it?"

His 3-word reply would be an imprint in my soul that would never again leave me: "It's in you."

Just as quickly as he appeared, he vanished, and I was left in the excited fear of my courage. Now I was no longer in fear of not having courage, I was in the realization that I had grit, fearlessness, and strength in me that I had never confronted before, and that scared me because I knew life was about to undergo a tremendous change. I could not imagine what that would look like. I knew I had to act now while my courage was strong.

I went to sleep that night with a wave of calm blanketing my entire being. I knew what I had to do. The next day I announced to my husband that I would be moving out and, within a week, moved into my new townhome with my daughter. This was likely the first time I had ever claimed a boundary and followed my own longings. I did not have all the details, but I trusted this decision. I had thought about this for a long time and even had conversations with my daughter's father about what it might look like, but until I declared my intention and followed through, I didn't really know what it would feel like.

It turned out that the courage to declare my boundaries and untangle from my people pleaser gave me the exact dose of freedom that I had been craving. Freedom to be me for the first time in my life. Free from having to please others. Free from someone else's schedule, routines, and expectations of me. I had never lived completely alone and had been in a relationship since I was 17. This was going to be my time to get to know myself. I got to rewrite a new page of my menu. Who is Diana when there are no expectations of her? I felt immense relief having moved into my own space. I decorated it exactly as I chose to, adjusted to a routine of co-parenting my daughter with her father, and continued my healing journey.

I still felt fear, but my bravery was stronger. I feared financial repercussions. I feared the impact that this relationship severing would have on my daughter as her father was angry and involved in courts for 2 years, and we were unable to communicate for many years. (Eventually, we found our way to being content in each other's presence and celebrating our daughter together).

The first Christmas since the separation was a wake-up to what I had left behind and how my life would be forever changed. On Christmas day, right as the clock struck noon, my daughter and my dog drove away with her father in his Jeep™, leaving me with my tears of abandonment. I was alone on Christmas day for the first time in my life. The one day that had been so sacred, so predictably safe in my home growing up. I sat on my stairs and sobbed deeply. I didn't know what to do with myself. Eventually, my sister came over, and we went for a run, watched a movie, and shared Thai food. I made it through that first holiday, and all the ones that followed became easier. That day required me to rewrite the holiday menu page and my expectations around them.

Although I missed my daughter when she was with her father, I began to enjoy my quiet, alone time and channeled my energy into my health and well-being. I had been physically active and, at times, competitive since the age of 17, but stretching and breathwork were not part of my wellness routine. I was introduced to yoga. Yoga and I did not have a friendly relationship at first. I watched the other 30 people in the hot yoga room with smiling angelic auras (which, I discovered, were glistening with sweat), perfectly sculpted bodies, and able to hold the poses. At the same time, I stumbled all over my mat, cursed the salty sweat in my eyes, and judged everyone in the room as egotistical as they stared at themselves in the mirror. I brought my competitive energy into the yoga room, intending to "beat this yoga" thing. In truth, it took courage to return to the hot yoga room again and again because yoga whipped my butt and my ego. Yoga showed me how to cultivate a deeper relationship with my body, my mind and my spirituality.

In my yoga practice, I observed how my mind would check in and check out. I could feel the tension and release of my body without having to talk about it as I did in therapy. I now know this to be a somatic practice (Soma = body) whereby I get to be in my body and allow the stress stored there for decades to breathe, find space, and move out. I soon grew to love my yoga practice and its healing qualities. For the first time, I was conscious and fully in my body, and I grew to welcome and crave the experience. There were days that I pushed my body to stay in poses beyond its capacity and judged myself for not being "good enough" despite being a trained athlete, and then I would soften and forgive myself for my perceived imperfections. Overall, yoga was a life-changing and life-teaching experience. While meditation was an amazing practice to slow down, observe and calm my mind while becoming a witness to life itself, yoga was my opportunity to deepen my relationship with my body. Gratefully, yoga gave me the space to release much of my undischarged energy and tension from a lifetime of being disconnected and dissociated from my body. There were days where my practice ended in tears for no known reason and practices that took me to quiet places within my breath. I could lean into not attaching to the appearance of the pose and learn to feel the pose and its gift in each moment.

With each bead of sweat dripping from my body, I observed myself releasing the tension, the drama, the fears, and the barriers of my heart. I began to deepen my self-inquiry. How could I begin to soften the walls that protected the caves of my heart? I began to fall in love... in love with myself and with my life. I saw the patterns of life that had to play out the way they did because of the menu I was served. I sent compassion to all of it, the beautiful, put-together Diana and the ridiculously messy one, now dripping with sweat. I felt my heart begin to crack open and allowed some light to come in. As the light came in, light reverberated outward. The edges of my heart were softening, and I let others see me in my messiness. Yoga taught me to make vulnerability a daily practice. On my mat, I practiced being in connection with all that showed up, and off the mat, I found my way to a novel experience of being in a community.

I made friends. Real friends. Deep, meaningful relationships for the first time. To be a friend, I learned to be vulnerable and share parts of my life that I had kept secret my entire life. I made time for these new friends and enjoyed our REAL talks about REAL life. I began to remove my emotional and physical masks (because one cannot wear makeup in hot yoga without the makeup melting). The more I kept it off, the more authentic I became. I shared my inner world. I shared my fears. I shared my joys and my dreams for life. And, each share was equally received as I had begun to be part of a community for the first time in my life.

The courage to be authentic allowed me to find my way into a community of people who received all of me and loved me. I learned to create and nurture the tribes of sisters. I would often be the one to gather them, and in their presence, I found myself deeply relaxed.

I remember hearing a story about an actor doing a Ted Talk. Someone in the audience asked him, "Why do people love you so much?" His response:

"Because I let them."

As I found the courage to allow my masks to come off, my heart softened, and I began to let others love me.

This is when I met my first real love, Dan, who would be my partner for the next 15 years, through the greatest and most ecstatic moments and the most profound and most painful season of my adult life.

People who witnessed the inception of our relationship would reflect on how, over a few weeks, our yoga mats started to find their way closer to each other. One day, I invited him to go skiing and started crushing on him. We did partner yoga together and went for long walks. Then, one night he came over to 'teach me the guitar,' and we talked for 10 hours. We were inseparable from that day onward. He was 12 years younger than me but had wisdom and maturity beyond his years. Although the age difference would remain a source of insecurity for me for most of our relationship, we were well-matched. We practiced yoga together, we cooked and watched movies together, and we made love often. I was delighted by his ability to express his emotional ranges. He became a good friend to my daughter as she effortlessly welcomed him into our family bubble. His profession was a firefighter, and I loved the contrast between his gentle nature at home and his commanding presence at work. Whenever I needed him, he was always there. He was my best friend.

The day he told me he loved me, it was through a text message soon after we started dating. No one had told me that before except my first husband, once, on our wedding day, in his vows. Stunned, I slid down the wall to my knees and didn't know how to respond or what to do. I was 39 years old and paralyzed by the potential of love. I was overcome by fear. In my world, love hurts. I sat on the floor for a long time, curled into a ball, rocking back and forth. I asked myself, could I trust love? Could I not only open my heart but keep it open? I didn't have a healthy imprint of a loving relationship and didn't know if I could trust myself and my heart to this gentle man. The truth was, I loved him as well and would need to find my brave heart to allow him to love me fully. And I practiced this for many years. It was a mature and unconditional love. I chose to have the courage to receive and feel love for the first time in my life.

I loved this part of my life and the love story we created, resulting in our marriage and the blessing of our beautiful son. I courageously practiced keeping my heart open to give and receive, being a patient and loving parent, and, for many years, living a dream life that included many laugh-filled moments.

I welcomed courage on my menu to keep my heart open and to receive love. The courage to take financial risks and open up my own businesses. The courage to step onto stages in front of 100s of people and teach from my place of truth. For many years that followed, I remembered the encouragement from Jesus "courage is inside you." Almost 2 decades later, through an unexpected life transition, I walked away from everything familiar in my world and moved across Canada. During my travels to my new home, my daughter set up my

WIFI, and she chose the password. When I called her to ask for the password, I was reminded that my courage was not just for me but for the settled imprint that I got to leave with my children. The password that she set up for me? "I AM BRAVE." Bravery now appears on my menu with permanent ink.

Re-alignment Steps:

1. Ask your heart what it needs to open to life and love, and where you can step into your divine courage, knowing it is in you? If you close your eyes and ask, *where is my courage? Where can you feel it?*

2. *Where have you been courageous in your life before? What hard things have you already done?* Knowing you have already done hard things, take a deep breath and trust you've got this too. You have survived 100% of the hard moments of your life.

3. *What is your imprint of love? Do you recall the first time you heard the words "I love you?"* and were you the one speaking or hearing those beautiful words.

4. Write your epitaph as if your family and friends are reading it at your celebration of life. *What do you want them to say?* Use that as your guideline to live your life today and each day.

5. *If you knew you were to die tomorrow, what dreams or longings remain inside you?* Today, take a step toward those things.

6. Be careful what you ask for and how you ask for things in life. There are many times that I manifested something clearly and received it through a painful experience. For example, if I ask for courage, I may have to lose everything to cultivate my courage to get up when life has fallen apart. Today, when I pray for something, I include the following *in the highest and the best for all involved and that no one is hurt in the making of this manifestation.*

Chapter 6

The Waves of Life

*Your experiences do not define you; they
inform you and can catapult you to your
deepest purpose.*

Over the next few years, I continued to practice yoga
daily, became a certified Yoga instructor, and began
teaching it. I loved teaching with themes, making the classes
physically and energetically transformational, and planting
seeds to awaken hearts and alter conditionings. Exploring
my childhood conditioning was something that I turned to
daily. A wise teacher told me that freedom was only possible
when we were free of our conditioning. When I taught yoga,
I moved in a flow of ease and grace, free of conditioning. I
was beginning to be in a relationship with the parts of me
that had been hidden. The parts of me were creative, free,
courageous, wanting to live life on my terms and curious
about what those terms might be.

Dan and I talked about opening up a hot yoga studio. I
knew something was calling me to this part of my life with
a powerful whisper. I was being asked to share my truth, my

heart, and love through my teachings. It all seemed exciting and possible when I began this journey of entrepreneurship. We decided to build 2 new studios.

Initially, I got caught up in design, marketing, sales systems, and schedules. It was exciting. To make it all work, we agreed that I would resign from my school board job and use part of the cash payout of my retirement funds to build out the structures. The rest (several $100,000s) would go into a Locked-in Retirement Account (LIRA), which was self-directed, meaning I could invest it anywhere I chose. My husband wanted to invest it in our "friend's" financial business, and I saw no reason to question the legitimacy of the business, the friend's credentials, or my husband's presumably informed choices.

When I recall that day, I know my body was telling me something was wrong. It was not a clear "yes" for me; here was the people pleaser coming out again, and she overrode my feeling of nausea. I signed the paperwork and transferred most of my retirement income to this business. I didn't really understand the transaction (which, it turns out, was illegal), nor did I ask the right questions. I trusted my husband's decision. I trusted these friends. I didn't trust myself or my body telling me something was wrong.

Our Yoga studio was called Inspire Yoga. On the first day of operations, we had a large open house with a ribbon-cutting ceremony and media coverage. We had a lineup out the door (truly, people had been trying to line up for weeks once they found out what the business was going to be). I kept hearing, "if you build it, they will come." We made $40,000 that first day and witnessed an amazing, loving community begin to form. It was magical. I knew my dharma was to build heart-centered communities; it took little effort to do so. I worked around my kids' schedules, taught a few classes a week, and worked late into the evenings planning workshops, doing marketing, and all the behind-the-scenes work of running a business. Within a few months, I began a Yoga Teacher Training Academy. I took small groups through deep-dive personal development journeys disguised as Yoga and was honored to witness my students transform before my eyes and fall in love with themselves and each other. I was called the "Love Architect." Through it all, I was fortunate to practice yoga, meditation, and breathwork daily. I felt privileged and extremely grateful. I was now a Lululemon™ Ambassador, and I taught classes of over 100 people at times and, with each class, weaved spiritual and life coaching into the asanas (postures) to help empower people. My students loved that perspective. It was always authentic as I taught what I needed to learn each day. I pulsated between feeling content and grateful and trying to release the fear and tension of being a business owner with the responsibilities that came with it.

We were now living in a beautiful cul-de-sac large home with wild and wonderful gardens, a relaxed environment, and a community that filled my soul. I was content with the two studios, and life was fulfilling for the first 2 years.

Eventually, the studio expenses became financially overwhelming, and my husband's solution to that problem was to quit his firefighter job to access his retirement funds and open studios # 3 and #4 to increase our cash flow and build an Inspire Yoga empire. Everything in my body yelled, "No, don't feed the (spiritual) ego!" But, once again, I didn't listen to myself. My people pleaser went along with that decision. One of the studios was secured with a second mortgage on our home which meant that we were now putting our children's home at risk. The other to our investment properties. We borrowed money from everyone we knew to help us out. I take full responsibility today as I had the power to say "no" but didn't. My people pleaser came out to play, and she cost me everything I had worked my entire life to secure. We had now been in business only 2 years and were in deep trouble. And, to top it off, we partnered with a reputable and very wealthy woman who not only made us empty promises for one of the studios but betrayed us and ended up having claim to our family home through our business partnership (again, taking full responsibility for those decisions).

Within 6 months, the sacred doors of each studio closed, one at a time. It was like a portal to my heart closing each time. I dove into a deep pool of fight/flight survival responses and could barely catch my breath some days. I knew that response well, and during these months, I found myself back in old patterns. I forgot to breathe. I forgot to meditate. I forgot to practice yoga. As the studios were attached to our personal assets, I knew it would be weeks before I would have to walk away from everything we owned. I didn't know how I would pay any of my house bills. I had little funds to buy food. And there was this million-dollar massive debt that I tried to ignore. I had to remind myself to keep breathing, but, more often than not, I completely forgot. There came a time when the power was turned off in one of the largest studios, and we had to teach outside in the park. We were unable to pay our contractor teachers, and they slowly walked away. One at a time, the studios began to close, one in the middle of the night because my shame would not allow me to face my clients. I chose the timing for the other studio doors to close so that I could face my community and not hide in shame. It was hard. It was necessary. It was integrity. Soon, there was only one studio left. The original one. Unable to pay the teachers, we taught all the classes while knowing that the financial impact of the other studios closing was now inching close to our familial home.

Within weeks, we could not pay our own bills, and our gas was turned off at home. Without hot water or heat. I encouraged my 15-year-old daughter those days to stay at her father's home as much as possible, embarrassed to explain why our utilities were turned off in our beautiful 3000 sq foot home. I was now living in constant tension that things would get worse, and they did.

I was waiting, constantly and anxiously, for the inevitable loss of everything that I had built my entire life. I would avoid opening mail in fear that it was another notice of an unpaid utility bill and another service would be cut off. One night, while making love with my husband, a brief release from our constant tension, I broke into deep sobbing tears as the fear in my mind was bigger than the desire to stay in my body. There were days that I wanted to check out of my life, leave this body and planet, and begin to plan my escape. The only thing that kept me here was the thought of my children growing up without a mother. I was in deep pain and began disconnecting from my spiritual practices. I lost faith in life itself.

Eventually, we had to surrender our beautiful home,

investment properties, and vehicles. We had one little investment property that we call "the cottage." It was a tiny 100-year-old cottage with a peaceful conservation property that overlooked a large river, and we had rented it out to mostly yoga teachers. When it seemed that was our only place to land, one of my friends who had lived there told me, "it will be a healing space for you." I couldn't see it at the time. I was full of resentment and anger over this move. I had to get rid of most of our furniture and belongings as there was very little space for us, let alone our stuff. My husband spent the first summer knocking down walls, removing all the mold and mice feces, and trying to patch up the roof. Over the years, we had snakes, raccoons, stoats, and thousands of mice as unwelcome guests. It was in such bad shape that, when we had to file an inevitable bankruptcy, the bank did not want to touch it as it was appraised below the value of the little mortgage. We went from a 3000 sq ft beautiful home in a lovely subdivision to this tiny shack (and I can hear the ridiculousness of that statement as I know many millions of people are homeless, and I had a home). We moved our minimal personal belongings, one truckload at a time to this little cottage and tried to pick up the pieces of our unsettled life. My son changed schools, and at age 7, we convinced him this was for the better even though we didn't believe it (we did our best to shelter him from how tough things were). My daughter, now 16, tried to convince me that it would be a good move, that we didn't need all the stuff (what a teacher). Dan began to build bedrooms for us in the basement with whatever recycled material he could find discarded from construction sites, as we could not afford the material to do renovations. We moved into the "cottage" in the summer of 2013 while clutching... no... gripping with white-knuckled fists... our one remaining studio. Eventually, we had to let go of the grip, and it slipped away.

When the last studio closed on Oct. 24, 2013, I felt my world collapse. I received a phone call at 6 am from one of my teachers that the studio locks had been changed. I wanted to go into hiding. I had let down all my students, staff, and the contract teachers who had been my friends. I felt immense responsibility to our teachers, members, and community. I never considered my family's needs on that day. My mind was spinning. I was overtaken by shame and fear. What would people think? How could we reimburse membership fees? Where could we find $10,000 to reopen our doors? The familiar heavy and dark cloak of shame took over. I knew that cloak, and it willed me to pack up, move away and never return. I was spinning out of control and in complete fear. I rushed to the studio to place a messy handwritten sign on the door: "We are working with the landlords to reopen the doors for you, our community. Thank you for your patience" and remembered a tap on my door 2 nights prior and a visitor that would knock some sense into me.

The tap on the door on the cold Tuesday evening was unexpected. No one knew where we lived. I was home alone with my son, and we simply never had company as I was so embarrassed by this little shack. When I answered the door, a strange man dressed impeccably introduced himself as "John." He was a neighbor who lived at the top of the valley in one of the mansions that overlooked our little shack. He wanted to rent a space in our driveway while his driveway was being refinished. I found it funny that he came to us randomly as there were neighbors much closer to him, and he had to walk about 10 minutes to get to our driveway. Still, I offered him our driveway, free, as a neighborly gesture. I knew this man was the owner of a series of gyms that had closed, and there was scandal around their closure, but I didn't pry. He thanked me, and I didn't see his car for a few days. Until that morning when I got the call that the locks had been changed.

I opened the curtains that morning and "John's" car was there. The one and only day that he parked in our driveway was that morning when I was startled out of sleep to be told the studio locks had been changed. I left a note on his windshield: "John, our business was closed today, and I don't know what to do; I wonder if you could please call me, I need help." Later that day, John called me. We met at 6 am the next morning in his home gym and while he worked out and I briefed him on our business situation and personal financial situation, he looked at me firmly and said, "you have no business worrying about the studio and trying to reopen it while your family and personal home are in crisis. Move on." This was a hard realization, but I knew he was right. To this day, I recognize that John was an angel, sent to give us a firm kick and remind me where I need to put my priorities. My family was at risk of being homeless, and I was trying to revive a hopeless business. I knew I had to put my own oxygen mask on first.

Three months later, we filed bankruptcy as I sat slouched in my chair, shamefully gazing at the amount of debt that I had acquired and unsure how I would come through this season. This dark monster of shame was dangerously close and very personal now, more than ever, in my life. Some days, that darkness almost took my life. I was tired of sitting in the darkness, of feeling sucked back in each time I was able to come up and gasp for air. I oscillated between the depth of drowning and wanting to swim for my life, and my yoga studies, ultimately, became my lifeline.

In yoga philosophy, there is a concept called Spanda. Spanda is the understanding that the divine flow of life goes in waves, up and down, around and into dark tunnels that eventually give way to light. Once I was able to come up for a breath, I remembered that concept, and it became my lifeline. The more I remembered this theory, the more I could feel myself being able to strap on my metaphoric surfboard, ride the plunging wave crash, and have faith that I would find my way through the wave eventually, even if I could not see the shore.

Reflecting on that hard season of my life, I can feel the pain and meet it with compassion for that younger part of me who was in a deep survival state doing all that she could for her family's survival. Breathing through all the fear when she remembered to breathe. Gasping for air when breath was hard to access. Carrying the shame every day as a heavy shackle and still showing up for life, for her family, and for her work. I can hug that younger version of me today and feel her release some of that burden. She got up every day, opened the blinds, and said "it is today," with a wilful hope in her voice. The younger version who meets the mature ME today and is reminded that I am not defined by my situations in life. That I am friggin resilient. That I have survived 100% of the wave crashes of that season and of life.

Spanda, riding out the ups and downs of life, rooted in faith, became an important ingredient on my menu.

Re-alignment Steps:

1. Sometimes (or often), we have little control over life. What we can control is our responses to life. If you can commit to a daily spiritual practice, when the waves of Spanda crash down, you will have some tools to navigate without drowning and tools to come up for air. Find your spiritual practice and commit to that practice daily (meditation, breath-work, yoga, prayer).

2. Be willing to talk about your shame. One of the problems that I experienced was that the heaviness of my shame prevented me from reaching out to others for support or being willing to talk about it. Keeping the shame quiet, hidden, and in the dark spaces of your life makes it grow and intensify. Alternatively, shame cannot survive being spoken. Once I was through this dark season, I began to speak and write about it. The first few times were hugely uncomfortable, met with wiggles in my seat and avoidant eye contact. In time, I became more comfortable relating these difficult times of my life, giving them a voice, and allowing the shame to be in the light. When shame is spoken, it is given light and permission to dissolve. As I shared, many people would come up to me after a speech, class, or event and say, "just like me, and I've never told anyone." Our society conditions us not to talk about the difficult and challenging

moments, but we have an opportunity to change that limiting belief, knowing it is the pathway to healing when we find the courage to talk about our dark experiences. This is the new "Just Like Me" movement.

3. I use a mantra often from an Australian Aboriginal tribe to remember that this moment is not forever. I say, "It is today." And each day, I get to start anew. Remembering that today will not last forever and the waves will continue to flow allowed me to get up each day. And then, it is up to me to make the changes, choices, and actions that allow tomorrow to be different.

4. Notice your communication. When I was in deep fear and shame, my communication was painfully negative. I would use words like "never, worry, can't." My posture reflected defeat, and it was difficult for me to see any light in the tunnel of darkness. A simple technique that I share with my clients is to change your "worry" to "wonder." Worry is a word that stimulates stress response in your neurobiology, and you start to see more things to worry about. If you can, simply remove the word "worry" ("I'm worried that I won't have enough money, I'm worried that the kids might not arrive safely, I'm worried that I'll be alone for the rest of my life..etc"). Replace each of the "worry" with "wonder," and you begin to open a portal to your brain that ignites possibilities and

creativity. You can begin to see solutions when you are not flooded with stress in your body (which prevents creativity and feelings of contentment and connectedness).

Chapter 7

Breathe and Everything Changes

When all else fails, turn toward your
breath and trust it to transform the
experience of your life.

Several months later, we were settled into the little "cottage" and trying to figure out how to survive. With the studios closed, neither of us working, and no money in the bank, we were surviving day to day in deep fight-and-flight mode, unsure of how to move forward.

It was a cold and dreary Sunday morning in December. The sky was grey, the clouds lingering low above my head. I was shivering, and my tears were beginning to freeze. *Breathe,* I kept repeating. *Breathe, and everything changes.* But nothing changed. I couldn't find my breath. I was gasping for air. I paced back and forth in the muddy field. After having now lost the 4 businesses, my retirement income, my investment properties, my cars, and my home, and having just filed for personal bankruptcy, I had no money to pay for gas or food, let alone pay my bills for the little "cottage" home that the bank allowed us to keep. It was no longer animal-infested and mold contaminated, but the construction was still fully unfinished. Unfortunately, we could not pay the mortgage and received a notification from the Sheriff that we were in default on our mortgage payments again. The notice indicated they could come any time, repossess the home, and put us out on the street.

When we invested my retirement income in our 'friend's' business, I was told that those funds would be transferred to a Locked-in Retirement Account called a LIRA, and, typically, one cannot access these funds. This investment came with the promise that our funds would have enormous growth and, in exchange, we would be able to borrow funds at a low-interest rate to help us keep the studios afloat should we need money. With the studios closed and no income, no savings, and the risk of losing our only roof, I needed those funds to keep us alive.

I began the process of applying to the Ontario Securities Commission to access my LIRA due to "Financial Hardship" (the only way to withdraw funds from this retirement account). With shame, grief, and through many tears, I explained how I was in this situation and why I needed the money. It took weeks of documentation, waiting, and wondering when I finally received the approval in the mail to access my LIRA; I took a big exhale. It was a big win. I would get my money, pay back my overdue mortgage, and have some money left to finish the renovations on the home and get some food.

Unfortunately, I found out my "friend" was banned from doing financial business in the province where we lived due to previous illegal activity, and had registered his business in a different province in Canada. The order to release my funds was not recognized in that province, and they could not honor this request. No matter who I called, cried to, and begged, I could not access my funds. There was nothing that anyone could do about it. So, on that Sunday morning, in total despair and gasping for breath, I did the only thing that I could do... I called his wife, a long-time friend of mine, and begged for her help.

"We need money. I am desperate. I feel hopeless. I don't know what to do. We have been friends for many years and gave you a job when you needed one. Please, talk to your partner and tell him he has to give us some money. Anything. I'm begging you. We have nowhere to go. No money coming in. You have to do something. " The phone was silent. My sobs turned to yelling. I was shaking. I felt terror. I had spent my life building my safe home, investments, and retirement income. And now, it was all gone. My businesses gone. My friends gone. I shouted, desperately trying not to let it sink in. "I trusted you. I trusted your partner. You both betrayed me; help me." My survival was at her mercy.

Within 2 days, they transferred me $10,000. It was just enough at that time to catch up on our mortgage and fill our fridge (the rest of my investment was never to be seen). I realized how little I had been breathing until that moment. That pivotal moment showed me how unconscious I had been for the last several months and what I had been missing. My breath. I had not been breathing. I had not been practicing yoga. I had not been practicing regular gratitude. I had not been practicing faith. This little bit of money felt like a massive win, and I was able to discharge some of the tension that I had been carrying in my nervous system for the time being.

Soon, I returned to my daily yoga practice, meditation, prayer, and breathwork. I began to teach a few yoga classes in gyms, schools, and parks. Within a few weeks, I received a phone call from my previous school board asking if I would consider returning to work there. I immediately said yes. As I found my way back to my breath and practice, I saw possibilities awaken in my life. Some days I would come home and curse the decrepit home we lived in, and in the next breath, I would gratefully thank the Universe for giving me a roof even if it leaked.

I returned to my gratitude practice waking up each morning saying, "thank you, thank you, thank you." *Thank you for my health and my family. Thank you for being able to serve these deserving nonverbal children as a Speech-Language Pathologist. Thank you for allowing me to teach yoga. Thank you for being able to put food on the table. Thank you for giving me a roof over my head when many do not have one.* Every morning I would reset with "It is today. Thank you for my breath."

I made it through that dark winter, and as I welcomed spring, I realized what a gem of a property I was sitting on. Although it was a tiny cottage in the city, it was on a conservation lot with a river in the backyard. I took long walks and pauses by the river. I found myself healing in that space as I did what I could to beautify the gardens, a symbol of hope with each new perennial. I took a few local stay-cations with family and friends that summer, bringing back some play into my children's and my life. I recognized how long I had been without play, and my nervous system longed to feel better.

At the end of the summer, I took stock of my cottage. My husband tried his best to fix the house, but little was finished because of his overwhelm. The roof was repaired and no longer leaked; however, many of the ceilings and walls were missing drywall and were covered only with insulation and a vapor barrier. Elephant tusks of spray foam were coming out of every seam of the walls. The stairs were a fall risk without banisters. The kitchen counter was a piece of plywood, and the rest was pieced together with whatever we could find at the time from dumps, construction sites, and recycled building stores. There was a part of me that was proud that we reused EVERYTHING to build the house and a part of me that craved to see it finished.

As my hope and motivation grew, so did my capacity to co-create my reality. I began to look at casting calls for various HGTV home renovation shows. Most of them required a significant financial contribution from the homeowner, and I was not in a position to apply to those shows. There was one that got my attention. It was called "I Wrecked my House" and required no monetary input. I watched the pilot's episode, which included 4 homes that were "wrecked" by the homeowner. Halfway through the show, one home was featured as the "winning" home that received a $50,000 renovation. I put in an application.

A few days later, I received an email from the production assistant to submit a video. I had to tell my husband that I had filled out a casting submission for that show, and he would be required to admit he "wrecked our house." He was not impressed but played along. I put it out of my mind until, later in the fall, I was driving home from work and stopped at a coffee shop to wait out the traffic and enjoy a tea. While waiting for my tea, I noticed a few missed phone calls from an unknown number. The calls were incessant, so I decided to answer. The person at the other end introduced himself as the show's producer and announced that our family and home had been selected. I was pleased that they had chosen us, but in the back of my mind was telling myself not to get too excited as I only had a 25% chance of receiving the renovation.

As he continued to talk, I heard him say that I would have to sign a contract, vacate the premises for a week, and meet with production staff within a few weeks. I stopped him and asked, "what are you telling me?" He replied, "you are getting the $50,000 renovation." I felt my tears fall as I laughed out loud and jumped up and down in the coffee shop. We won. Remember, I am a powerful manifestor (just like you).

We met with the production staff and designers and then moved out for a week. We recorded some video footage and "B" roll at a local hotel and waited in anticipation for the "reveal" day. Finally, one week later, we were getting miked up in the trailer and filmed walking down the street. I felt my breath quickening while my body shook from the cold and impatient anticipation. I approached the door. I slowly turned the handle. I unhurriedly stepped inside. I paused. I gasped. I relaxed my shoulders and felt gentle and grateful tears forming.

It was perfect.

The drywall was all finished. The ceilings edged in beautiful crown molding. The kitchen was simple and elegantly complete. And, they used our own reclaimed wood for feature walls and mantels. They replaced our worn-out furniture with beautiful new pieces custom-made for our space. They had turned my shabby little cottage into a beautiful, warm, loving home.

In that moment, I found my first full breath in over a year as my tears kissed my cheeks.

I remembered in that season the power of my relationship to my breath with gratitude, which allowed me to re-align through this difficult time and opened me up to the possibilities of transforming a tattered and tired broken house into my loving home. In truth, the transformation of my home was symbolic of my life. This difficult season showed me the power that I have when I awaken to my true co-creative skills of manifestation and a deep practice of acknowledging how powerful the breath is in each moment.

The powerful author, Ekort Tollee says:

"One breath is an entire meditation."

One breath can change your entire neurophysiology. Alter the chemicals that are discharged in your body and bring you back to the present moment. Today I know this to be the truth, and today, I remember to:

Breathe, and Everything Changes.

It took me a long season to be able to ride the wave cycles and not be consumed and stuck in the wave. Once I could change my perspective by seeing the beauty around me in that little cottage, practicing gratitude, and remembering Spanda, I began to see beauty all around me and call in a more peace-filled presence. That was the gateway to slow down the wave cycles and all the thoughts and fears that came with it. Then, I learned to enjoy the ride and see the light and possibilities with faith that would guide me through future seasons.

I added 3 qualities to my menu that season: breath, creation, and faith

Re-alignment Steps:

1. We often take our breath for granted. It is a life-giving gift, and our relationship to our breath can change EVERYTHING. When you take deep, slow, and conscious breaths (ie, you are aware of your breath), you begin to slow down the release of the stress neurochemicals that respond to hyperarousal (fight/flight) reactions (sympathetic nervous system) and begin to activate the parasympathetic nervous system (relaxation system). If you can add an audible sigh to your exhalation, you deepen your relaxation by toning the vagus nerve, which responds to sound, humming, and sighing.

2. Your nervous system is the communication channel between the body and the brain. When you activate conscious breathing, you can begin to soften the kinks in your nervous system, allowing a freer communication channel between your body and your brain. Breathe in and out gently. It's not woo-woo.. it's science.

3. Here are a few Breathing techniques to relax your sympathetic nervous system. Try them on and see which one works best for you. The wonderful thing about breath work is that it is free, can be done anytime, and requires no equipment for guided breathing practices. As you breathe, pause in the space between the inhales and exhales.

- Ujjayi Breath is the breath of yoga. It is a steady inhalation through your nose and out through your nostrils. It requires a slight constriction through the back of the throat so you can smooth out your breath and allow an audible quality to your breath that sounds like "the ocean" and feels like you are trying to fog up an imaginary mirror through your nose. Repeat 10 times with equal inhales and exhales.
- Square breathing: Inhale through your nose for a count of 4. Hold for a count of 4. Exhale for a count of 4 through your mouth. Hold for a count of 4. Repeat 10 times.
- Alternate Nostril Breathing: pinch your nostrils with your thumb and index finger (in true yoga style, it is the ring finger and the thumb while the index finger and the middle finger rest on your middle forehead or 'third eye,' find a placement that works for you). Pinch your right nostril closed and inhale through your left, pause, pinch your left nostril closed, open your right, and exhale through your right nostril. Keep your left nostril closed. Inhale through your right nostril. Pinch your right nostril closed and exhale through the left. Repeat for a count of 10-20 rounds of breathing.
- 3 part breathing: lying down, place one hand on your belly and one hand on your chest. Inhale ⅓ of your breath to fill your belly (like you are

inflating a balloon), and pause. Inhale another ⅓ to fill up your chest area, and pause. Inhale the final ⅓ to fill up the space between your collarbones and up to your throat. Gently exhale through your mouth from top to bottom. Repeat for 10 rounds.

4. If you find yourself in a collapsed or depressed state, you actually need more arousing breath and movement to arouse your nervous system. One practice that helps to stimulate awakening in your body is Kapalabhati breathing:

Inhale and exhale all the air in your lungs. Inhale halfway, then do gentle and quick exhales as you snap your belly in. The inhales take care of themselves. Repeat for 30 breaths, then take a deep inhale. Repeat.

Other ways to stimulate your nervous system are to move your body, dance, walk briskly, go outside, and feel the rain, the wind, the coolness, or the sun on your skin. Brush your skin gently with a nylon brush or gently tap your body with your hands. All these will help you to come back into your body.

5. What you focus on expands. This is science-based. It happens through a little part of the brain called the Reticular Activating System (RAS), which looks for confirmation of whatever you focus on to show you more of THAT. So if you are focused

on presence, love, and gratitude, you will see more of that. If you focus on suffering and lack, you will see that. This is essentially the brain practicing the law of attraction. I often focused on my pain and felt so overwhelmed by my suffering.

When I began to focus on gratitude, I found more things to be grateful for. Begin each morning with a simple gratitude prayer (mine is simply "thank you, thank you, thank you."). Then, write in a gratitude journal at the end of each day. This will encourage you to look for things to be grateful for throughout the day, knowing you will write these down. The RAS now becomes your gratitude friend showing you all the millions of things that you might have to be grateful for today.

Chapter 8

Breaking the Silence

*It is in the arena of life that we get confronted with
our greatest disowned parts, and our work is to love
those parts of ourselves to experience and reclaim
our wholeness.*

I stepped into deep co-creation for the years that followed.
I became aware of my responsibility in my life, the power of
my manifestation, and becoming clear about the parts of me
that were ready for deeper healing. I began to follow the
breadcrumbs of my life to see how I had manifested some of
the pain that I received by not being clear, not using my voice,
and letting fear guide me. After doing therapy, meditation,
energy work, and reading every book on childhood healing while practicing mindfulness and studying my
mindset, I decided I was ready to go deep into my
unconscious. I had read Debbie Ford's book, *The Secret of the
Shadows*, 15 years earlier but was not yet ready to confront
the deepest parts of myself that were in hiding and still sat in
my spiritual ego of wanting to feel good, light, and bright. It
was time to get messy.

As our menus are formed and the unconscious (below the

surface of our awareness) is programmed, we learn to UNbe-come what we were born to be (divine miracles). Usually, most people then begin striving for perceived perfection that creates a fragmented or false self. Perfection often motivates these false selves: achieve perfect grades, find the perfect partner, buy the perfect house/car/clothes, and climb up the perfect corporate ladder. Society is also really good at supporting those false beliefs: Success looks this way, aging looks this way, babies must behave this way, and on it goes.

Along that conditioned journey, we begin to lose touch with our own truth; we begin to disconnect from our authen-ticity. And so the seeds are planted to become who you are taught to be from a very early age. The Ego Identification is formed and becomes your belief about who you are.

The problem with inflated ego identification is it needs to create strong masks for survival in this culture of perfection. It creates masks to hide all the fears that you are not enough: Not pretty enough, not smart enough, not thin enough, not accomplished enough. And soon, this ego identity, which is always rooted in something being wrong with you, begins to make choices that counter your natural and true SELF. Your true identity is put aside so that you can fit in the world. Be accepted. And be loved. This means that your authentic truth, expression, and heart is needing to conform and shapeshift to feel safe in the world. Your truth now is masked using very strong defensive mechanisms and compensating strategies that keep you 'safe' in each moment: a closed heart, the need to be right, playing roles that you believe others want you to play, avoiding feeling, a strong desire to control your environment, intellectualizing everything (like overtalking to avoid feeling) and even using humor to deflect discomfort. Remember my Ice Queen? She was birthed through the need to be seen as perfect, to protect being hurt when she expressed her truth. She had to close her heart to live in the world... for a time.

As we begin to put on our masks, it takes effort to keep them there. Your true self hides in fear that the world will not love the real parts of you, the parts with slight imperfections on your face, body, or bank account. The parts that are unsure, tense, anxious, and in fear of being recognized as an imposter. How does this all begin? As we reviewed in Chapter 4, it begins by expecting your children to be perfect little creatures. Compliant, quiet, and in control all the time. Hence we place these values on the menu of our little ones, and they become adults who have no idea who they are, what they want, and how to be authentic in the world. Even if abuse was not your norm, there are subtle ways that parents with the best of intentions manipulate children to become perfect little beings through typical parenting reactions. And I say that lovingly because they don't know better.

The imprints (positive and hurtful, rules and beliefs, judgments and stress responses) left on children become powerful impressions that determine their menu and how they view the world. They become inner disturbances that require a lot of energy, and we try to ignore them—until we can't anymore.

Without shining a light on the menu and the unconscious programming and disturbances, these will eventually be passed on to future generations. And the cycle continues until, one day, one of these children; perhaps it is you today, says, "STOP." I will no longer unconsciously impress these beliefs, reactions, disturbances, and stress patterns onto the menu

of my life, relationships, children, and world. This is the day
you get to dive deep into the study of your life, including
your unconscious. Until then, the menus will be running
your life, and you will not be aware of the impact it is having
on you and those around you because it is below the level of
awareness, or Unconscious. The unconscious holds the deep
unprocessed pieces of our past and memories. These thoughts
and feelings can manifest in everyday life and in unexpected
situations, often caused by a trigger (see trigger tracking at
the end of this chapter).

Let's review: the unconscious programming that you
received prior to age 7 largely determines 90% of the way you
engage with life. Your operating system informs and controls
every experience you have in your relationships, with yourself
and others. Your menu deeply influences it, and until you cast
a light on it, it remains unseen. This is the birthing process
for your shadows, the parts of yourself that are unseen and
kept in the dark.

The Shadow Self was first coined by Carl Jung in the 20th
Century. He describes the Shadow as "that hidden, repressed,
for the most part, inferior and guilt-laden personality whose
ultimate ramifications reach back into the realm of our animal
ancestors and so comprise the whole historical aspect of the
unconscious." It is, essentially, the unconscious parts of the
personality that our ego doesn't want to identify or claim.
Some call them our disowned parts that we would not want
the world to see. They hide in our blind spots.

Imagine that the shadows are those parts that have not
seen the light of day because they are so hidden. As Debbie
Ford referenced in the title of her book, The Secret of the

Shadow, they are the deep dark secrets that have remained a secret for most people most of their lives. They are so secret that we don't realize they exist. And, not only do they exist, they are part of the rich fabric of our being that once rejected, leads us to be fragmented and feel like something does not belong when the truth is something is missing. The parts of you that hold wisdom, truth, richness, and the juice of life.

Until we recognize, reclaim and integrate or fall in love with our shadows, we will continue to feel incomplete in life and believe something is wrong with us.

I saw the misalignment in who I was, who I wanted to be, and the division between the two. I made a commitment to myself that if I wanted to change my life, it was up to me. And it would begin right now because nothing changes until something changes. I continued to explore the menu of my life, especially the pages that were hard to read or in invisible ink. I studied 'shadow work' and did 'shadow practices.' There were so many ingredients in my menu that were rooted in shame, guilt, and fear, which contributed to and came from the powerlessness of silence that I experienced as a child.

In order to reclaim all parts of myself, including my shadows, and rewrite these uncomfortable parts of my menu, I needed to cultivate a welcoming and compassionate relationship with all of my feelings. I decided that if I longed to find my voice, express myself, and reclaim my wholeness I had to have the courage to become intimate with all parts of me. And I found JOY in it all.

Joy is not a sensation or a feeling. Joy is simply the umbrella under which all emotional ranges rest when in present-moment awareness. Happiness, jealousy, anger, sadness, excitement, and fear. These are all labels that we give to the physiological sensations of our bodies. When each of these emotions can be witnessed without making them wrong, we are in present moment or joy. It is like you are stepping outside of yourself, noticing the sensations and the emotional ranges. I began to move into the sensations of my body to discern the emotional range that was willing to come through at this moment. I softened and allowed the sensations to come and go (remember Spanda?) and not attach to the thoughts or stories that I created around the sensation. It's not that I didn't feel, I actually felt more, but I didn't allow the feelings to define or impair me.

I learned there are no "bad" feelings, simply a range of emotional-energetic experiences that we have been taught are 'good' or 'bad' (through our menus), and suppressing any emotional range results in a reduction of the emotional-energetic range that we have the potential to experience in our lifetime and the creation of more shadows.

One shadow range that was deeply ignored and denied in me was the emotional range of anger. As a child, it was not safe to feel or express anger, and when I witnessed it from my father, it was a weaponized rage that sent me hiding under covers. I was familiar with the research that touching my anger was a required part of my shame release and would allow me to connect to my passion and my silenced voice. But I was terrified to experience this. What if I unleashed my anger, and it turned into a lifelong rage that could never be contained again?

My default response to anger was to shut it down, put on meditation music, and calm myself. After all, I am a Yogini with an unhealthy childhood imprint of anger. I knew, in theory, that not having access to rage or anger resulted in my being needy and a people pleaser, unable to state my boundaries (reference chapter 4) clearly. Accessing this emotional range would allow me to reclaim my silenced voice to release my shame and guilt, and use my passion to ignite my voice for good in the world. My mind saw this unfolding as it needed to. My body quivered at the idea.

I left Canada and took myself across the pond to the Netherlands to find a safe space to play with my shadow ranges. I did it on a gray day in Amsterdam during a Heart IQ™ circle. I touched not only my anger but my deep fury. I witnessed these expressions leave my body as messy, loud, primal sounds of uncontained rage that had been confined for decades. I don't know how long I was in that state, but once I returned to my present reality, I immediately felt the familiar shame. What did I do? Would I be shunned, kicked out, or judged? Instead, the strangers in my circle received my anger with love, encouragement, and celebration. I felt an immediate relaxation in my entire nervous system and spaciousness in my throat. At that moment, I felt my wholeness and completeness. My anger was not "bad" or "wrong." It was a necessary expression of what was bottled inside me, pushed to the basement of my emotional range, never to be revealed… until now. Having my anger lovingly witnessed normalized it and allowed me to take a deep exhale.

When I welcome the time to stop and feel all my emotions AND express them in a healthy manner as they arise, what comes out isn't scary anymore. It is clear, it is on purpose, and it is veiled with passion. And from that passion grew the increasing clarity that I was on the path toward reclaiming my voice. Touching the emotional ranges of anger allowed me to find my voice to express my excitement, joy, love, and gratitude.

In Sanskrit, wholeness is referred to as Purnatva. And we are always whole and complete; however, when we deny parts of ourselves (our shadows), we sever our wholeness. On this day, I reclaimed all parts of myself, knowing that there was nothing that did not belong. I decided that I was worthy of feeling and expressing myself fully and realized that anger channeled through the heart is simply my passion for life. In a world that is so fractured and unable to feel wholeness, I asked myself repeatedly: "How can I use this newfound passion for good in the world?" I fully believe that the problem in the world is not that we are angry; it is that we are not angry enough to make a difference, use our voice to express our passion, and make a change in the world. The question then remains: "what are you angry about enough to make a difference in the world?" And turn THAT into a passion and use your voice for THAT cause.

Within a year, I was invited to speak on a stage with The Global Changemakers™ sponsored by Mindvalley with a commitment to help entrepreneurs to become healthier in their emotional and energetic systems. I went on to co-create powerful communities through my Yoga Teacher Training program, helping people find and express their unique gifts and voices in service of something bigger in the world. I confidently began to offer my powerful teachings, merging the ancient teachings of yoga philosophy with current neuropsychology, shadow work, positive psychology, and mindset in coaching, education, healthcare, and corporations.

I was finally creating a life filled with purpose and passion and loving every moment that allowed me to use my voice for good in the world.

Re-alignment Steps:

1. Take time, daily, to sit in stillness and notice the sensations in your body. *What parts are warm, cold, tingly, tight, spacious?* Simply take the seat of the observer and notice without judgment.

2. Find a community to talk about your pain, shadows, and anger. You will hear me repeat this in this book: Men NEED men's groups, and women NEED Sister groups to hold the space for them to be witnessed in their pain and in the parts of themselves that were not welcomed. These are not groups that go out and gossip, bitch, drink or play sports. These are groups where you can sit in your truth and the pain of your truth and simply be acknowledged and held without anything needing to be fixed at that moment. The love you receive is the medicine when skillfully delivered. A shadow needs a light (community) to be seen. The light can be amplified in a community. Many people believe that nothing will change until they hit rock bottom and suppress everything. That becomes a toxic inner world that will leak into your relationships. Your parents may not have been able to encourage you to talk about what was bothering you, and you learned to keep quiet. As you mature and decide that you wish to do it differently, find a group that can hold all parts of you with love and compassion. PS: your partner is NOT that person. Your partner

cannot be expected to hold everything for you, your lover, friend, provider, protector, and all the roles you expect of them. Waking up and being willing to work through your shit means finding communities that can 1. Hold you accountable 2. Provide you with the space to express, and 3. Offer you unconditional love, no matter what you bring. Then, you cleanse those unprocessed emotions/expressions and bring the best part of yourself to your relationships.

3. Journal daily about your reactions vs. your responses in your daily interactions. A reaction is usually unconscious. Ask yourself, "where did that come from" and be tender with the part of you that brought that up. You are on a learning and healing journey (for life). Then, ask yourself what you need to be able to move toward a compassionate response versus reaction (e.g., maybe you are working too much and are overwhelmed and need to take planned breaks in your day. Or perhaps you need to talk to another about something you have been holding inside; we call these withholds and will talk about them more in the next few chapters).

4. A practice that I love to do is called Shadow Characterization. I write about my deepest shadow, the part of me that I never want to bring into the world or want others to know. I write down the qualities of that part of myself, all the ugliness,

bitterness, and fears. I write about the behaviors that this version of me, at her worse, projects into the world, and I draw a picture of her. As soon as I do that, I bring that unconscious part of me into my consciousness, the shadow into the light. Then I can imagine what it would be like to be her, even briefly, and what gifts she might offer in my life. For example, I have a shadow character called 'Wicked Wanda.' She is the part of me that is so fearful of being alone, on the streets, unkept, begging for love. She is old, ragged, and incredibly messy and doesn't care about anyone but herself. I can see her gift when I can love that part of me that can be messy, selfish, and attached to the wanting-more-in-life. The gift of Wicked Wanda is to motivate me to work, volunteer, and be responsible for my financial stability. She is the part of me that can be self-compassionate and understanding when I am tired and remind me to rest and that everything will be ok. She is also the part of me that remembers never to turn away from others struggling in their lives. She is truly a blessing. Now it's your turn. Write out the character traits that you never want the world to see. Indulge and go deeper into the discomfort.

5. As you track your reactions, notice when you blame others for how you feel. Be willing to take responsibility for your emotional states and feelings. It is so common to say, "she made me....

(angry, sad, frustrated) or "he always makes me feel… (angry, like a failure, unworthy). Instead, change your language to empowering communication "I feel….". As you own your feelings, you take back your power and begin to mature into self-responsibility, realizing that others are NOT responsible for your feelings. They simply might be the beautiful messenger and a catalyst for your inner experience that was hooked by their external trigger. The hook is in you, and you are responsible for that healing. A very responsible and mature communication practice is "in your presence I feel…" and state the sensation (the body experience rather than the emotional label, which can sound blaming).

6. Awareness is the key. If you find yourself constantly looking for your shadow, especially as the wounded shadow, it can become all-consuming and take away from your present experience of being in a relationship with others. There is such a thing as being addicted to healing and making trauma the primary character of your life story. That will always take you away from the present moment, where true healing occurs. Be aware of your constant narratives of what was done to you. Instead, be willing to feel with compassion what is present now that feels betrayed, hurt, abandoned, and love THAT. Be present to your innermost experiences in relation to life and allow the trigger that needs

to find you, find you. We do not heal the past by dwelling there but by living in the present. It is OUR sole responsibility to bring loving awareness there and see how we are making others responsible or trying to make them accountable for our present moment lived experience. And still, others can be a blessing as they provide you with triggers that show you exactly where the wounds remain unhealed.

7. Trigger tracking is a great way to help move from the unconscious to conscious responses. When you feel a trigger or a reaction to something or someone in your environment, become curious about it and name it. It is often easier to begin with a small trigger, like someone you don't know well saying or doing something that leads you to feel irritated (notice how I phrased this… others are not responsible for your feelings, they simply elicit feelings in you that are triggers being activated). Notice how that trigger feels in your body. Track or journal the story that you are creating around the trigger (e.g., "he is so selfish") or the meaning that you create around the situation ("I knew I could not trust him"). In time, you might find that you can track a pattern of triggers and begin to disengage from your attachment to that trigger (essentially, let it go). When my daughter was 4, she went through a period where she was mean to her friend. I found myself deeply triggered by

this and made a judgment rooted in fear that she would be a 'mean girl.' As a result, I didn't handle the situation as skillfully as I would have wanted to until I began trigger tracking. What is being hooked in me that is creating a story around this? Once I was able to see how my "people pleaser and good little girl" were confronted by her less-than-kind behaviors, I could non attach to the story I was creating about her and deal with the behaviors with greater competency and kindness.

8. In relationships, when you choose not to have difficult conversations because you are running a story that prevents you from being honest, it leads to cumulative tension. Over time, this tension becomes a trigger. One of the ways to un-armor your triggers is to be willing to have difficult conversations and share what you have been holding from bringing up in conversation with the other. We call this a 'withhold' conversation. What are you withholding that you can now share with the other? It would begin with a request, "I have a withhold to share, something that has been triggering me. Do you have time or capacity to listen?" If they agree, share your experience of the event and how it makes you feel. Then, if the other is willing, you can make a request. This modified practice is considered "non-violent" communication (based on the work of Marshall Rosenberg). It might sound like this: "I have been aware of a

trigger that has been coming up for me. It shows up when…. "(this is radical personal responsibility, not blaming statements). "When {insert trigger} happens, I feel….." (what are your emotions or sensations in that moment, eg., tight, tense, like I cannot use my voice, disempowered) and I imagine that (what is the story you are running in your mind). (e.g., "I imagine my feelings don't matter"). "Could we find a solution that works for both of us?" I have used these often; they are one of the most conscious ways to resolve conflict and soften the trigger in you.

Chapter 9

Harvest the Gold in the Grief

There is a golden nugget waiting to be harvested even in the darkest moments of your life.

I was so busy focusing on creating a life filled with purpose and passion that I didn't realize how fractured my marriage was becoming until it was too late.

While I traveled, for work and with my children, my husband chose to stay home, alone, and work on his new Yoga studio, a business that I did not support given our previous experience with yoga studios and the impact it had on our family. When we were home, he would often separate or isolate himself from me and then spend long days and nights at the studio. Often, I would only see him when I went to the studio. Sometimes I was denied access to it if he was angry with me so I would not see him for weeks. We had counseling, and I begged him to let me into his world. Instead, we drifted further apart.

In March 2020, my son, daughter, her boyfriend, and I were in Iceland. I remember the flight so clearly. It was a red-eye, and when everyone was asleep, I looked out the window and was mesmerized by the beautiful dance of the Aurora Borealis, the northern lights. Their green, pink, and blue shimmer was a miraculous and privileged vision. I tried to wake up my son, but he didn't budge. I thanked the Universe for gifting me with that shimmering sight and knew this would be an unforgettable trip. By the time we landed, we heard the news—a global pandemic had been declared and the world was going into lockdown.

After a refreshing stop at the Blue Lagoon Spa, we booked our return flight home making this a short, long-distance weekend. It was a memorable weekend as we watched people transition from a carefree and friendly disposition to being cautious, keeping their distance, and closing their stores. I knew the world would never be the same. I never imagined how much that thought would be a foreshadowing of my life.

We knew that, upon our return, we would have to quarantine. We arranged for my husband to stay at his mother's house while my daughter, her boyfriend, my son, and I stayed in our little home. We made it an adventure—trying new recipes, playing games, and learning what it meant to "shelter in." I enjoyed this extended and uninterrupted time with my children. We all thought it would only last a few weeks to months at best and cherished each moment. What I didn't know was that it would be the last time my husband would stay in our home. Within a few weeks, our marriage, which was in crisis already, ended, and we stopped communicating altogether. I was shocked, lonely, confused and found myself returning to old numbing patterns. I didn't have the capacity or the knowledge to manage the current climate in the world and my failing relationship, so I became FINE and got busy with work, my kids, and my routine.

Like most parents, I was responsible for setting up my family for success during the lockdown to ensure that school was done and we had adequate workspaces in our little home. I even created online meeting schedules, so we did not interrupt each other. We planned daily workouts and shared experiences. Every day, I showed up and did what I had to do. I pivoted my Yoga Teacher Training program and coaching to online and taught my young private Speech Pathology clients how to do speech therapy virtually. At the same time, I searched for meaningful and appropriate activities to support their communication. I had longed for this time at home, having been so busy for eight years. I felt a sense of gratitude. But, in my heart, something was missing; my husband. I dreamed that he would turn around each time he walked away, engulf me in his safe arms, and take away the ache that crept in during the long nights sheltered at home. Overnight, I became a single mom (for the second time in my life), responsible for the wellbeing of my family alone, managing the fear of Covid 19, and he walked away. I had to be FINE.

A few weeks passed, and our newly separated family got into a routine. As I slowed down, I began to pay attention to the health of my senior cat. It was becoming evident that he was not doing well. Patches had been with me through some major transitions in my life. He was a model of resilience, having gone missing for three months and eventually finding his way home. I was startled awake one morning with Patches lying still on my bed, having lost control of his bladder, clearly in pain. I made the short drive to the vet, snuggled him, and said goodbye as he took his last breath, my tears landing on his soft black and white fur. I would miss his presence, his weight on my belly as I slept, and his little meows that, I swear, sounded like "mom." I shed a few tears that day but returned to work quickly as I had a day packed with scheduled meetings. More FINE.

Spring gave way to summer, and as the days became longer, we started to have some fun outside. Playing Nerf™ war, baseball, and lots of basketball. I noticed myself laughing playfully and relaxing into this gentle schedule. Although there was a lot of laughter in my home, when I meditated at night, I often sensed the global collective fear and grief, and I knew to release those feelings through a moan, a sigh, a movement, or a yell. My kids were used to these unpredictable expressions. It was something I had done for years. I didn't anticipate how real that collective pain would soon become an expression of my deep anguish.

Early one Monday morning in June, I saw several missed calls from my sister and niece. They lived near my father, who was six hours away from me in a nursing home. I had been monitoring the COVID-19 numbers in his nursing home and expected they would call me to tell me he had tested positive for COVID-19. I was not prepared for my niece's words when I called back, "Opa died." I dropped the phone, let out a curling scream, and began to sob. I was supposed to see him at the end of March but couldn't because of COVID restrictions. This was unexpected. My son ran to me and immediately engulfed me in a full-body embrace, the pressure of his body temporarily soothing my nervous system as I found myself gasping to breathe. My father and I had a complicated relationship, but

I was proud of how we reconciled in the last 15 years, having opened my heart with grace, forgiveness, and love for him. Again, I became FINE, busied myself, and prepared for an unwelcome virtual memorial.

During the next few months, I found myself needing more and more time alone. I had less control over my tears, and my grief started to overtake me. I would go to bed early, sleep in late, and walk for hours a day. Often, I would sit on my bedroom floor, demoralized, crying. My daughter, skillful in how to hold space for people, would often find me there and slide down the wall to join me on the floor. She never asked me, "What do you need?" or said, "It's going to be okay, Mom." She just sat with me in silence. She was my greatest support as I was fully isolated during the shutdown. She sat with me most of that summer until the time came for her to follow her heart, and she moved 4,300 kilometers away.

She had wanted to live in the mountains for years, and this was the perfect time for her to transition to create and live her dreams. I told her we would come to visit every few months and, eventually, her brother and I would move there. We had a tearful goodbye. As I watched her vehicle and trailer drive away, I felt like a part of my heart was left with her, which I expected. But, I was unprepared for the intensity of the wave of grief and darkness that soon engulfed me. I felt like I had just lost my only lifeline. I was desperately alone and painfully lonely. I could no longer be FINE.

The darkness called me in, "Come and sit here in your body. Be in this space. Touch your grief." Although I had been touching my shadows, my anger and my boundaries, the one experience that had been denied was my grief. This opportunity of a global pandemic invited me to slow down and bring compassion and a loving presence to the pain of my grief. I knew that suffering resulted from resisting pain, so I had only one option left: embrace the pain and be fully present with my grief.

If:

Pain x resistance = suffering

Then:

Pain x Presence is the recipe for Freedom.

Each morning, I slowly peeled back my heated blanket from the small sliver of bed that I continued to occupy while the other side remained empty and lonely. I gently awoke, intending to greet my grief with kindness and curiosity, "Good morning, Grief; what do you need today?" Sometimes it wanted to walk or dance softly. Sometimes it wanted to stomp and push against a wall. On other days or minutes, it appeared as a moan with big, loud, and messy sobs. I learned to turn on the faucet of my grief in digestible degrees. I gave it the most loving attention and treated it like a friend who needed my time, patience, and nurturance. I knew much of this grief was recent, and an equal amount was old and unprocessed from a young girl who had lived a life of neglect, abuse, heartbreak, and loss.

Slowly, as I attended to this deep sorrow inside me, I welcomed all the sensations that needed to be expressed or moved through my body. I found myself allowing each emergent moment without trying to escape, fix, deny, condemn, or change it. I realized that so much of my suffering in the past was due to my resistance to my discomfort, but when I welcomed my pain and opened the portal to its truthful expression, I allowed myself the freedom to embrace it all. There was nothing wrong. I was allowing all healing to have its time and reminded myself that it would be a lifelong journey, and now was the time for this healing.

Releasing grief in this way requires a strong conscious intention to feel, embrace, and release pain. It has less to do with the story and more to do with the impact of the story on your body. The story is real. I never want to deny that. But the story's impact is what the body holds onto and needs to release to feel well again without numbing. Tell the story to feel the grief but do not deny the grief by staying in the story. You will know the difference because the embodied release of grief will feel good. You may feel tired, yet complete, fully breathing, and relaxed. Like you just released a heavy weight from your heart. This is the embodied expression of joy-filled grief. Take your time.

In our society, we put a time limit on the healing journey of grief. Whereas some communities celebrate grief with rituals, time, and community support, in North America, most workplaces offer between 1-5 days of time off from work to grieve the loss of a loved one. And most people are given NO time to grieve heartbreak at the end of a marriage or relationship. They are told, instead, "You will get over it. Time will heal. It wasn't meant to be. And everything happens for a reason." Those phrases do NOT help. What helped me was people honoring my need for space. Sitting with me silently when I cried. Not asking me where I was going when I went out for my 4th walk of the day or what I needed because I didn't know what I needed most of the time. What helped was my daughter putting down a plate full of lunch because she noticed I had not eaten again. What helped was others not asking me what I was doing in my office or why I was dancing with wildness at 10 pm on my back deck to the sound of whatever music allowed me to move the rigidity through my body and ended in an ecstatic solo dance with music blasting through my ear pods. There is no set time to end grieving. It may be appropriate to call in your lifeline—coaches, counselors, friends, and to find solace in the knowing that all healing has its time.

Over months that felt like years, my grief started to transform. As I welcomed it fully with love, it softened. Soon, I became aware of something awakening in me, a deep hunger and yearning for life. It came as little nudges at first. I started to map out a vision for my future, where I would live, and my life. I found the right coaches to help me through my transition, did deep trauma healing, and reflected on how those trauma wounds set me up for unhealthy attachments and expectations in my life and relationships. I began to see the nuggets of gold in the darkness. And slowly, I began to harvest the wisdom of those nuggets: love, gratitude, humility, patience, and deep respect for this grief process. These could only come from the courage I cultivated daily to sit in the unknown of grief.

It was a tough year. In four months, I lost my husband, my cat, my father, and, for a while, my daughter. In the next 10 months, I left my stable job of 32 years, sold my house that had become my beloved home after all, and moved to an unfamiliar community, 4,300 kilometers away, to start anew at age 56. That journey to the mountains led me to a curious and new life experience where my daughter reminded me, "I am Brave," as she selected that phrase for my Wifi password. I began to design coaching and yoga programs for healing rooted in present moment loving presence. Now, I get to help others through their grief journey, and each time; I heal a little more myself.

I know that grief is not a linear process, and everyone's healing is different. For now, I feel complete in my grief and am not surprised when a song or a memory triggers a longing to be held by Dan, or some sadness weighs down my heart. Today, I pay attention to these sensations and take extra time to process my grief. Sometimes tears fall. Sometimes I just wrap myself in my weighted blanket and slowly sip my cup of tea or watch a sappy love story. Then I smile; I made it. I made it through this most grief-filled time. One of my favorite speakers, Les Brown, says, "When life knocks you down, try to land on your back. Because if you can look up, you can get up. Let your reason get you back up." After this year of grief and growth, my 14-year-old son was my reason because I was keenly aware that everything I went through, he was going through. I had to do this deep work for both of us.

Grief is a temple water energy that longs to be expressed, moved, and felt. My only job was to turn on the faucet to let it flow in small amounts that I could manage while ensuring I fulfilled my other responsibilities, especially the solo parenting responsibility that I had for my son.

There is a Japanese tradition called Kintsugi, known as the "golden repair." It is the Japanese art of repairing broken pottery by mending the cracks with golden dust. Once repaired, the bowl is stronger and more beautiful than before. I know my season of Covid was my opportunity to mend my heart with Kintsugi as I stayed in the gift of my discomfort until it revealed my uncrushable strength and love. The gift of believing when I could not see the way as my tears were too heavy. The gift of transforming my life with clarity has allowed me to consciously choose where I live, love, work, and play. Through this year of grief and all that I've grown from experiencing, I have been blessed with so much gold as I allow the cracks in my heart to be gently repaired. With each gold stroke, I remind myself that my heartbreak is a measure of my capacity to love wholeheartedly. Love and life do not come with any guarantees. Love anyway.

My new mantra is that I can "feel good feeling bad," and I now carry that mantra when faced with challenging emotions or experiences. It is a reminder that all sensations, when welcomed and not denied, when witnessed through the observer's lens, and when fully felt from a willing heart, can soften, heal, and transform. When we push away, deny, blame, judge, project, avoid, numb our sensations, and turn to being FINE, we create the tension in our bodies that diminishes our life force. Instead, I chose to take out my surfboard and ride the peak of that wave that lasted for most of the summer and fall of 2020 and winter of 2021. Once the crest of the wave started to merge again with the ocean, once I started to feel more stable, clear, and empowered in my truth, I realized that my grief had not swallowed me. I was still alive. And there was so much richness that came from my release of grief. So much goodness was revealed in me with generous, ease in my heart, and clarity in my mind. And, on the other side of that wave, when I rode through it and remained present to it, I experienced many revelations and yearnings. I took out my pen and paper and started rewriting the next chapter of my life. I drafted the first line of the first page with one word: SURRENDER.

My menu now adds the following: loving presence, co-creator, transformation, uncrushable strength, choice, beauty, belief, trust, and tender heart.

Re-alignment Steps:

1. It's okay to get help. Grief needs to be witnessed. Avoid hiding your grief in the corner of your bedroom. Find someone to share your grief with, and allow yourself to be held in that tender space. By allowing yourself to be witnessed, grief will be met with love, and you get to bring it out of your body. Connect to a therapist, coach, grief group, a circle (men with men, women with women ideally), or a friend. In some of my deepest and darkest moments, I had a few people on speed dial for a zoom call to walk me away from the edge and through the darkness.

2. Ask yourself: "What am I unwilling to feel?" Focus on the sensations experienced in your body rather than needing to name emotions (e.g., I feel heavy in my heart is easier to admit than I am in a state of deep grief). That way, you do not overly identify with the emotional range and acknowledge it through the lived body experience.

3. Cultivate a self-loving kindness practice. Include the parts of you that shine with light and those of you that hold the darkness. Let it all be wrapped in your loving arms and expressed through your open heart. There is nothing that doesn't belong. You can place your hand on your heart or any other body part that is having a sensation and practice saying, "You, too, belong here."

4. Where in your life can you harvest the gold in your moments of darkness? The gold that shows up as wisdom, trust, patience, loving presence, and self-compassion even amid grief? How can you use your life experiences as stepping stones to your growth, strength, and full potential?

5. What hunger lies inside you, veiled by unexpressed emotions, that has the potential to become your birthplace for transformation? Through it all, can you wrap it with your loving presence to allow your life to thrive with clarity, meaning, deep reverence, and joy?

Chapter 10

Living with Surrendered presence

*"Surrender is not giving up on life; it is
giving up on trying to control life."*

My mom received her angel wings on February 12, 2010, after a gentle and relatively quick surrender to brain and lung cancer. For the 6 months leading up to her passing on that gloomy February morning, my family and I decided to keep her home and took "shifts," dropping into the role of her care provider for the 6 months preceding her passing. I bathed her, fed her, and shopped for her. I washed her hair and held her frail hand, worn from many years of unprocessed pain and betrayal. We sat and talked about life, often through tears of laughter and regret.

It was a physically and emotionally demanding experience as I lived 6 hours away, had a young family, and worked. My life became very scheduled—consisting of working for 6 days, caring for my young family, driving to my parent's home, and spending 4-5 days caring for my mom. I would then have to commute the 6-hour drive back home and settle into my family/work routine... Just as I felt alive again, I would be driving back to care for her. The drive to her home was often a fist-clenching drive through winter storms trying to abort my mission. The drive home was equally treacherous, with my vision obstructed by my tears as I witnessed her losing her strength to live.

She passed away gently in the night with our family gathered in her home. I felt the relief that she no longer suffered and the agony of losing my Mommy. With her letting go of the reigns of life and death, my mother left me a legacy imprint of the gift of surrendering when nothing is left to hold onto.

After her passing, I realized I was exhausted. I took a trip with some friends to the kitesurfing capital of the world, Cabarete, Dominican Republic. If you have ever kite surfed, congratulations. I wish I could say, "me too," but the truth is, I never made it off the beach. I tried. I tried with all my effort, strength, and determination. What I learned about kite surfing is that the harder you try, the more powerful the resistance becomes, which means creating the ripe and perfect condition of being flung in the air on an uncontrolled journey, or dragged across the beach with a magnified force that is equally dangerous. Each day I would go out with a coach and survey the beach. I breathed gently as the sea rolled back and forth while the heat of the glistening sand baked my toes, and the mighty wind mustered all its threatening force to create the ideal conditions for kitesurfing. After a quick demonstration, I was offered the kite bar. I confidently began to pull on the bar, but every time the wind caught in the kite, it would pull me backward, forward, sideways, and to the ground. With each gust, I did what I always did in life. I grasped harder. I held tighter. I tried to control it by seizing the bar with clenched fists. The more I clutched with all my force, the more power I fueled to the wind in relation to the kite.

It was instinctual for me to hold tight with all my might when something felt challenging. I had learned very early on that I could control life by working harder, faster, and more than anyone else. Unfortunately, working harder and resisting the kite simply resulted in my being dragged, on my face, 100 feet down the beach, with my coach racing behind me, trying to grab my feet to stop me. I giggle today at that vision. After many tries, I remembered the lessons from my mother through her illness. *You cannot control life, and sometimes all you can do is let go of the reins and surrender to your destiny.* I softened the hold on my bar until I was barely holding on with 4 fingers. Soon, the kite began to dance in the wind in response to my tender hold. I took a big exhale and thanked my mother for that lesson. I never did get off the beach that week. Let's just say that my inner wisdom was certain that it would not end well. However, I never forgot the lesson of surrender and letting go of controlling life from that kite surfing experience.

Over the following many years, as we moved in and out of owning our businesses, losing our businesses and almost everything we owned, and feeling my marriage slip away, I would begin to catch myself returning to my habit of grasping life, longing to control what was out of my control. And each time I did, it would not end well. I would remind myself to consciously practice softening my fists, relaxing my shoulders, taking deep breaths, and trusting in the experience of life. I practiced letting go of what was not mine to hold onto and remembering that the only things that I could truly control in life were my responses. In 2017, while in my circle retreat in Amsterdam, I was gifted a fully surrendered experience that, today, remains as one of the deepest impressions of a full surrender for my body, mind, and soul.

It was the final day of the circle retreat. I had played small throughout, watching others claim space for their deepest healing and needs. Prior to the retreat, I had spent 5 years in a state of intense nervous system activation, living in a state of fight/flight trying to control life when I could not even control my breath at times. When I registered for the retreat, I knew that I needed to pause life and find my way back to myself. Although I had many daily practices that allowed me to release a little steam each day and gave me the capacity to teach and serve, I was out of touch with what I needed to thrive in life. This unknowing followed me to the retreat. When the retreat began, I felt content being there, witnessing the courageous participants processing their desires and their pain simultaneously. Each day I stayed curious about what I might want to experience and express and had few answers. I wondered how others could be so clear and how I could be so bound in my doubt, fear, and ignorance of what I needed. Beyond the healthy imprints from others taking space in the circle, the nourishing food, and the opportunity to rest without any responsibilities, why had I come here? The answer was downloaded to me, gently and clearly, on the last day, at the last hour.

I had seen others battle for the space in the circle so as soon as the space opened up, I shot up my arm and jumped to my feet. I was ready. When asked what I yearned to experience, I expressed, "I want to experience a full surrender," followed by, "And I know how it will look." The room laughed.

I wanted to experience surrender on my terms and with my careful, comfortable, controlled plan. The facilitator asked me if I trusted him. "Of course," I humbly lied as I immediately regretted taking this space and time.

I was brought to the stage, in the presence of this intimate group of 40 people that I had come to know with a blend of mixed feelings; jealousy, admiration, judgment, and, most of all, love. I was guided to the stage with a stool. I was invited to stand on that stool, and once standing, I surveyed the people below me, all of us silently curious. I could hear myself breathing. I felt shy, unsure, and had a massive vulnerability hit. I drew my eyes to the ground, which seemed far away. Over 10 feet down. I was asked to select 12 men to stand in front of me. Men? I didn't really trust men. Most men had abused me, ridiculed me, and betrayed me. Could I trust these men whom I barely knew? I selected the men, and they stood, making 2 rows in front of me. They crossed arms, and a blanket and pillows were placed over their horizontal scaffold. I was asked to turn, so my back faced them. The song *Let me Fall* by Josh Groban began to play. I started to understand what was being asked of me. I was about to do a trust fall, backward, into the arms of these men. The ultimate act of surrender and trust. The music penetrated my ears, each verse louder and louder. My entire body began to tremble. My fists clenched. Tears streamed down my face onto the stool. I have no idea how long I stood in fear with the narrative that this was to be my certain and imminent death. My mind went into resistance, but my body knew this had to be. I had not only asked for full surrender; I had ached for this.

The facilitator stood before me, gently encouraging me

as he held onto the stool. I inched my heels back until there were no steps left. The song continued, *Let me fall, let me fly, there's a moment when fear and dreams must collide.* Through my heavy sobs, I silently counted in my head, 1....2....3...Go.

I fell back and heard a curdling scream release from my body as I landed in the arms of the men, safely and quickly. My first thought was, *that's all?* I had created so much tension, fear, and a death narrative—and within an instant, it was over. I began to laugh at myself and ruminated over all the times in my life when my mind created stories of fear, tension, stress, and worry over nothing. Times that I tried to control and curate life itself when it was not mine to manage. I thought we were done, but my process continued.

The men gently lifted me overhead and softly walked me around the room while the song continued, *And if I fall, there's no reason to miss this one chance, this perfect moment...* I melted into their strong hold. I surrendered and trusted their powerful hearts as I sobbed, this time, tears of joy. I was held in a way that I had never been, and I felt my nervous system, body, and heart fully release. After a while, they tenderly placed my feet on the ground while continuing to hold me. They formed a circle around me and lovingly guided my body from one to another while every muscle in my being was fully relaxed. I fully surrendered my body to them as I was soothingly passed around their circle. The last words I heard from the song were, *I will dance so freely, holding onto no one.*

Eventually, they helped me find my feet, and we all moved into stillness. I gazed into each of their eyes. One was a successful entrepreneur, one was a writer, one identified as a regretful rapist, and all were angels for me at that moment and in my life. I looked around the room. I felt my vulnerability and that of all the other women who were now weeping. I got to embody and experience what all these women craved in their lives. I found the gift of letting go of control. It takes an immense dose of trust and willingness to open up your hands to *let go and let God.*

When one grows up in an unpredictable home, with neglect and abuse, it is common to work really hard to control life, emotions, and relationships. And gripping life to manipulate it and everyone in it leads to more tension and disappointment. I often ask myself, what is in my control and what is outside of my control to determine where I can be self-responsible.

I discovered that this is what is in my control:

- How I respond
- How I react
- How I feel (emotions)
- What I put into my body
- When and how I move my body
- What and where I get to work
- How I get to serve in this lifetime
- How much love I pour into my relationships

I then understood that this is what is outside of my control:

Everything else.

And, the only thing I can do with that *everything else* is to let go and surrender.

Because of my trauma wounds and my attachment wounds,

it is very difficult for me to surrender (as it might be for you), and I had the belief that surrendering was an act of passive non-doing. Sometimes it is. And often, surrendering is taking the time to do the work that has to be done and then letting go of the way that it shows up as your destiny.

As I was navigating my grief journey and the complete untethering of everything that I knew would be my life in 2020-2021, my main practice was surrendering to life itself. I would recall my riverbank experience and tell myself, *this moment is your life.* I listened deeply. When my body needed stillness, I stopped. When it needed movement, I moved. When I needed to breathe, cry, yell, or love deeper—I followed those impulses and allowed myself to be penetrated by life. I dropped all care about what others thought of me and started to live fully and authentically. Surrender is only available when you are willing to find a state of loving awareness. To be in a relationship with your body, mind, and heart and know what it needs because you not only hear, you listen deeply.

Moving across Canada with only my son, dog, and cat, I left behind my familiar, loving relationships, my home, and my work. I stepped into the abyss of life with full surrender. As I closed the door to my beloved 'cottage' and hugged goodbye to the man that I still loved, every cell was relaxed. I was in surrendered awareness and excitement about the wonder of life itself. With each step and each mile, I knew with certainty that I was supported, that the Universe had my back and that I was always divinely guided. As I follow the breadcrumbs of my life, I see how life has always happened for me, and when I fully surrender to it, life truly happens *through* me.

Surrender is not actively giving up. Surrender is a full-body, tender experience that infiltrates our being when we let go of control. If control is the disease fed to us and results in tension, disappointment, trauma, armor, and defense—surrender is the wisdom medicine that we need.

When we release control and surrender to the life waiting to reveal itself to us, we awaken beyond our separate selves and get a glimpse of the larger truth of who we are: whole and expanded conscious beings. Instead of arguing with life, we create the inner art of presence and the ultimate freedom rooted in forgiveness and love.

Surrender is on every page of my menu as a heading and a footnote.

Re-alignment Steps:

1. Practice tracking your body. What and where is your habitual holding of tension? It requires stillness to be able to feel it. What some of my clients often notice is that, in the stillness, they become aware of other parts of themselves and emotional states that were not present before. For example, when one becomes still and relaxes their nervous system, they may be able to recognize an underlying state of fatigue that was always there but ignored when lying beneath the business of life.

2. Invite breath to soften the parts of your body that are holding tightly. Relax your hands, soften your jaw, and drop your shoulders while releasing any judgment that your current state is wrong. It is simply informing you that something is tense. Your body is an excellent communicator when you listen.

3. Release the *shoulds* that may have been imprinted in your life. Your life is unfolding perfectly. Notice if you are holding on too tightly to something that may no longer be yours to hold, or never was. Be willing to see life as feedback, not failure.

4. When practicing meditation, become aware that you are thinking. This is a skillful means of meditation, and there is nothing wrong with you noticing what you are thinking. The practice of being aware that you have unwelcomed and distracting thoughts is mastery in meditation, as it means that you are

not lost in your thoughts; you are, instead, a witness to them. Then, simply practice placing those thoughts on a cloud and visualize them blowing away.

5. Surrender your story of not being enough, especially when comparing to others who are all perfectly imperfect—like you. These stories usually show up through communication in subtle ways. When you catch yourself in your story, replace it with the following, *I am perfectly imperfect... just like you/them, etc.* Or, *I cannot do this... YET.* Reframe your negative comments to positive ones; for example, *I never get it right* to *I'm learning to* ... When adding a comment, feedback, or announcing your presence, avoid using "just" (e.g., "it's *just* me" or I *just* wanted to add that..."). The examples I have shared are simple and powerful ways to amplify your communication to remember that YOU ARE ENOUGH.

Chapter 11

The Sacred Journey of Forgiveness

*Forgiveness is remembering that everyone
is doing the best they can given their
conditioned imprints, their resources, and
their capacity in every moment.*

As I follow the breadcrumbs to my life with beginnings that
found me alone, untouched, and abandoned from my first day
on this planet, it is not surprising that I was holding so much
tension in my body for most of my life and a miracle that I was
so high functioning and still here. No one provided me with
the critical imprint of love and safety that a newborn, or a
growing child, requires to feel protected in the world. This
was the first of many attachment imprints of neglect, fear,
and pain that would define my future relationships, and it
would be decades before I would see how it would play out in
my adult life. Surrendering lent itself to softening the edges of
my heart. There was no longer anything to protect. I was a
mature woman and was responsible for how my heart showed
up each day. As such, I realized that my journey to healing
needed to include my journey to forgiveness. On the one hand,

I do believe that everything happens for the evolution of my soul; therefore, there is really nothing to forgive. However, on a human level, some things occur in our lives that we hold tightly in our hearts and prevent us from being present in life.

Forgiving someone is an act of self-love. It is to purify your heart and free it of the bitterness stored deep inside your heart's cave. Forgiveness is coming to understand that the other did the best they could, even if it is incomprehensible on a human level. Hurt people do hurt people, but in a way, it's not their fault. They could not have done anything differently at that moment, even though we would love to argue they could. I believe everyone (you and me included) is a miracle and has essential goodness at their core, but our experiences lead us to create harm on this planet, and to others.

As we talk about forgiveness, please know that it never means the other's actions were ever ok on a human level. NEVER. But this is beyond whether it is ok or not ok. It's simply an acknowledgment and acceptance of reality. I had a teacher who used to say: "It is what it is, so what are you going to do about it.... Yogi?" In other words, you have a personal responsibility to look at what prevents you from being fully in life with an open heart and do THAT work. You are living in the past when you hold tightness in your heart and keep replaying what the other did to you. I hold no judgment if that is your choice, but please know it is a choice.

Forgiveness also does not require you to share your forgiveness with the other person, as it is for the benefit of your heart and well-being. A forgiving heart is a pure heart.

My forgiveness journey began with my father. For five

years, I kept our contact minimal to process my childhood trauma and understand how my childhood imprints impacted my decisions and attachment styles as an adult. At the time, I was practicing and teaching yoga. It would have been easy for me to simply say the three common words: "I forgive you." However, it was not that simple or direct. Doing so would have been a spiritual bypass that would not have allowed me to feel and subsequently release the pain, tension, and fear trapped in my body. All that anguish needed somewhere to go. I worked on releasing daily. Through my tears of realization, I mourned the death of that little girl's innocence. I learned how to reparent her and give her what she needed to feel safe, loved, and meaningful in the world.

When I trusted my capacity to remain in a loving connection with my heart while in my father's presence, I eventually felt ready to visit him. I remember the warm summer day as I walked into his home, filled with the scent of my mother's home cooking. I was transported back to my childhood for just a moment, the moment blending the comfort of a home-cooked meal with the confusion and fear that often accompanied it.

I sat down at the kitchen table to eat dinner and heard the familiar bark of his orders to "get me a glass of milk," mixed with urgency and anger. I felt the return of tightness in my chest and tension in my nervous system, yet, I chose to take a breath and pause. I activated *my heart* power and stepped into my sovereignty during that pause. I simply replied, "NO," and went back to eating. I spoke my truth lovingly and clearly. I said *no*, not to be hurtful but to claim my adult boundaries. Cultivating forgiveness for him allowed me to release my fear of his actions and accept who he was while being true to who I was. My father received my "no" as it was intended, as a way to show him how to treat me, and before I knew it, he apologized. He apologized to ME! My forgiveness of my father allowed me to release my tension, him to release his, and we were able to reframe our relationship, which permitted me to see him in his truth:

He did the best he could, given his conditioned imprints, his capacity, and his resources in every given moment.

When my father passed away from COVID-19 in 2020, I could not be with him. However, I felt complete in our relationship, and even with his advanced dementia, I knew he was complete with it, also.

Although it was easy to *blame* my father and focus all my forgiveness and healing work on the suffering he caused, I realized that the pain of my mother's neglect was more traumatic. It had sourced my confused, conditioned imprint of love, safety, and connection. As all humans do, I formulated my belief systems and attachment patterns based on my childhood imprints. My experiences resulted in a fear-based attachment and the need to cultivate protective strategies to keep me safe from abandonment and neglect. One of these strategies was to shield my heart and keep people at a distance, hence the Ice Queen. My trauma around neglect and abandonment had resulted in my having to sheath my heart to avoid feeling the pain of past and future abandonment.

I then chose to turn my attention to cultivating forgiveness for my mother, not only for neglecting me but for setting me up to be abused by my father and for teaching me, by numbing her own feelings, that it was unsafe to feel fully. She taught me that the only way to walk through the world was with a protective mask on to hide the darkness that she lived in. It was a difficult forgiveness journey. Where I saw my father as a bully, I viewed my mother as a victim, making me question how much control she had over her life. I became curious about her wounds, her trauma, and the generational trauma passed on from her mother that I may have unknowingly carried. I could feel how much energy went into holding down that wattage of grief, disappointment, pain, and anger and how it prevented her and me from feeling fully alive and in joy. I took time to let that tension escape from my body. I held my little self and called on a support team of caring angels and trained practitioners to hold space for the various wounded parts of me to be welcomed, integrated, and freed.

Through this generational healing work, I released the known and unknown wounds, including my mother. I wondered how my mother might have experienced life and parenting differently without carrying this deep and dark ancient pain. I experienced a deep softening for my mother's little girl and all parts of her that had been disowned and unwelcomed in her life, and I fell deeply in love with all those parts of her.

In her final days on this planet, my mother acknowledged her inability to be fully present for my sisters and me. She apologized in a letter, encouraging me to use my voice for good in the world and to love fully. The truth is I had long ago forgiven her and could see clearly:

She did the best she could given her conditioned imprints, her capacity, and her resources in every given moment.

Next came forgiveness for all of the others that had caused me pain:

The man who sexually abused me at 18

My first husband who encouraged me to have an abortion of a child that I wanted to keep

My classmate, who, in graduate school, called me a slut

All the teachers who didn't see what a miracle I was in their classrooms

All the friends who had betrayed me while going through my financial and business hardships, including the couple who stole my retirement income

Friends and family over the years who decided that our relationship was disposable

My recent husband, whose own wounds danced with mine in a way that tore us apart

I made the conscious and deliberate choice to compassionately and gracefully release resentment towards them all by feeling them all and cultivating compassion and understanding.

I practiced the Hawaiian prayer of forgiveness, the Ho'oponopono prayer:

"I'm sorry. Please forgive me; thank you. I love you."

I remembered that they all did their best given their conditioned imprints, capacity, and resources in every given moment.

I learned that forgiveness could not be willed but that it could be practiced. Sometimes it is messy. Sometimes it is confrontational. Sometimes it is gentle. Yet, it is always healing.

I turned my forgiveness inward on myself and the little girl in me who was spiraling out of control as the pandemic collided with the end of her marriage, and lost all sense of safety in her world. I forgave myself for not seeing the demise of my marriage before it was too late. I forgave myself for not being the wife that he needed. I forgave myself for demanding more from him than he could offer me. I forgave myself for needing him so much, feeling so abandoned, and defaulting to anxious attachment each time he withdrew. I forgave my reactive little one for hurting him when she was in pain and didn't see his pain was also pure and real. I followed the breadcrumbs to my first day of life, alone in a hospital, and turned to deep compassion and understanding for this little girl who lived in me and didn't know better and would deny her voice and her feelings most of her life for her survival. I felt all the feelings she would not have had the capacity to feel in her early days and throughout her childhood. The feelings that prevented her from joy in her life. The feelings that kept her armored because the pain would have been too much for her developing system. I sent her love and understanding. I forgave her perfect imperfections. In the end, forgiveness didn't lead to joy; forgiveness led to relaxation.

Forgiveness has been my most sacred work, and it continues to be where I place my attention when I find myself in judgment, fear, unsafety, and pain. Forgiveness has become my emotional and energetic clearing house. I know that every day that

I am doing the best I can given my conditioned imprints, resources, and capacity in each and every moment.

Self-forgiveness requires that you recognize that your

choices result from your conditioning and that you always did your best at the moment. As the wonderful author Maya Angelou says:

"When you know better, you do better."

Forgiveness is not only your responsibility but your gift to your heart and soul. You are stepping into holy spiritual territories when you forgive others for the harms, injustices, and atrocities they cannot recognize. When you forgive yourself for being perfectly imperfect based on your own imprints, you become one with the sacredness of your soul.

Today, my menu is filled with forgiveness for others and myself.

Re-alignment Steps:

1. Take time daily to be in your body and feel what is longing to be nurtured and released. Self-safety is essential and received by your nervous system when you move, touch, breathe, and make a sound. Given the option, consider slowing your movement down, take long breaths with audible exhales, and be willing to release whatever sound is stuck in your body. When you find yourself alone, know that you can hug yourself.

2. Read the children's book, *The Little Soul and the Sun, a Children's Parable* by Neale Donald Walsch. It will help you to create a different narrative and relationship with those who hurt you. In that story, the 'Kind Soul' graciously agrees to help the 'Little Soul' on his journey to come to earth to practice forgiveness. The Little Soul excitedly agrees when the Kind Soul says, "In the moment that I strike you and smite you, in the moment that I do the worst to you that you could ever imagine—in that same moment...remember Who I Really Am. Because you see, I will have been pretending so hard, I will have forgotten myself."

3. Repeat this prayer daily: "Spirit, guide me to release the contracted pain and tension of my old stories so that I may create a richer, more expanded narrative guided by love and forgiveness. "

4. Write a letter of forgiveness to your younger self

for holding onto the pain and protecting your heart. Be gentle, understanding, and compassionate with your self-forgiveness journey. Tell them: "It's okay; you did the best you could, given your imprints, capacity, and resources in each moment." Holding on was your self-preservation, and you needed it at that moment. Perhaps you don't need it anymore as a mature, wise soul? Perhaps there are days that you will need to armor to get through the day. Being aware or conscious of it all is your guide to freedom.

5. Sit in quiet meditation or gentle movements and imagine life with freedom in your heart. From that state, write a letter of forgiveness to the person that betrayed or hurt you without the need to send it. Be willing to see them with empathy as a younger version of themselves who did their best *given their imprint, capacity, and resources in each moment.* If you need support while doing this, call a friend, a coach, or a therapist.

Chapter 12

Integration is a lifelong journey

*Life is like a kaleidoscope, and our journey
is to return to see all parts as parts of the
greater integrated whole.*

It is June 25, 2021. The final chapter of my relationship and my life as I knew it. I sent the moving trucks ahead to my new home 2 weeks ago and have been living minimally for the last few weeks, enjoying the simplicity of life and allowing this to be an imprint of what is possible and how little I truly need for my contentment.

These last few weeks have been a churning of emotions. On the one hand, I am planning a reset in my life—a new opportunity for my son and me as we move across Canada, 4,500 KM, beginning with a 6-day drive. On the other hand, we are leaving his father, my husband, my friends, my work, and all that I know as familiar, comfortable, and safe. Many people do not understand or support this decision. At some moments, I don't fully understand myself. I do know that, for 5 years, I have felt a calling in my heart to move to the mountains, and this is the time. My husband encouraged it and knew it was the best decision for our son even though he would no longer be present in his daily life. Deep down, I knew that to be true. Moving to a very small community in the mountains by the ocean was like a dream come true.

And still, my heart ached at the reality that this move meant the inevitable permanent end to my marriage, the loss of my beautiful little home that saved me, and life as I knew it.

I kept my energy high those days and did what I needed to do to put one foot in front of the other with this plan. Our home had sold, and we would transfer ownership in just a few weeks. I spent the next 2 weeks saying goodbye to my dear friends. My husband came around more and spent time with our son and, surprisingly, with me. I would savor these final moments with him and with us as a family. I held onto our hugs a little too long and watched him walk away with a familiar longing in my body each time. I reminded myself that I couldn't make him want to be with me.

My lawyer called on the day we were to leave our home for good and begin our long drive. The buyers had backed out. The house would not sell on that day. I remembered 2 little words that a friend had used to describe 2021:

Plot Twist

I smiled. Of course, this would be the final plot twist to this phase of my life. I hugged my husband one final time and got in the car with my son, dog, and cat, ready for our journey across Canada.

I took a big exhale, put the car in drive, and knew that this was just another plot twist in my life that would turn out ok because *it always turns out ok*. Sometimes better than ok. And, often, better than I could have written it.

Three days later, we were driving through the beautiful prairies of Saskatchewan when I got the call; the house had been resold and for a better offer. This time there was no need to exhale as there had been no holding of breath. I knew it would all work out.

On that long and beautiful drive, I had a plethora of time to reflect on my life. All the pain that I experienced and how my relationship with pain had transformed in the last 10 years. I remembered my formula:

pain x resistance = suffering.

My pain was not as great as some and, in so many ways, more than anyone should ever have to endure in a lifetime. And yet, my suffering was, and always is, within my control.

Therefore, I am reminded to choose the alternative formula

Pain x loving presence = freedom.

Freedom from suffering. Freedom from conditioning. Freedom to rewrite my menu from my sovereignty and the courage to always wear my crown.

While driving through the rolling hills and beautiful lakes of my home province of Ontario, I congratulated myself that I have learned to witness my pain and all parts of my life, my body, mind, 70,000 thoughts daily, and most deeply, my spacious heart. When I take this stance of witness consciousness, observing it all, there is nothing wrong. There is simply an observation of what is with non-attachment, grace, ease, and a pearl of deep wisdom. I allow my breath to create the changes that alter my entire physiology, my mind, and my relationship to life.

By the time I reached the halfway point of the drive, I was in an area of Canada called the prairies. I had been told this part of the trip was boring, but I admired the landscape with flat and yet billowy yellow wheat gently swaying in the summer breeze. I smiled, feeling and reflecting on all the parts of me, the parts of me that I loved and admired for her strength, resilience, and courage, for her ability to love so hard that the pain of loss was so deep. The parts that I was told were not welcomed and had been written with invisible ink in the menu of my life. In that moment, I committed to making any revisions to my menu sealed with visible ink so that I could live a life of transparency, wholeness, authenticity, while loving all parts of myself. I look forward to discovering more parts.

As I traversed the first sign of mountains, I brought up the energy of my needy little girl who craved to be seen and heard and promised always to give her a voice and allow her voice to be the voice of all unheard children in the world. And her voice would never be a 'power over' voice but a voice of reason where reason is needed.

When I crossed the threshold of my new province and was greeted by a rainbow kissing two mountain ranges, I called in my fearful, anxious, and out-of-control little one who was scared to be alone and unloved, and I loved her with every ounce of my energy. I reassured her that I was committed to offering that unconditional love whenever she needed it.

Driving into my new community, I welcomed the Ice Queen, thanked her for protecting me when she did and allowed the warmth of my heart to continue to melt her. I committed to welcoming her to return anytime I needed protection from what could be a cruel and uncaring world or people who had forgotten who they were so deeply that they treated me unkindly or unfairly or simply to soften the pain of the world in my heart so that I could digest it more slowly. Not forever, but for as many moments as I needed to recenter, find my footing, and see the grace in all situations.

I turned the corner and pulled into my new driveway. I took a long way home, and the place of home is that place where I feel my wholeness and freedom. Freedom from my conditioning. Freedom from the ingredients that were placed on my menu. With that freedom comes excitement, which might have been interpreted as fear in a different phase of my life. What will it look like and, more importantly, what will it feel like, and how can I integrate more of my healing into my daily life?

In 2022, my soul word was INTEGRATION (I choose a soul and leadership word every year). I had it engraved on a bracelet to remember. I knew I wanted to integrate all of my work; communication, conscious leadership, relational work, self and co-regulation, neuropsychology, positive psychology, and shadow work. I thought that the year would be just about integrating my professional life. It was that and so much more. It was an acknowledgment of the need to integrate all parts of my spiritual and emotional healing into my Being.

Whereas psychology and personal development are typically about discovering yourself, like reading a recipe for your life, spiritual integration is about embodying and *living* the uncovered gifts you've been given in relation to life and being willing to see it as nothing but divine perfection. It requires us to read the recipe, make the recipe, taste the recipe, adjust the recipe, and then savor the recipe knowing there could never have been a different recipe.

As I have embarked on this spiritual journey, it has been an invitation to taste all parts of my menu, savor it as slowly as I could, and allow all of my taste buds to come alive in connection to each morsel, even when they felt uncomfortable and stung. Now, I get to decide what I choose to add to my menu and which items I wish to lovingly discard, having tasted their bitterness and deciding to let them go. Integration includes tasting all of my menus and committing to continue to be in relationship with my menu, checking in regularly to ensure that the invisible stuff is not spreading to other pages. This is how I allow life to be experienced from a fully embodied lived state and see it all as the greater sense of loving universal life.

Through Integration, I took the time to welcome home all of me with the presence of a mature, loving, and compassionate parent that stepped forward to re-parent the wounded, scared and abandoned parts of me. Often it looked like I was doing nothing, when in fact, I was doing so much in my non-doing state. This was where the magic happened, and I gave myself 2 full years for that magic to transform my nervous system and my heart.

I committed to being the parent I never had and was the one who self-soothed all parts of me with a "Dear loved one, you will be ok, and it's ok not to be ok right now." I reparented:

- *my mind, practicing non-attachment to my thoughts*
- *my nervous system with daily self-regulation practices*
- *my body with the grace that she is getting older and still is a vessel to honor and nurture*
- *my heart and the spaciousness of her depth that held 10,000 highs and 10,000 lows over the years*
- *all the emotional ranges and the sensations that give rise to them, for they all belong and create the capacity to broaden into even more when met with love*
- *the shadows or disowned parts that I now curiously attend to as they show up in my relationships without attaching to having to go look for them*
- *the triggers that came out of the unprocessed pain*

My mature and wise self embraced all that came and held it with love and acceptance because to deny what it is would be insanity. Instead, I held space for it all with a non-judgemental acceptance, created changes that were within my control, felt all the hard feels, and I reached out for a helping hand when needed, which was a first in my life as my trauma response to life kept my hands to myself and not ask for help. I stepped into my self-agency, my self-responsibility, my self-acceptance and my self-love.

As I continue on my journey toward integrating all parts of myself, I bring forward all the following parts to be part of my experience, seeing them as being on a continuum of life. As such, I choose to embody:

My inhales, and my exhales

My humanity with my divinity

My divine steady masculine presence with my divine wild feminine presence
My understanding of compassion, surrender, forgiveness, and courage with my lived experience of all of these
My concept of letting go with the practice of letting go with love
Movement with stillness
Light with dark
The beauty and the messiness
Gratitude with disappointment
Fear with Trust
The divine emptiness in me where quiet resides and the infinite divine spaciousness that fills the void of stillness

And so on, and so on, as life flows.

This deep integration of all the parts of me is now calling me to fall in love, with myself, with my life, with the unknown, with the familiar, with the fear, with the ecstasy, with the pain, and with life itself. *Do I have to like them all?* Absolutely not. But, I can love them all, feel into the moments and *allow* love to be revealed in each moment of the reset of my life.

When I allow myself to be in full spiritual integration with this human body that is a vessel for my soul, I remember to step into my divine sovereignty and live the life I was sent to live, with gratitude and understanding that life can be a Big Hot Beautiful Mess, and I signed up for it. And, along the way, I may not like it but I can love myself through it all.

Then, I let go some more and release my attachments to how life unfolds. I remember I am not here to stress, fear, play victim, or blame. I am not my mind, and I am not my body. All of these are temporary blessings that allow me to experience the pulsation of life and remember that I am complete always.

Integration is welcoming all of life and what it brings without attaching to any of it. Doing this deep work has, in truth, been the deepest spiritual practice of my life. It is constant work of integrating the past with the present and my longings for the future. Of recognizing my triggers and my defaults. Of being able to step back and say, *Not today, I'm Sorry, Where are they right,* or "*I am a miracle,*" and meet whatever comes up with strength, discipline, conviction, and compassion.

As I move into 2023, I take the space to sit in silence until I can release the stories that there is something wrong or missing in the void. In fact, I have come to appreciate the void and seek it often. Sometimes I am still in it. Sometimes I choose to release something different that might be bigger, louder, and messier and free me from the shackles that came from living my life with someone else's menu. There is nothing to do in my stillness, no one to be. I simply "am that I am." It came without labels. It came without stories. It came without thought. It came without a prescribed menu. In fact, in my spiritual integration, the menu is as empty as it is full. The void is delightful and spacious. And I get to fill that void of what was judged as a wrongful feeling of "empty" with the spaciousness of Love.

My menu now includes integrating all my parts with love, profound stillness, radical acceptance of what is, humility, and loving compassion. I know I am OK and sometimes better than ok. Sometimes I may still return to FINE, and even that is OK as I hold myself tenderly in that state. Then, I remember I am still whole. And I soften.

Re-alignment Steps:

1. Stress can not coexist with grace. It is essential to commit to self-regulation practices, including breathwork, meditation, stillness, and being witness to your thoughts, as discussed throughout this book. *Nothing changes until something changes.* When you can relax your system and trust that the Universe has your back and always has, the next decision in life will be grace-filled. We all experience the paradox of tension and ease, grace and pain, surrender and fight in life. When you can see all these apparent paradoxes as simply a single moment in the nonduality of life, you can relax your system at that moment, thereby removing the dualities (and the subsequent stories that arise from that) and softening to the experience with Grace (even if just for that moment... and the next moment....and the next moment... as a practice of life).

2. Remember, you are the embodiment of the universe. She went to so much trouble to create you. Don't take yourself or life so seriously that it feels hard or harsh. Instead, add a dash of being seriously playful to each day.

3. Practice being present to all of life, the parts you welcome freely, and the times you resist. This witnessing presence is the key to unlocking life's

fullness and all it offers with Grace.

4. Return to the center of the center in the center
(usually in your heart but some traditions experience this soul center in the Solar Plexus). In
Yoga, we call this Madhya, the unshakeable and
unchangeable you that was there the first day when
your parents picked you up, thanked God, and
began their journey of conditioning you. There
is a YOU that is pure, untouched, and pure light.
That YOU remains here today if you are willing to
look deep enough to dust away the cobwebs of your
heart and remove your armor. If you are willing
to trust and are open to love. Place your hands
on that center and repeat, "I am." "I am." "I am."
until you can feel your unconditioned, beautiful
and spacious heart.

5. Remind yourself often that you are a soul having a
human experience, and this body has a timestamp.
Take care of it. Take care of you. When your divinity meets your humanity, you give yourself the
freedom to experience life through the eyes of
Grace.

6. Go back often and look at your menu. Put on your
Courageous crown and modify the ingredients
from the place of divine sovereignty that you are.
If you are not feeling whole, complete, in alignment, and relaxed, life is telling you that it is time
to create change. That change always starts with

you. And, in the end, be willing to find moments of pause in the void and allow your menu to dissolve until you can be in the vastness of "I am that I am" without labels, pain, stories, longing, etc. Simply be in the vast presence of your soul.

Chapter 13

Your Call to Freedom

You are me, lovingly disguised as you.

A part of me remains in judgment that it took so long
to find my way to the home of my heart, my freedom, my
sovereignty and my self love. But, deep down I knew it could
not have happened any differently. It had many curves, detours
and bumps. Often, just as I thought I had reached the peak of a
mountain, I found myself tumbling back. I had to allow many
aspects of who I thought I was and the attachments that came
with those to die so that I could give birth to the unidentified
me, ready to fully step into the life I signed up to experience.
I got up, dusted myself off (after a few days, weeks, months,
and sometimes years), turned on my courage, and kept moving
from the darkness into the light. One foot at a time. Some
might say I am resilient. I believe we are all resilient. None
of us truly knows where we are going, but we wake up every
day, place our feet on the ground and welcome each new day
without knowing what truly will come of it. That's resilience.
We all fall, and we get back up. That's resilience. We all have
heartbreak at some time; the work is to be willing to remain
open to love. That is resilience.

Your process of awakening is already in motion. You cannot do it wrong. You are already on that journey. It is called LIFE. Deep listening ensures you don't miss what is really important to you and that you make decisions along the way that align with what is most valuable and authentic and lights you up. Then take THAT action. I call that Inspired Intuition. It requires that you recognize when you are out of the spontaneous flow of life and get yourself out of the way. Perhaps it's a disturbance like a big boulder in the river blocking the flow. The truth is, with the disturbances in the water, the water will know to go around the boulder. You cannot stop life; you can simply create a resistance to it that may feel a little more challenging, and you can begin to consider that even THAT is the right experience at this moment. How do you know? It's the experience you are having at this moment.

In life, there is no way "out" but through, including the fear, the pain, and the resistance. You don't need to magnify it in your experience to repeat it for decades; rather, what appears to *be* in the way *is* the way. If your fear is in the way, that is the way. Listen and inquire into it. What are you afraid of? What is your heart longing for and in fear of? Embrace the whole of your experience. Let go of the reins and allow yourself to flow with the current of grace rather than against it.

When you feel blocked in life, there is nothing wrong; there may simply be a misalignment and a nudge to go deeper, do something different, and be patient, as your soul may not yet be ready. In the exact perfect moment, the dam will burst, and you will experience the shift that makes it all perfect. Everything else is a preparation for that moment. Can you sit with the whole of your experience? Notice when you grasp with the mind and argue with the timing of life. Listen. Take time to process and emotionally digest to allow the ripening of your life.

THIS IS THE WORK.

The work is to return to our natural states of love. To do the deep work to heal our traumas, our pain, our fear, our grief, our stress, our judgments, our divisions, and everything that prevents us from showing up fully from a place of love and seeing the humanity and the divinity in ourselves and the other (whomever that other might be that you have created a divide). That is what we are called to do. That is what the world needs. And, that is what I reminded my son on April 21, 2021, at 1:30 in the morning.

I was awakened by a whisper coming from the end of my bed. I looked at my clock. It was 1:30 AM, and I was startled out of a deep slumber on this cold and dark April morning. "Mom, when will life go back to normal?" This was one of three questions my 14-year-old son asked that night. I took a big exhale. As you now know, life would never be normal for us again. We had spent the better part of 13 months in isolation and alone in our little home. He was doing remote learning, and all the losses that I felt were also part of his story. We were planning our move across Canada, our house was up for sale, and he rarely had contact with his father.

My son's voice reached out in the darkness, his anxious blue eyes looking for answers as he repeated, "When will life go back to normal?"

I tenderly reflected on this past year and paused before thoughtfully responding. I gently reached for his hand and said, "Things may go back to some level of normalcy for some people, but we get to create our new normal. I don't know exactly what it will look like, but I do know that we will live the outdoor life that we have dreamed of, and we GET to embrace this adventure." I felt myself excitedly anticipating this new season of our lives and writing my menu along the way. He seemed satisfied with this response. Phew. A second question followed.

"What is the meaning of life?"

This wise question from a 14-year-old who, just a few hours earlier, was laughing as we watched an animated show together. My sweet, curly-haired boy who used to sleepwalk his way to my room before these deep worries filled his mind. I remembered that his entire family, life, and world, as he knew it, had changed.

I took a deep breath, wondering if he was ready for the truth. Then, I trusted in his wisdom and replied, "The meaning of life is whatever you make of it." I let the answer settle on his heart and watched as his brow relaxed, seemingly content with my honest response.

His final question, filled with both hope and courage, "Why are we here?"

I paused to look at his curious eyes and wondered what response he sought from me. His soft but firm gaze affirmed that he was referring to the big philosophical question about the purpose of life itself.

As my eyes met his, I gave him a big hug, smiled proudly, and remembered the final teachings in the Yogic Text, the

Bhagavad Gita. In the story, the God representation, embodied as Krishna, is having a conversation with his cousin and friend, Arjuna, who is having a massive crisis and wanting answers urgently to a decision that is leaving him with an uncomfortable integrity and vulnerability conflict. After 17 chapters of dialogue in the book, Krishna says to Arjuna, "Whatever you do, do it because you love me." In other words, make LOVE the reason that trumps all reasons. My answer was quick and clear: "We are here to love my son; we are here to love."

And, just like that, with the innocence and acceptance of an untethered Being, he was back in his room and called to me, like he does every night through the walls, "Thanks Mom, good night, I love you." "Goodnight, Ben, I love you too," I replied with motherly tears of pride in my eyes.

It took me a while to go back to sleep that night. Life is curious. I had mine planned out, and something completely different was birthed through me that was not on my menu. I was gratefully reminded of the blessing of life on that night by my son. I trust that I have been given the gift of life wrapped with deep meaning, beauty, love, and freedom. The freedom of surrendered presence. The freedom of being in my discomfort until it revealed my uncrushable strength. The freedom of believing when I cannot see. The freedom to recognize that I am a miracle, just like you. That you also, know the depths of pain and can act out of that place, just like me. That you are doing the best you can given your imprints, capacity and resources, just like me. That you have wounds that cannot be seen but call out to be healed and have the greatest chance of healing in connection with others and through life, just like me. You are finding your way home to your 'heart print,' just like me, and along the way, you have the freedom to rewrite your menu too.

My journey has guided me to recognize that my homestead, every day, is my heart. I had to experience all that I did to remember to tenderize my heart, separate it from my mind and judgments and the imprinted menu ingredients and be in the presence of all of life, my pain, and my healing until all that was left was love. I spent many years trying to get above my pain. The deepest loving experience that I could give myself was to journey into my heart center and sit in its divine stillness to feel it all and disentangle from my stories, from my pain, from my projections to others, and from life itself. Now, in the stillness, I welcome the integration of all my healing to settle into my body. And though it looked to the outside that I was doing nothing, the healing was integrating with perfect wisdom in my body, finding the path to alchemizing it into love. The way through was into my body.

My inability to feel for most of my life led me to a protective strategy called dissociation, or not being in my body. It protected me. Sometimes it might still sneak in as I return to my familiar mind space to justify my life when I fail at controlling it. My "unconscious" moments usually come with suffering (remember: pain x resistance $=$ suffering). The medicine is to be in my body, awaken in each moment I forget. To find stillness and, for even one second, the void that is filled with all of my aliveness. Until the mind takes over again and argues that reality. It is simple and can be difficult until it becomes a regular practice. As a spiritual warrior, it is essential.

'The Work' is to stay present in life, receive it with a kind curiosity, investigate it, and soften it into your own loving presence. Soften until you recognize that you are already fully divine, perfect, and whole, and the practice of dropping into presence provides you the freedom to feel all the feels and remember that you are not your experiences. To move through the frozen. To digest the undigested pain of your life. To find the precious layers of yourself that are patiently waiting to be reclaimed. *Do you dare to go there to feel it?* Can you be vulnerable and resolute in life to not only hear but listen to your innermost wisdom and truth, adjust your GPS of life to flow in that direction, and allow the magic of your love to be uncovered when you attune to the callings of your soul?

This is your call to freedom. The more you answer the call, the greater the experience of feeling in harmony with life. In time and with practice, you will create a new way of being in all of life with ease and a sense of grace. It is a practice of returning to yourself by undoing the menu of your life because beyond all your experiences, thoughts, fears, pain, and ecstasy, at the deepest layer is your essential nature which is pure, unchangeable, and unshakeable. This, your divine conscious being, is the only common element to all of your life. It has always been there. It will always be there, even when you have been so busy doing life. The only question is will you remember to notice its gentle presence?

Although my experiences were not always graceful or welcomed, my life has been Grace-filled and unfolded with divine perfection. It came with many servings of tears, despair, loneliness, fear, betrayal, loss, disappointments, and equal moments of softness, generosity, deep connections, and abundance. All of it is in service of my soul's evolution. When in pain, I wanted to curse it, blame it, and fight it along the way. Yet, the pathway to freedom was to love it all. Love was always the answer.

When I started my personal development journey, I searched for my pain. I found it. Then I decided I wanted to *turn my pain into purpose, my mess into my message, and my shit into sheer teachings* and continue to make that the drishti or focal point of my life. I was driven to create something out of my suffering. That, in itself, caused me more tension and kept me focused on MY pain. I chose not to turn my pain into my purpose but to heal my pain with a loving presence and make that my purpose. Now, with a bigger vision of ensuring that the meaning I create in my life is one of service, I offer my loving presence to the collective pain in the world because it has never been just about me. People will hurt you, love them anyway. Even if from afar. Because that is what the world needs, and every time you remember to love, you get to reclaim your authentic nature and serve that energy with the world. We are all interconnected, and what we put into the world impacts others on all levels.

A peach (and many other fruits) produces a plant hormone called Ethylene. This is what gently nudges it along its ripening-sweetening journey. The most miraculous thing is that once one fruit begins to release the Ethylene for its own evolution, it influences all the nearby fruit on that tree to also ripen and sweeten, not in spite of the one fruit but because of it.

Each of us is a part of the sweet fruit of life and throughout our lives, we share our own version of "ethylene" with the world and create impact through our very presence. Sometimes it is kind and conscious. Sometimes it is weaponized and comes from a state of forgetting. Freedom is knowing you have the opportunity in each moment to connect back to your center, call your energy back in, resist reacting, take a pause and breathe, notice your triggers, take radical self-responsibility, be loving, be present, be empathic and remember that we are all doing the best we can. This is how we awaken a unity consciousness where we remember we are all interconnected at some level, like the fruit, to one divine menu of life. A life that can be sweet, soft, and deeply rooted in an ancient truth that remains just as real today as it did thousands of years ago:

I am you lovingly disguised as me.

Today, I know there is no destination or pressure to heal, for healing is simply synonymous to following all of the loving impulses as I sit in life's experiences. There is nothing to transcend, overcome or strive to achieve. There is simply moment by moment life that calls me into it's joy, it's pain, it's love, all for the delight of it. When I release the need for it to be different, I am free to be in the stillness of that moment. This is the quiet presence that holds the space for me to heal my trauma, my pain, and my mess until I can meet it all with love and pour LOVE into life. I choose freedom from the conditionings that were placed on my menu. Freedom from the limiting beliefs, judgments, and constant thought patterns about things that are not even real in my life. Freedom from all the pain that came when I resisted it. Today I know The Call to Freedom naturally arises through the practice of loving presence, which is for my evolution and the evolution of all beings.

In that loving space, my spacious heart beckons me to awaken to my freedom every moment of every day and ask:

"What would LOVE do?"

And as often as I can remember, I will serve THAT medicine from the menu of my life.

Re-alignment Steps:

1. Here is my signature Re-Align to Thrive™ practice. It is designed to awaken you to healing in your life from a place of loving-kindness. An audio version of this embodied meditation can be accessed in the resources section of this book.

Remember that you are a miracle and be willing to see the miracle in others. You were born with the essence of the Golden Buddha, of light and love itself. Your life experiences do not negate that ever. What you have done and what has been done to you never takes away your essential and intrinsic goodness. The Universe went to so much trouble to create you (seriously, 1 in 400 billion odds), and you are here today, reading this, perhaps not in spite of all that you have gone through but *because of all you have gone through*. Big Breath.

Explore what emotions and energetic experiences are present in you in the form of sensations. Sensations are the language of the body and can inform you about how you are doing. Rather than attach to the emotions, label the sensations and sit with them for a few moments (e.g., instead of "I'm sad," tell yourself, "I notice my heart feels heavy and my shoulders are drooping.").

A Allow whatever surfaces to be part of your experience. Soften and hold space for all of your sensations and experiences. The research shows us that when we identify sensations (not emotional labels), there can be a shift within 90 seconds. There is no need to attach to the sensation nor to the shift. Simply observe it with compassion and kindness. Trust that it is all part of your embodied journey.

L Love each sensation as it arises as a loving communication from your body about this moment, your life. Love yourself no matter what comes up; your life experiences do not define you. Use a mantra: "Life is happening FOR me." "I am the loving creator of my life." "I can realign to thrive in my life." Recite these daily. In between acknowledging each sensation, take a deep breath, and exhale with a loud sigh. Relax your shoulders, and continue the exploration of the sensations of your body.

When you practice being the REAL you, contemplate these next 3 questions:

I Inspired Wisdom: What is your Inspired Pop Up when you ask the question: "What does love (my heart, life, the Universe) want me to know right now?" When you ask this question and listen deeply to the wisdom of the response, you train yourself to stay with the moments that are painful and trust that they will show you the path to your deepest purpose. Place Inspired Wisdom on your menu.

G Grateful: What are you grateful for in this very moment? By practicing gratitude, you allow yourself to cultivate more things to be grateful for and gain a new perspective on all of life. Be grateful for all the experiences, as they catalyze change in your life. Place gratitude on your menu.

N Need - What would you need right now to be the embodiment of loving presence and freedom? Ask for help, take a rest, let go of the attachment, and remember you are a miracle and on the right path. Please know that, on the human path, it is normal not to feel love and freedom all the time, so let's just normalize that truth. Then, ask yourself *what do I need right now to resource my capacity for love and freedom?* Ask for THAT. And place THAT on your menu regularly.

2. Below is a mantra in Sanskrit that I recite daily for the freedom and happiness of all beings. As one committed to your own freedom and love, consider saying this daily (in English or in Sanskrit):

Lokah Samastah Sukhino Bhavantu

In English it translates to:

*May all beings everywhere be happy and free, and may
the thoughts, words, and actions of my own life
contribute in some way to that happiness and to that
freedom for all.*

Dear loving soul, as this book comes to an end, allow it to be your *Call to Freedom* and an awakening of loving presence in your life. Re-Align your heart daily with your deepest longing to be love, to live from love and to receive love. Place this message on your mirror and read it daily:

"I, (your name), am LOVE. A more loving child of the Universe has never lived. I am LOVE's prayer of becoming and its answer. I am here to love without limit, to awaken each time I fall asleep, and to reclaim my freedom. Everything I have experienced has been a stepping stone for this day, and I am proud to be here, reflect on my love with grace, and step forward with the courageous wisdom of the adventurer I am and always have been. My love has forever altered the course of history. I am LOVE embodied."

Pain Melts Into Love

Diana Lockett

When you find your exhale in the divine perfection of life
There is a moment where there is no need to hold onto strife
And In that fabric of your soul
you know that everything was needed to awaken the whole
Through this perfection of that unfold
All the tears and the pain are a harvest of gold
And alas, your pain simply melts from above
Until all that remains is the gentle power of love.

Resources

Heart Meditation

https://bit.ly/RealignwithHeartMeditation

Re-Align to Thrive™ Practice

https://bit.ly/Realigntothrivetoday

I have read 100s of books on healing, personal development, spiritual awakening, and integration. The following list is some of the ones that I turn to again and again:

1. *The Little Soul and the Sun:* A Children's Parable by Neale Donald Walsch (Author), Frank Riccio (Illustrator), 1998

2. *The Mastery of Love:* A Practical Guide to the Art of Relationship, A Toltec Wisdom Book by Don Miguel Ruiz and Janet Mills, 1999

3. *Waking the Tiger: Healing Trauma* by Peter A. Levine Ph.D. and Ann Frederick, 1997

4. *Insights to Intimacy: Why Relationships Fail & How to Make Them Work* by Christian Pankhurst, 2016

5. *Healing the Child Within: Discovery and Recovery for Adult Children of Dysfunctional Families* (Recovery Classics Edition) by Charles Whitfield, 1987.

6. *When Things Fall Apart: Heart Advice for Difficult Times* (20th Anniversary Edition) by Pema Chodron, 2016.

7. *Bhagavad Gita*, A new Translation by Stephen Mitchell, 2002.

8. *Conscious Uncoupling: 5 Steps to Living Happily Even After* by Katherine Woodward Thomas, 2016.

Acknowledgements

It takes a village to birth a book, and I send love and gratitude to all the wonderful humans who said YES to being in my village:

My children who patiently waited while I wrote one more chapter
My Editors: Alex Blake and Mimi Safiyah
My Graphic Designer: Liana Khabibullina
My Book Designer: Dania Zafar
My Web designers: Ian Coll and Katie Smertherman
My Launch Consultant: Chisom Ezeh
Photo Credit: Ian Coll, www.Cedarsprucefilms.ca

About the Author

Diana is a 5x International Bestselling Author and International Speaker who uses her superpower of vulnerable storytelling to allow her audience to soften into their own loving presence. As a visionary Conscious Communication Leadership Consultant and Coach, she creates safe spaces that invite leaders, teams, and educators to Re-Align to Thrive™ to transform their corporate teams and classrooms by accessing inspired wisdom and inspired action. The result is an environment where participants feel relaxed and safe to communicate confidently and clearly and build compassionate relationships rooted in collaboration, innovation, education, integration, and cooperation.

Diana is a mother of two incredible humans who have been her greatest teachers. She lives in the beautiful mountains of British Columbia, Canada, where she is inspired daily to meditate, practice and teach yoga, build community, and be in nature.

To Contact the author for group, personal, educational or corporate leadership training/coaching, please visit

www.dianalockett.com

33947602R00103

Antioch

•Aleppo

Latakia

MW00618665

Hamidiya   •Homs

Tripoli

LEBANON

Beirut

Baalbek

Beit ed Din

Zahle   JABAL ASH SHARQI

Rasheiya

Damascus   •Irna

Merj Uyun   Qatana

Ein el Shara

S

JEBEL
ED
DRUZ

Busra

ISRAEL   JORDAN R.   PALESTINE

Ramallah   •Amman

•Jerusalem

Bethlehem

J O R D A N

·ersheba

P A L E S T I N E

OLIVE
OIL

EUPHRATES R.

S Y R I A

N

W   E

S

Scale of miles

0   25   50   75   100

map by palacios

THE ART OF SYRIAN COOKERY

Author's mother Maheeba showing Syrian foods. Top row—Fried Kibby, Baked Eggplant, Kibby Stuffed with English Walnuts. Second row—Meat Pies, Raw Kibby, Stuffed Squash. Third row—Stuffed Grape Leaves, Kibby Stuffed with Laban, Spinach Pies. Fourth row—Syrian Bread, Black Olives, Cheese.

THE ART OF
SYRIAN COOKERY

*A Culinary Trip to the
Land of Bible History—
Syria and Lebanon*

HELEN COREY

DOUBLEDAY & COMPANY, INC.
GARDEN CITY, NEW YORK

The Orthodox Church consists of a number of so-called "autocephalic" or autonomic churches, the oldest of which are the four Eastern patriarchates of Constantinople, Alexandria, Antioch, and Jerusalem.

These different organizations, although independent of each other ecclesiastically, agree in doctrine and, essentially, in form of worship; and together they constitute what is called the Holy Eastern Orthodox Church. The Syrian Orthodox churches fall under the patriarchate of Antioch.

The eight bodies comprising the Eastern Orthodox churches in the United States—the Albanian, Bulgarian, Greek, Rumanian, Russian, Serbian, Ukrainian, and Syrian churches—are headed by a bishop or archbishop under the spiritual jurisdiction of the Mother Church in their ancestral homelands. The titular head of the Syrian Antiochian Orthodox Archdiocese of New York and North America is the Most Reverend Archbishop Metropolitan Antony Bashir.

ISBN: 0-385-00295-5

LIBRARY OF CONGRESS CATALOG CARD NUMBER 61–18785

20   19   18   17   16

Syrian Antiochian Orthodox Archdiocese
OF NEW YORK AND NORTH AMERICA

239-85TH STREET
BROOKLYN 9, N. Y.

September 1, 1960

Miss Helen Corey
% Mayor's Office
Terre Haute, Indiana

Dear Helen :

I have read the manuscript of your book with
great interest. This book will strike the fancy of
all good cooks and should be required reading
of all our Orthodox Catholic people. This is
the only book of its kind that faithfully portrays
the religious and cultural significance of various
foods our people have eaten since the dawn of time.

You may use this letter in your book as a recommen-
dation for the use of the book in all our parishes.

With our blessing and all good wishes,

Most sincerely,

Metropolitan Antony

Metropolitan Antony

ACKNOWLEDGMENTS

To my sister Kate, who tediously tested the recipes for accuracy (over the past three years), goes my deepest gratitude.

Special thanks go to my dear cousin, Ruth Betros Fisher, for general information found throughout these chapters.

A warm acknowledgment goes to Mayor Ralph Tucker of Terre Haute, an epicurean, for his encouragement and patience.

Words are not adequate to express my appreciation to all those friends who contributed their time and guidance in compiling this book.

I respectfully dedicate this book to my mother Maheeba, whose inspiration prompted its writing and who was patient enough to explain her favorite recipes so that they might be presented in an accurate and straightforward translation of cooking in a typical Syrian kitchen.

PREFACE

Arabic cooking is like Arabic dancing—vivid, exotic, enchanting. Seasoned with herbs and spices, moistened with olive oil and butter, rolled in cabbage and grape leaves, food no longer merely abates hunger but becomes a picture of fragrance and charm to satisfy sight, smell, and taste.

There is no difference between Syrian and Lebanese foods. In America these foods are most popularly known as Syrian foods. However, since Syria was under the rule of Turkey for centuries, some of the drinks and foods are Turkish. This is why the coffee served in Syria and Lebanon is called Turkish coffee.

A part of my heritage, these recipes have been handed down from mother to daughter for generations and followed by instinct—a little of this, a pinch of that—and flavored to please the palate, though the ingredients were never accurately measured.

As my sister and I gathered these recipes from my mother, Maheeba (Mabel), she recalled many scenes of her native land; of certain *haflis* (parties), of friends, of the rich aroma of Turkish coffee poured into a demitasse, of the historical background of Arabic script and the makings of exquisite damask cloth.

When we lived in Canton, Ohio, as children, my sister, brother, and I used to get a great deal of pleasure watching my father and his friends take turns smoking the *narghileh* (Turkish water pipe) as they relaxed during the evenings, exchanging stories of their journey to this country. The *narghileh* had the sound of bubbling water and an incense aroma filled the house from the Persian tobacco that was used. Our *narghileh* was made of beautiful cut glass with an oriental brass stem, and the smoking pipe that was attached had an almost cobra look with its many variegated colors. The smoke was being drawn through cold water to reduce the strength of the nicotine. The guests were served Turkish coffee and the hostess was ready to play the part of a fortuneteller. The cups were inverted and left to stand so that the coffee sediment formed a pattern on the inside of the cup. Then the cups were turned up again and the hostess interpreted the future of each guest from the pattern in his cup.

I have included in the book features on the religious significance of foods, Syrian-Lebanese festivals, weddings, Easter, Epiphany, the preparation of wine and bread for Holy Communion, and a complete Lenten section.

This is an adventure in foods you will want to repeat over and over again. While these customs and traditions still prevail in the land of my ancestors, I felt that you would enjoy opening a few doors to this ancient land, reflecting the mingling of traditions between those days and modern times.

All of the ingredients used in the recipes are available in this country. A Shoppers' Guide in the back of the book tells where they can be purchased.

CONTENTS

Recipes CAPITALIZED in the text may be located by consulting the Index.

LIST OF ILLUSTRATIONS

Majority of photographs taken by Bob Kadel, Terre Haute, Indiana

INTRODUCTION

From the Land of Promise

From the shores of the Mediterranean—land of the Son of God, land of prophets, patriarchs, and apostles—throughout Syria and Lebanon, the same generous hospitality and an open door await the guest.

In the large cities of Damascus, Beirut, Jerusalem, and the villages of Irna, Ein il Shara, Katana, Heena, and other regions the greeting *"Ahlan wa sahlan"* welcomes the visitor and the barrier of strangeness is gone; he is among friends. The familiar phrase *"Nishkor Allah wa-silt bil salami* [Praise the Lord you arrived safely]" is repeated by host and relatives as they receive visitors from abroad.

As introductions are made, one becomes aware that many proper names are derived from names of the Deity. For instance, my brother's name is *Abdullah* (Albert), which means the Servant of God. My father *Mkhyal* (Michael) is addressed *"Boo Abdullah* [the father of Albert]," and my mother is addressed *"Im Abdullah* [the mother of Albert]." Arabic-speaking people are taught from early childhood to show respect for their parents and their elders. A young person never addresses an elder by his proper name, but rather as *"Umtee* [Auntie]" or *"Umee* [Uncle]."

Early morning visiting is usual as everyone gets up before dawn while the air is fresh and cool. A brisk walk to a friend's home gives one a chance to view a paradise of fruit trees. As the guest arrives, coffee and sun-ripened apricots, grapes, and honey-filled figs are placed on tables inlaid with mother-of-pearl. Early breakfast is the time for gossip—and sampling the dainty dishes. A few hours later, at home, regular breakfast consists of coffee, olives, *zahter* (thyme with sumac), scrambled eggs covered with *Kamoun* (powdered cuminseed), *kareeshee* (cheese), and bread, which is considered the "staff of life" in the entire Middle East. From this bread and cheese alone a Syrian can make a complete meal.

The canteen of the Middle East is the *breek*. It is an earthen jug with a narrow neck; in the wide base there is a small spout. The art of drinking from a *breek* is to pour water into the mouth without touching the lips to the spout. Water is kept cool by evaporation through the pores of the jug. Taking the place of water on some occasions is *shraab* (a mixture of fruit juices), or *nbeeth* (wine) served in silver cups inscribed with Arabic mottoes. Many other earthen vessels serve as household containers for oil, honey, wine, rice, wheat, pickles, flour, and olives.

In Damascus the many bazaars fill the streets and alleys of a whole section of the city. Vendors, yelling *"Halee dirsak ya walad* [Food for sweet tooth, young one]," sell *halawa* (a delicious paste made with sesame seeds) and *kathamee* (roasted chick-peas). The youngest of the vendors can be seen walking alongside his donkey carrying beets and other provender. You can hear him chanting out the phrase *"Dafee butnak ya birdan* [Warm your stomach, cold one]." A visitor can walk down the *Souk el* (Street of) *Bezourieh* in Damascus and see many of these vendors. Nearby on the *Souk Arsouniyah* and *Mahidien* are shops jammed with *narghilehs,* hardware, and Arabic instruments.

Native women fill the streets, going to and from the market place carrying urns, woven baskets, and bread on their heads, delicately balancing them without the support of their hands. Streets in the villages are very narrow and crowded. Men are seen hammering out gold, fashioning chains and necklaces and other pieces of art with the same crude tools used by their ancestors.

Tradition and habit are deep-rooted with the Arabic-speaking people. Most of them are hereditary farmers and in some of the villages they find it simpler to follow the ways of ancestors than to venture to use new implements for tilling the land. The cow and ox are used for pulling the plow, which has a long pole with a steel point. However, in many areas Western methods are being utilized for tillage. Damascene or Beirut cows serve the immediate family needs but do not pay for themselves commercially. The usual source of milk has been largely the goat and the sheep, which are much cheaper than a cow.

Scribes sit on oriental rugs in front of buildings in Damascus, mastering the difficult art of gracefully written Arabic script. Writing from the right side to the left, little marks placed above and below a word indicate vowels. When my sister, brother, and I were children, our parents sent us to the Orthodox church hall following grade school classes where we learned to read and write the language from Arabic scholars *Yusuf* (Joseph) Sabb and *Hunna* (John) Shaheen. Our first lesson taught us that this was one of the richest languages in the world.

An exotic type of entertainment has been brought to America from the Middle East. At the *sahras* (parties) guests are treated to Arabic rhythms poured forth by *derbukkis* (drums), reed, and lute. Dancers whirl and sway to the music, and the guests join in the dance of the *dubkee*. Troubadours of the twelfth and thirteenth centuries accompanied their ballads with the lute, which was an original Arabic instrument called *il oud*. Al Ghazali, a philosopher, wrote: "He whom the spring with its blossoms does not move, nor the lute with its strings, is corrupt of nature."

Prior to a wedding, festivity lasts for a week at the home of a bride. Women take turns singing *zalagheet* (wedding songs) with verses such as "*Ah wee, ahla sahla bil thyoof, ah wee, niskee il ahal wal thyoof* [Welcome to the guests, a toast to the parents of the bride and groom]." The guests are served pastries, pistachios, almonds, sunflower and pumpkin seeds. The candy-coated almond signifies a sweet and prosperous life.

Approval of the marriage is mutually agreed upon between families and relatives of the bride and groom, and they are allowed to see each other only in the presence of the family.

In Syria, one day prior to the wedding, gifts of goats and lamb are sent to the home of the bridegroom to be made ready for feasting hundreds of guests. Meats are cooked all night long in a huge *khalkeeni* (kettle) holding hundreds of pounds of meats, some of which are stuffed with rice, spices, and butter. *Kibby* (ground lamb blended with wheat, onions, and spices and baked in butter) heads the tempting array of foods. Platters filled with *Roz* (rice dotted with browned orzo), *Batinjan mihshee* (baked eggplant stuffed with lamb and pine nuts),

Some of the most popular Syrian foods. Top row—Fried Kibby, Baked Eggplant, Kibby Stuffed with English Walnuts. Second row—Meat Pies, Raw Kibby, Stuffed Squash. Third row—Stuffed Grape Leaves, Kibby Stuffed with Yogurt, Spinach Pies. Fourth row—Syrian Bread, Black Olives, Syrian Cheese.

and *Warak inib mihshee* (diced lamb, rice, and spices rolled in tender grape leaves and mellowed with lemon juice) are served on tables adorned with shining damask cloth. If the wedding takes place in the summer the foods are placed on bronze and silver trays and laid out on sheets on the roof. Guests take turns climbing the stone steps to partake of the feast.

The flat rooftop of a Syrian house serves many purposes. When wheat is washed it is spread on the roof to dry under the sun, placed in an earthen barrel, and stored for winter provisions. In the same storeroom are bunches of garlic and onions, dates, figs, and apricots strung together, all suspended from the ceiling.

These dried fruits are sold at the colorful market places of Syria and Lebanon. Especially tempting are the varieties of apricots grown around Damascus. The apricot is pressed and dried and sold in thin cakes called *qamardeen*. An extensive variety of nuts is available, along with cheeses, and breads covered with sesame seeds or topped with golden-brown chickpeas. Used in many foods is the *snoober* (pine nut), which comes from the umbrella pine cones. The cones are placed on the rooftop and then the nuts fall out and are ready to be eaten or stored with the other provisions.

Following a wedding ceremony, it is customary for the groom to present his bride with a gift before she enters her new home. Upon entering, she notices a small section of *ahjeen* (dough) pasted above the door's entrance by the mother-in-law. If the dough sticks to the doorsill until the bride enters, it means a long and happy life for the wedded couple. A familiar saying to the couple at the end of the wedding feast is "*Nikshalak arees* [May you be blessed with a boy]."

On the wedding night the guests and bridal party stain the palms of their hands with henna, clenching their fists to absorb the stain, which acts as a reminder of the gay festivities. The henna dye is made from the leaves of the henna, formerly called camphire tree. Women stain their hair and fingernails as well as the palms of their hands with this dye.

Syrians and Lebanese have a few superstitions. When an infant is first seen, the person looking at the child will puff into the child's face after complimenting the parents of the child. If a well-wisher should *seeboo bil ein* (cast the evil eye upon the child) the puffing will dispel the evil eye. This is done because it is believed that those possessing the evil eye are not aware of it. If a child becomes ill, and the parents feel the evil eye has caused the illness, an elderly woman of the village is called in to say special prayers over the child; as she prays, she holds a bullet sizzling in a skillet over the child's head to rout the evil spirits.

At Eastertime in the Orthodox Catholic Church a large catafalque covered with roses is used to portray the bier of Christ. To pass under this catafalque is considered to insure good luck throughout the year. Parishioners make the sign of the Cross as they pass under the bier, and at the end of the service a rose from the bier is distributed to each person by the priest. Following divine liturgy every Sunday, the congregation receives *Kurban* (Holy Bread) from the priest. Great care is taken not to drop any particles, for this is considered bad luck. If a piece should fall on the ground, it is picked up and in reverence pressed to the lips and taken home so that it will not be stepped upon.

The most common form of *Khobaz* (bread) eaten by Arabic-speaking people is a flat round loaf, as thin as wrapping paper and approximately sixteen inches in diameter. A knife is never used to cut the bread; it is torn by hand into small pieces used as scoops to hold foods. Appetizing morsels of *Shish kebab* (lamb on skewers) are placed in the bread and dipped in a dish of *Laban* (yogurt). The Bible refers to *laban* as a precious asset of the Land of Promise, since it flowed, not with milk and honey as in the English translation, but with *laban* and honey. Sealing friendships with the "breaking of bread" in the Middle East has been a tradition since ancient times and is practiced today in the homes of Syrian-Lebanese-American families.

The Syrian's daily habits and conversation center around the Church. It is unheard of to leave on a journey without making the sign of the Cross and saying, "*Be ism Il Ab, Wal Ibn, Wal Rooh Il Kodos* [In the name of the Father, the Son, and the Holy Ghost]."

The greeting "*Ahlan wa sahlan*" awaits you in the homes of second- and third-generation families of Syrian-Lebanese descent in America—and on your departure you will be given

an often-heard blessing from parent to child, and from friend
to friend—"*Allah koon ma'eck* [May God be with you]," for these
traditions and cultures exist here today as they did in the land
of my ancestors, the Land of Promise.

THE ART OF SYRIAN COOKERY

SPICES AND HERBS

Definitions—Arabic Translation

Spices and herbs exude an aroma that a gourmet appreciates as much as the taste. Taste and smell are so closely related that it is difficult to tell when aroma ends and flavor begins.

In ancient times spices and herbs were the only known medicines. Caraway tea was sometimes used in the nursery to relieve colic, the seeds being a mild laxative. Coriander seed was an antidote against scorpion bites, and its incense was believed to expel evil spirits. Hippocrates praised mustard for its healing qualities. Today's mustard plaster dates back to the old treatments for respiratory ailments; even mustard-perfumed baths were said to help a cold. A sprig of anise was believed to ward off epilepsy, and an anise plant near the pillow of a bed was supposed to restore youth and beauty. Anise is still used to treat throat irritations.

My mother's modern kitchen contains all the spices and herbs used in the recipes. Herbs and spices may be ordered from markets listed in the Shoppers' Guide. Maheeba, my mother, reminds you to use spices and herbs discreetly, for only you and your family know how much seasoning you like in your foods. Keep in mind the old rule of all cooks: when in doubt, season to taste. But do not change the basic ingredients in the recipes.

Spices include all seasonings from the bark, root, stems, seeds, or fruit of aromatic plants and trees growing in tropical countries; common spices are allspice, cloves, nutmeg, ginger, saffron, and cinnamon. Always dried, they are sold in two forms: whole or ground.

Herbs are soft plants grown in a temperate climate. The recipes in this book call for mint, basil, parsley, thyme, bay leaf, and marjoram.

Seeds come from spice and herb plants and trees. Anise, cardamon, coriander, caraway, cumin, and sesame are used in these recipes. Some aromatic seeds grow in America, but larger quantities are cultivated in Africa, Europe, South and Central America.

Preserving herbs. If you grow herbs in your garden, use them in fresh form. To preserve, pick off the tops and perfect leaves and scatter loosely on a tray. Put the tray in a dark, dry place. Drying should take from 3 to 4 days. When dry, crush the leaves and place in labeled jars.

Following are the spices and herbs that should be kept on hand:

Bakdownas (Parsley). Rich in vitamin C. For salads, soups, and garnishes.

Bhar hub wa na'im (Allspice). Dried berry of pimento tree. Tastes like a combination of cloves, cinnamon, and nutmeg.

Ha-bek (Basil). Leaf of annual plant cultivated in Mediterranean areas. Dried, ground, and powdered for *salata,* soups, and garnishes.

Hub-al-hal (Cardamon). An aromatic pod-shaped fruit with seeds inside. Used in Turkish coffee.

Hub-et il baraky (Black Caraway). Biennial herb with aromatic fruit known as caraway seed. Used in *Talamee* (Syrian Bread). Imported from Lebanon, Denmark, and Indonesia. A mild laxative. Added to tea, relieves the colic.

Junzabeel (Ginger). Zanziber plant grown in semitropical countries. Use whole in health drinks.

Kamoun (Cuminseed). Originally from Egypt. Slightly bitter flavor. Brings out the flavor of scrambled eggs. For indigestion, use 1 teaspoonful in powdered form, and follow with a glass of water. Annually exported by the ton from Turkey, Syria, and Iran.

Kirfee (Cinnamon). Cassia cinnamon grown in the Far East. Dried bark is sold in two forms: sticks or ground. Used in spice drink called *Miglee* or *Finjan Kirfee.* This is traditionally served to visitors of a newborn baby.

Kizbara (Coriander). An herb with aromatic seeds rich in vitamin C. For meats and vegetables. Tasty in a dish called *Fooleeyee* (Fava Beans).

Mahleb (Black Cherry Kernels). Use in *Talamee* (Syrian Bread) and *Ka'ick* (Anise bread).

Mardakoosh (Marjoram). From the mint family. Aromatic and slightly bitter. For soups, salads, and meats.

Ma-warid (Rose Water) and *Mazahar* (Orange-blossom Water). To flavor pastries, puddings, and cakes. When not available, substitute vanilla flavoring.

Na'na (Mint). A fragrant plant. Leaves, fresh or dried, for flavoring soups, meats, salads, and beverages.

Simsum (Sesame Seed). To flavor pies, cookies, rolls, and pastries. Sesame oil used for making *Baba ghanouj* and *Tahini* sauce. Tons of this seed go into *Halawa,* a mouth-watering Turkish candy.

Thume (Garlic). From the lily family. For flavoring meats and salads.

Warak al gar (Bay leaf). Aromatic leaf of sweet bay or laurel tree. To flavor soups and meats. Historically, used as an antiseptic during epidemics to boil with clothing.

Yansoon (Anise). Fruit of small annual plant which dries into the form of a seed. For *Ka'ick* (Anise Bread) and Anise Tea.

Zahter (Thyme). Pungent. Dried, fresh, or chopped for salads and meats. Blended with sumac into powdered form and used in Lenten pies.

ARABIC MENUS

The menus below are typical Arabic meals for each month of the year.

JANUARY DINNER MENU

Vegetable soup
Raw kibby
Cabbage rolls
Combination salad
Syrian bread
Coffee
Rice custard

FEBRUARY DINNER MENU

Kibby with yogurt-rice sauce
Meat pies
Stewed cauliflower
Syrian bread
Coffee
Stuffed figs

MARCH DINNER MENU

Eggplant stew
Spinach salad
Baked fish—*Tahini*
Coffee
Miskee sweets

APRIL DINNER MENU
(Palm Sunday)

Shrimp cocktail
Assorted relishes
Baked stuffed fish
Baked eggplant
   —Sesame-oil with lemon
Tomato-onion salad
Turkish coffee
Turkish delight

MAY DINNER MENU
(For a perfect outing)

Marinated broiled chicken
Fried kibby
Wheat garden salad
   (*Tabooley*)
Lettuce
Cool drinks
Cake

JUNE DINNER MENU

Raw kibby
Roast chicken
   —Rice-giblet dressing
Syrian bread
Stuffed shredded wheat
Coffee

JULY DINNER MENU
(Picnic)

Baked kibby
Yogurt pies
Charcoal-broiled lamb
  on skewers
Corn on cob
Wheat garden salad
  (*Tabooley*)
Grape or lettuce leaves
Soft drinks
Watermelon

AUGUST DINNER MENU

Stuffed grape leaves
Yogurt
Fava beans with lamb
Rice-orzo dressing
Beet salad
Coffee

SEPTEMBER DINNER MENU

Tomato juice
Stuffed squash
Fried kibby
Lamb liver
Salad
Turkish coffee
Cake

OCTOBER DINNER MENU

Lamb with yogurt
Spinach pies
Pickled turnips
Tea
Sesame pastry delights

NOVEMBER DINNER MENU

Assorted relish tray
Turkey—Rice-giblet dressing
Stuffed grape leaves
Baked eggplant
Nut-filled cakes
Almond rolls
Coffee

DECEMBER DINNER MENU
(Christmas Day)

Fruit cup
Roast duck
  —Giblet bread stuffing
Baked kibby
Stuffed cabbage leaves
Salad
Assorted pickled vegetables
Diamond pastry delights
Coffee

APPETIZERS

Maza

Syrian and Lebanese artistry with appetizers is unexcelled. The eggplant, when baked or steamed and peeled, is prepared several ways as part of the *maza*. The pulp is mashed with sesame-seed oil, garlic, lemon juice, and salt. Flat loaves of Arabic bread go well with the different spreads. Miniature *Kibby* (the national dish of Syria) and *Sfeeha* (Meat Pies) are prepared in advance and stored in the freezer for unexpected guests. Just heat and serve to tempt an appetite. *Joban* and *Laban dahareej* (Syrian cheeses) are musts on the *maza* table.

Here are some dishes for any group or party. For the centerpiece of your *maza* table, fill a platter with Flaming Apples. Surround the centerpiece with dishes of Meat Pies, Pickled Turnips, black olives, Garlic Eggplant, choice Raw Beef, Syrian Bread, and other delicacies.

RAW BEEF   *Lahum nee*

- ½ pound grade A beef, ground
- 1 large onion, chopped
- ½ teaspoon pepper
- ½ teaspoon salt
- 1 teaspoon dried coriander (optional)

Knead ingredients together. Serve as appetizer with Syrian Bread. Goes well with anise-flavored liqueur, *arak*, also known in the United States as anisette. *Serves 3.*

FLAMING APPLES   *Tafah moulahheb*

In stem end of large red apples, scoop out hollow about 1½ inches deep. Line hollows with aluminum foil and fill with brandy. Place Fried Kibby balls on the ends of toothpicks and stick around apples. Light brandy and serve at once. (Kibby balls are made with same ingredients used in *Kibby neeyee*—shape into small balls.)

NOTE: Brandy fire will not spread or burn, even when spilled on cloth.

Joban. (Syrian Cheese)

SYRIAN CHEESE *Joban*

    1 gallon milk
    2 junket tablets

Heat milk to lukewarm. Melt 2 junket tablets in milk. Mix with hand and set about 10 to 15 minutes. Stir again with your hand or with a wooden spoon. Set 10 more minutes until *Joban* settles on bottom. Pour into colander and shape smoothly with your hands (cupping the hands) to make sure all water drains out. Sprinkle with salt. Reserve liquid for making *Kareeshee*. *Yield: 5 Joban, 5 inches in diameter, 1½ inches thick.*

COTTAGE CHEESE WITH LEMONS
Kareeshee mi limoon

> 1 quart liquid from *Joban*
> 1 quart milk
> Juice of 2 lemons

Heat liquid from *Joban* on low fire until warm. Add milk. When milk rises, add lemon juice. Cook on low fire until cottage cheese gets thick. Pour into colander to strain off excess liquid. *Yield: 2 cups.*

COTTAGE CHEESE WITH JUNKET TABLETS
Kareeshee

> 2 quarts milk
> 2 junket tablets

Heat milk to boiling point. Remove from fire. When lukewarm, add junket tablets. Return to low fire until cheese gets thick. *Yield: 2 cups.*

YOGURT CHEESE   *Labanee*

> 2 quarts yogurt
> ½ teaspoon salt

Pour yogurt in muslin or cheesecloth bag. Tie top of bag in knot and hang on nail or kitchen sink faucet. Put a pan under bag to catch liquid. Set overnight. Excess liquid will drain off and yogurt will become firm enough to spread. Remove cheese following day and place in dish. Sprinkle salt on top. Spread on flat loaves of Syrian Bread. *Yield: 2½ cups.*

YOGURT BALLS   *Laban dahareej*

> Yogurt Cheese
> Olive oil

Roll Yogurt Cheese into balls the size of golf balls. Place in tray or dish. Allow to set overnight in refrigerator until firm. Place in glass jar and cover with olive oil. Keep lid on jar. To serve, place in small dish and spoon small amount of oil over Yogurt Balls to keep soft enough to spread on Syrian Bread. *Yield: 20 Yogurt Balls.*

Yogurt Balls, Black Olives, Yogurt Cheese, Syrian Bread.

EGGPLANT WITH LABAN   *Batinjan imfasakh*

2 large eggplants
¼ cup olive oil
1 cup yogurt
1 teaspoon salt
1 clove garlic

Skin eggplants. Slice very thin. Sprinkle small amount of salt on slices so that excess moisture will drain from eggplants. (This will prevent eggplant slices from absorbing too much oil when fried.) Fry in olive oil until golden brown. Remove from oil and mash. Add yogurt and mix well. Add garlic that has been crushed in salt. *Yield: 4 cups.*

SHEEP KIDNEY TOAST   *Kilwat ghanum ma'a joban*
- 1 pound sheep kidneys
- 1 teaspoon chopped parsley
- 1 onion, chopped
- 3 tablespoons butter
- 1 tablespoon Worcestershire sauce
- 2 tablespoons flour
- Salt and pepper to taste
- Bread crumbs
- Sharp cheese

Split the kidneys in half, removing outer skin and sinews, and mince them fine. Put parsley and onion in a pan with butter. Fry for a few minutes, then add Worcestershire sauce, sprinkle with flour, and cook for 2 minutes, stirring to blend in the flour. Add kidneys, salt, and pepper. Butter thin slices of toast, cover them with the mince, and sprinkle with a thick layer of bread crumbs mixed with a small amount of cheese. *Serves 4.*

COTTAGE CHEESE BALLS   *Shunkleesh*
- 5 pounds cottage cheese
- 5 tablespoons salt
- 1 cup melted butter
- 1 cup *zahter* (mixture of powdered thyme and sumac)

Place cottage cheese in cheesecloth sack. Tie top of sack in knot and squeeze out all moisture. Hang on nail or kitchen sink faucet for 3 days until cheese appears to be completely dry. Remove from sack, add salt, and knead well. Roll into balls slightly larger than golf balls. Lay on a clean cloth and cover with cheesecloth. Place in attic or in shaded area (in dry weather) for 3 days until balls are hard-crusted. Place in an airtight jar for 10 days. Mold will form around the cheese balls and the cheese will take on a dark color. The cheese balls are now ripe and ready for trimming. Trim off mold around balls and dip in melted butter. Roll in *zahter*. Place in glass jar and refrigerate. Serve with scrambled eggs or as appetizers with Syrian Bread. Yield: *20 Cheese Balls.*

NOTE: There is no substitute for *zahter*. This can be purchased by the pound from Middle Eastern stores listed in the Shoppers' Guide.

SAUCES

Marqeh

Sauces require special attention lest they be grainy or lumpy. Yogurt and Mint Sauce is delightful on green squash stuffed with a spicy mixture of rice and lamb.

These sauces are worthy of a poet's praise.

NOTE: Additional sauces may be found in the section on Lenten Foods.

YOGURT *Laban*

Recalling her childhood in Syria, Maheeba tells of how, while visiting an inn, she saw a goatskin hanging in an archway. A woman poured some *Laban* into a muslin sack to drain the water, making ready for a platter of *Labanee,* a spread used on flat loaves of Syrian Bread. Then two women poured the rest of the *Laban* into a watertight goatskin and swung the skin back and forth from a wooden tripod until the *Laban* turned to butter. The women told Maheeba that this method started long ago when a rider, after a journey, found his milk had been jolted into butter while the container dangled by his saddle.

Milk has long been fermented by exposing it to the air and waiting for it to jell. The fermented milk is then used as a starter for making *Laban*.

For centuries the principal food in the Middle East, *Laban* is served at most meals. In America, *Laban* is known commercially as yogurt, a Turkish word.

The Bible frequently refers to *Laban* as a healthful and filling food. It has been used for the treatment of burns and cuts and dietetically for stomach ulcers.

> 2 quarts milk
> 3 tablespoons commercial yogurt (known as *rowbee* or "starter")
> Turkish towels (or any heavy towel)

Heat milk on low fire until it comes to a boil. As soon as it boils, remove from fire and cool to almost lukewarm. It should be warm enough for the yogurt germ to spread, but not too hot to be able to immerse your finger in milk to count of ten. Then add 3 tablespoons yogurt and stir well. Cover pan with lid and wrap towel or cloth around pan to preserve heat. Store in warm place for 6 hours. Remove cover. After a few minutes, refrigerate. The yogurt will jell like pudding and, depending on the *rowbee,* will taste sweet or tart. If you are using the *rowbee* from yogurt that has been under refrigeration for a week or more, the results will be tart or sharp. If *rowbee* from fresh yogurt only a few days old is used, the taste will be sweeter.

This is a tasty complement to *roz* (rice) and *burghol* (wheat) dishes. *Yield: 2 quarts.*

YOGURT WITH RICE   *Laban-ee-yee ma'a roz*

    ½ cup rice
    3 cups water
    3 cups yogurt
    1 tablespoon flour
    1 teaspoon salt

Soak rice ½ hour in 1 cup water. Strain yogurt in colander. Add 2 cups water to yogurt. Mix well. Mix flour with small amount of water to make paste, then add to yogurt. Heat to boiling. Drain water from rice. Add rice and salt to yogurt. Cook on low fire for 5 minutes. Serve with Boiled Kibby. *Yield: 5 cups.*

YOGURT AND MINT SAUCE   *Laban-ee-yee lil koosa*

    4 cups yogurt
    1 tablespoon flour or cornstarch
    1 teaspoon garlic powder
    1 tablespoon dried mint

Stir yogurt well. Mix flour or cornstarch with water to make paste. Add to yogurt and cook on low fire. Keep stirring until it boils. Add garlic powder and dried mint. This is an excellent sauce for Stuffed Squash. *Yield: 4 cups.*

MARINADE SAUCE   *Marqeh lil shish kebab*

    1 clove garlic, chopped fine
    2 onions, chopped
    3 tablespoons olive oil
    ⅛ teaspoon thyme
    1 tablespoon chopped parsley
    1 bay leaf
    Salt and pepper
    ½ cup dry wine
    Juice of 1 lemon
    ½ cup water

Sauté garlic and onions in oil. Add herbs and seasoning and cook a few minutes longer. Pour in the wine, lemon juice, and water and simmer over low flame for 20 minutes. Remove from fire and cool. Try this over *Shish kebab*, fried fish, or vegetables. *Yield: 1½ cups.*

DRAWN BUTTER SAUCE   *Marqeh il samin*

    3 tablespoons butter
    2 tablespoons flour
    ½ teaspoon salt
    Dash of pepper
    1 cup water
    1 teaspoon lemon juice

Melt butter in double boiler. Stir in flour, salt, and pepper. Stir until thoroughly blended. Add water gradually while stirring and cook over boiling water until smooth and thick, stirring constantly. Add lemon juice. Serve over asparagus, broccoli, or fish. *Yield: 1 cup.*

SAUCE FOR ROAST LAMB   *Marqeh lil lahum ghanum*

    1 tablespoon fresh mint leaves
    1¼ cups wine (any cooking wine or sherry)
    1 teaspoon garlic powder (optional)
    ¼ cup lemon juice
    1 teaspoon sugar

Pick over fresh mint leaves. Chop fine. Mix together all ingredients. Stand in warm place for 2 hours. This is a tasty sauce to spoon over Roast Leg of Lamb. *Yield: 1½ cups.*

SOUPS

Shouraba

Soups have an international appeal. After seasoning the soup, the chef knows when he has reached perfection. As with wine, aging improves the flavor; soup dishes are usually better on the second day.

In Syria and Lebanon, soups do not usually form part of the menu when there is a multitude of cereal, meat, and vegetable dishes from which to choose. However, on cold winter days soup is prepared as the principal dish of the meal. Flavored with a combination of *laban* (yogurt), cracked wheat, and a variety of herbs and spices, the soup is sometimes preferred to other foods. Two of the most popular soups of the Middle East are Lentil Soup and Chicken Rice Soup.

NAVY BEAN SOUP   *Shouraba lubee by-tha*

    1 pound navy beans
    1 large onion, chopped
    2 cloves garlic
    ½ teaspoon caraway seeds
    ½ teaspoon rosemary
    2 tablespoons tomato paste
    2 bay leaves
    ¼ cup vinegar
    Salt and pepper to taste

Wash beans and put in pan. Cover completely with water. Bring to a boil and add remaining ingredients, except salt and pepper. Simmer 2 hours. Add salt and pepper and serve. *Serves 8.*

CHICKEN RICE SOUP   *Shouraba il roz*

    1 hen (sectioned for cooking)
    2 cups chopped celery
    Dash of allspice

Dash of cinnamon
Salt and pepper to taste
½ cup rice

Simmer chicken, covered, in water until tender. Add celery, spices, and seasoning. When celery is almost tender, add rice and cook another 5 minutes. *Serves 6–7.*

CHICK-PEA SOUP *Shouraba il homos*
1 pound chick-peas
½ teaspoon salt
½ cup olive oil
2 large onions, chopped
Salt and pepper to taste

Soak peas overnight in lukewarm water, with salt. Following day rinse well and rub peas between fingers to remove skins. Rinse again, cover with water, and simmer until tender. Add remaining ingredients and cook until done, about 30 minutes. *Serves 6.*

KISHIK SOUP
Kishik is a combination of *laban,* ground wheat, and spices. This mixture is dried for many days under the sun, then run through a sieve until it is a fine dry powder. It can be purchased by the pound from any of the Middle Eastern food stores listed in the Shoppers' Guide.

1 onion, chopped
Oil
1 cup *kishik*
3 cups water

Sauté onion in oil until soft. Mix with *kishik* and simmer for 1 minute. Add water. Stir until thick. This is a very nourishing and filling soup. *Serves 4.*

LENTIL SOUP *Shouraba il addis*
2 cups lentils
Salt and pepper to taste
1 tablespoon sweet butter

Sort and rinse lentils in water. Cover lentils with 6 cups water. Boil 30 minutes. When soft, strain through colander, working

through with wooden spoon. Work purée with hands until it is
very soft; add a little cold water and season; return to fire and
boil until it thickens. Then add butter, which has been brought
to boiling point in another saucepan. Most suitable for winter.
Serves 8.

LENTILS AND WHEAT WITH KISHIK   *Imjadara markoo'a*

    2 cups Lentils and Wheat (see Lenten section)
    1 onion, minced
    2 tablespoons butter
    1 cup *kishik*
    2 cups water

Sauté onion in butter. Add *kishik* and mix well. Add water and
stir. Add 2 cups cooked Lentils and Wheat and continue stirring
for 2 minutes over medium fire. *Serves 4.*

CREAM OF TOMATO SOUP   *Shouraba il banadoora*

    2½ cups tomatoes (canned)
    1 tablespoon minced onion
    ¼ teaspoon celery seed
    ½ teaspoon sugar
    ½ bay leaf
    1 whole clove
    ⅛ teaspoon baking soda
    2 tablespoons butter
    3 tablespoons flour
    2 teaspoons salt
    ⅛ teaspoon pepper
    2 cups milk

Cook the tomatoes, onion, celery seed, ½ teaspoon salt, sugar,
bay leaf, and clove together for 5 minutes. Sieve and then add
soda. Melt butter in double boiler. Add flour, 1½ teaspoons salt,
and the pepper. Add the milk and stir until thick. Add tomato
mixture gradually, stirring constantly. Heat 1 minute, stirring
constantly. *Serves 6.*

CREAM OF SQUASH SOUP   *Shouraba il koosa*

3 green squash (or zucchini)
2 cups milk
2 tablespoons Rendered Butter
2 tablespoons flour
Salt and pepper to taste

Stew squash in a little water until soft. Strain, measure, and keep hot. For 2 cups squash, use 2 cups hot milk thickened with butter and flour. Combine with squash, season, reheat, and serve. *Serves 6.*

VEGETABLE SOUP   *Shouraba il kuthra*

1 pound shin beef with bone
3½ quarts cold water
2 tablespoons salt
1 clove garlic, minced
½ cup minced onion
¾ cup diced celery
2 cups shredded green cabbage
1 cup diced carrots
1 No. 2 can tomatoes
⅛ teaspoon pepper
4 tablespoons minced parsley

Combine beef, water, and salt. Cover and bring to a boil. Skim. Replace cover and simmer 4 hours. Remove bone. Add remaining ingredients, except parsley. Cover and simmer 30 minutes. Sprinkle with parsley. *Serves 8.*

SALADS

Salata

Salads, plain or fancy, are always in demand. Syrian and Lebanese children and grownups walk along the streets eating head lettuce as we eat hot dogs. No picnic is complete without a special salad of *Tabooley* (see Lenten section), made with cracked wheat and vegetables and scooped into the mouth with a grape, lettuce, or cabbage leaf. Another favorite is a side dish of Cucumber-Yogurt Salad. Popular during the Lenten season and throughout the year, Syrian and Lebanese salads are prepared of endive, dandelion, tomatoes, and eggplant.

There is nothing so satisfying as *Salata kuthra*, the Syrian Combination Salad, with its olive oil trickling over all the vegetables and flavored with fragrant mint, used fresh or dried. The secret of the tasty Syrian salad lies in the expert handling of the seasonings.

COMBINATION SALAD *Salata kuthra*

    6 tomatoes
    2 green peppers
    1 bunch green onions
    1 avocado
    ½ bunch parsley
    1 bunch radishes
    1 cucumber
    1 tablespoon fresh or dried mint
    1 teaspoon garlic powder
    Salt and pepper to taste
    ⅓ cup olive oil
    Juice of 3 lemons

Chop vegetables, and combine. Add seasonings, olive oil, and lemon juice; toss and serve. *Serves 8.*

BEEF TONGUE SALAD   *Salata il sane*

1 small beef tongue, cooked
1 onion
Juice of 1 lemon
6 sprigs parsley
Salt and pepper to taste
½ teaspoon garlic powder
Olive oil

Slice and cube tongue. Add remaining ingredients and toss with enough olive oil to coat salad. *Serves 4.*

BEET SALAD   *Salata il shamonder*

3 large cooked beets, diced
1 onion, minced
2 tablespoons chopped parsley
Salt and pepper to taste
Olive oil
Vinegar

Combine beets with onion, parsley, salt, and pepper. Use enough oil to coat salad and one fourth as much vinegar. Chill and serve. *Serves 4–6.*

CUCUMBER-YOGURT SALAD   *Khyar ·mi laban*

1 large cucumber
1 clove garlic or ½ teaspoon garlic powder
½ teaspoon salt
1 quart yogurt
1 tablespoon dried mint

Peel and dice cucumber. Mash garlic with salt and add to yogurt. Add diced cucumber. Garnish with dried mint. *Serves 4.*

EGGPLANT SALAD   *Salata il batinjan*

    2 large eggplants
    3 tomatoes
    1 small onion, grated
    2 tablespoons chopped parsley
    1 cup oil
    3 tablespoons wine vinegar
    Salt and pepper to taste

Bake eggplants in moderate oven (350°) for 1 hour. Remove, dip in cold water, and peel. Dice and place in salad bowl, previously rubbed with garlic. Add quartered tomatoes, onion, parsley, oil, vinegar, and seasoning. Allow to marinate 1 hour before serving. *Serves 6.*

SALMON SALAD   *Salata il samek*

    1 No. 2 can salmon
    Salt and pepper to taste
    3 green onions, chopped
    Olive oil
    Lemon juice

Remove fat and skin from salmon, drain. Combine salmon, seasonings, and green onions. Moisten with olive oil and lemon juice. Chill. *Serves 4.*

TOMATO-SARDINE SALAD   *Salata banadoora-samek*

    4 tomatoes
    1 small can sardines
    Lettuce
    1 medium onion, sliced
    2 tablespoons lemon juice
    1 hard-cooked egg yolk

Peel tomatoes, slice, and chill. Drain oil from sardines, remove skin and backbone. Arrange lettuce on salad plate, place tomato slices on it, cover with sardines and onion slices, and sprinkle with lemon juice. Garnish with egg yolk, which has been pressed through a sieve. *Serves 4.*

NOTE: Additional salads may be found in Lenten section.

GAME, POULTRY, AND DRESSINGS

Jaj il arth ma'a hashwa

Syria has an abundance of game. Pheasant and quail are plentiful and have a mild flavor. Duck is also prevalent; the flavor varies with the diet and the time of year.

Good chicken is moist chicken, as every Syrian housewife knows. First, chicken is rubbed inside and out with spices. Then it is stuffed either with *Hashwa ghanum ma'a snoober* (a mixture of minced lamb, pine nuts, and lemon juice) or with a mixture of rice, minced giblets, and English walnuts. The chicken is trussed and placed in a large kettle to simmer until it is almost tender. Timing isn't checked by the clock; tenderness is determined by poking and pinching. The chicken is then roasted golden brown in the oven.

Pigeons and sparrows—roasted whole or cooked in a stew with rice, almonds, and raisins—are delicacies.

DUCK WITH WINE SAUCE   *But ma'a marqeh*

  1 duck
  2 tablespoons butter
  1 onion, chopped
  1 cup red wine
  1 cup tomato sauce
  1 cup water
  Dash of cinnamon
  Salt and pepper to taste

Wash and clean duck and cut into serving pieces. Sauté onion in butter, add duck, and brown on all sides. Add wine, cover, and cook for 20 minutes. Add tomato sauce diluted with 1 cup water, cinnamon, salt, and pepper. Cover and simmer until duck is cooked, approximately 30 minutes. Sauce may be thickened with a little flour if desired. *Serves 4.*

ROAST GOOSE   *Wuz*

    7–8-pound goose
    1 apple, quartered
    2 onions, quartered

Singe, wash, and clean goose. Stuff cavity with the apple and onions. Prick with a fork through the fat layers of the goose. This will help to draw out the fat. Place in shallow pan in moderately hot oven (375°) for 15 to 20 minutes or until fat starts to run. Remove from oven, pour off fat. Repeat this two or three times until fat ceases to drip. The bird is well cooked when thick portion of drumstick meat is soft. (For a 7–8-pound goose, roast 30 minutes per pound.) Do not add water and do not baste. Discard apples and onions after roasting. *Serves 6.*

TURKEY   *Habesh*

    25-pound turkey
    2 tablespoons baking soda
    ¼ teaspoon cinnamon
    ¼ teaspoon nutmeg
    ¼ teaspoon allspice
    ¼ teaspoon salt
    ¼ teaspoon pepper

Soak turkey overnight in pan of water to which baking soda has been added. Following day rinse thoroughly. Place in large kettle and parboil until tender. Remove from turkey broth and dry. Reserve broth. Preheat oven to 250°. Rub inside and out with spices. Place turkey in roasting pan with small amount of broth. Cover with aluminum foil. Bake in slow oven (250°) 2 to 2½ hours, basting occasionally with broth. When turkey turns golden brown, remove from oven. Triple the recipe for Rice-Giblet Dressing and serve with the turkey. *Serves 12.*

ROAST PHEASANT *Jaj il arth*

2½–3-pound pheasant
½ teaspoon salt
½ teaspoon pepper
½ teaspoon cinnamon
Salad oil

Clean and dry the pheasant thoroughly. Rub cavity with salt, pepper, and cinnamon. Bake uncovered in a moderately hot oven (400°) for 20 minutes. Place several thicknesses of cheese-cloth, soaked in salad oil, on the breast of the pheasant. Cover and bake in slow oven (250°) for 2 hours. Serve with Rice-Giblet Dressing. *Serves 3.*

FRIED RABBIT *Arnabee miklee*

2 rabbits
4 tablespoons flour
2 teaspoons salt
¼ teaspoon pepper
6 tablespoons salad oil
4 tablespoons hot water

Clean rabbits and cut up for frying. Combine flour, salt, and pepper. Dredge rabbit pieces until well coated. Brown on all sides in oil in a covered skillet. When well browned, sprinkle with hot water. Cover and simmer over low heat for 45 minutes or until tender. *Serves 4.*

MARINATED BROILED CHICKEN
Jaj ma'a limoon wa zahter

2 1½–2-pound broilers
½–¾ cup salad oil
¾ cup lemon juice
2 tablespoons thyme
1 teaspoon powdered garlic
Salt and pepper to taste

Split broilers down the back. Combine remaining ingredients to make a marinade. Pour on chickens and marinate 1 hour. Arrange chickens skin side down on preheated broiler, about 3 inches from heat; broil about 40–45 minutes, basting every 5–10 minutes with the marinade. *Serves 4.*

CHICKEN STEW   *Yukhnet jaj*

    1 tablespoon baking soda
    1 cup chick-peas (*homos*)
    3-pound stewing hen, cut in serving pieces
    4 onions, quartered
    2 large potatoes, cubed
    Cinnamon, salt, pepper to taste

Soak chick-peas with baking soda in water overnight. Drain chick-peas, cover with water, and add pieces of hen. Cover pan and simmer on low fire 3 to 4 hours or until tender. Then add onions, potatoes, and seasoning and cook 15 minutes more. Delicious served over Rice-Orzo Dressing. *Serves 6.*

ROAST CHICKEN   *Jaj mishwee*

    5-pound chicken
    1 tablespoon salt
    ¼ teaspoon cinnamon
    ¼ teaspoon nutmeg
    ¼ teaspoon allspice
    ¼ teaspoon salt
    ¼ teaspoon pepper

Clean the chicken. Tie legs together. Place in pan and cover with water. Add 1 tablespoon salt. Cover and cook until tender, about 40 minutes. Preheat oven to 350°. Remove chicken and rub cavity with spices. Roast in moderate oven (350°) for 30 minutes, using chicken broth to baste. Chicken will turn a golden brown. *Serves 4.*

ROAST CHICKEN WITH RICE-WALNUT STUFFING
Jaj mihshee ma'a hashwa roz

    5-pound chicken
    ¼ pound giblets, minced
    3 tablespoons butter
    1 cup rice
    ½ cup chopped English walnuts
    ½ teaspoon salt
    ⅛ teaspoon allspice

⅛ teaspoon nutmeg
⅛ teaspoon cinnamon
⅛ teaspoon pepper

Clean the chicken. Sauté giblets in butter. Add rice and stir constantly for 3 minutes. Remove from heat and add walnuts, salt, and spices. Stuff the chicken loosely. Truss, tie legs together, and place in a kettle. Cover with water and simmer until almost tender. Preheat oven to 300°. Remove chicken from kettle and roast in an open pan in slow oven (325°) for ½ hour or until chicken is tender. Last 10 minutes of roasting, glaze chicken with butter to turn a golden brown. *Serves 6.*

MINCED LAMB DRESSING *Hashwa ghanum ma'a snoober*

½ pound lamb, minced
¼ cup pine nuts
¼ pound butter
¼ cup rice
Juice of 1 lemon
Salt and pepper to taste

Sauté lamb and pine nuts in butter. Place in a bowl and add rice, lemon juice, salt, and pepper. Use to stuff a 5-pound chicken. Or omit the rice and use as a tasty dressing over a platter of *Kibby neeyee*.

GIBLET-BREAD STUFFING *Hashwa kiwanis ma'a khobaz*

2 cups cooked giblets
1½ cups boiling water
¾ cup butter or margarine
½ cup minced onion
¼ teaspoon pepper
1 tablespoon poultry seasoning
1½ teaspoons sage
1½ teaspoons salt
2 tablespoons prepared mustard
2 tablespoons diced celery
3 quarts day-old bread crumbs
2 tablespoons minced parsley

Chop giblets. Combine the boiling water, butter, and onion and simmer 5 minutes. Add remaining ingredients and mix well. Place in baking tray and bake about 30 minutes in moderately hot oven (350°); or use this to stuff cavity of an 8-pound bird. *Serves 6.*

Simmering rice and giblets in Rendered Butter and heating chicken broth to pour over the rice.

RICE-GIBLET DRESSING   *Roz ma'a kiwanis* or *Hashwa roz*

- 1 cup rice
- 1 teaspoon salt
- 3 tablespoons Rendered Butter
- ½ pound giblets, chopped
- ¼ cup pine nuts or English walnuts
- 2 cups chicken broth
- ½ teaspoon salt

Soak rice in warm water with 1 teaspoon salt for 1 hour. Rinse rice thoroughly in water and drain. Melt butter in pan and add giblets. Sauté giblets, then add pine nuts, stirring until golden. Add rice, stirring gently about 2 minutes. Add boiling chicken broth and ½ teaspoon salt. Cover pan and cook on low fire for 25 minutes. This recipe can be used to stuff cavity of a 4-pound bird. *Serves 4.*

RICE-ORZO DRESSING   *Roz ma'a shareeyee*

- 2 cups rice
- 2 teaspoons salt
- 3 tablespoons Rendered Butter
- ½ cup *orzo*
- 4 cups boiling water
- Cinnamon

Soak rice in warm water with 1 teaspoon salt for 1 hour. Rinse rice thoroughly in water and drain. Melt butter in pan and add *orzo*. Stir until browned. Add rice, stirring gently about 2 minutes. Add boiling water and 1 teaspoon salt. Cook on low fire in covered saucepan until water is absorbed, about 20 minutes. Sprinkle cinnamon over rice when cooked. This recipe can be used to stuff cavity of a 6-pound bird. *Serves 6.*

NOTE: *Orzo* can be purchased from Middle Eastern stores listed in Shoppers' Guide. A substitute is vermicelli. If using vermicelli, break into small pieces ¼-inch long.

RENDERED BUTTER   *Samin imfakis*

Rendered Butter is used especially in rice recipes and in baking *Kibby* and all pastries. This butter will keep for months, stored in jars or crocks and kept on a pantry shelf. It is more convenient to cook many pounds at one time rather than a few pounds. Sweet butter is *not* a substitute for Rendered Butter.

Melt 5 pounds butter. When it appears ready to boil, add ½ cup *burghol* (cracked wheat). Heat on low fire. When steam no longer appears, remove from fire. Set to one side for 30 minutes. Pour into another container. Salt and residue will remain on bottom of pan. (Flour may be substituted for wheat.)

MEATS AND OUTDOOR FESTIVALS

Lahum wal Mahrajan

Women of Syria and Lebanon know a thousand and one ways to make meats tasty. Marinated and seasoned with spices and herbs, meats are slowly cooked to bring out the flavor.

During the feasting season the head of the family goes to the country to bargain with a farmer for a lamb. At home the lamb is fattened for a week on mulberry leaves and malt. Then the family and the neighbors and relatives all gather to slaughter the lamb. The lamb is dressed and rubbed with a handful of spices and herbs and is tied on a spit and rotated over coals. As it starts to turn brown, the lamb is basted with hot fat. Sometimes lambs are stuffed with Minced Lamb Dressing and served whole on platters surrounded by fruit.

In this country the Syrians and Lebanese travel great distances to *mahrajans* (outdoor festivals) to see relatives and renew acquaintances. The *mahrajan* usually takes place in a park rented by one of the Syrian organizations. Booths featuring *Khobaz arabee* (Syrian Bread) and *Kibby kras* (Fried Kibby) are set up. The air is filled with the aroma of *Lahum mishwee* (Lamb on Skewers), and picnic tables are loaded with *Fatayer Laban* (Yogurt Pies), *Sfeeha* (Meat Pies), bowls of *Tabooley* (Wheat Garden Salad), and other delectable foods.

Hundreds of people arrive and merriment is in the air as the festival gets under way with Arabic entertainment. The older men always find time to relax during the afternoon as they gather at picnic tables playing their favorite card game of whist.

The famous Arabic entertainers Amer and Sana Kaddaj, Kahraman, Odette, Hanaan and Fadwa may be on hand to render Arabic songs. These *mahrajans* often find the famous *oud* (lute) player Joe Budway entertaining, with the Hamways beating the *derbukkis* (drums), providing Arabic music all day and throughout the evening. Young men and women are in gay spirits as they

stand in a curved line, holding hands, dancing the *dubkee*, swaying forward and backward, kicking the right foot out and down
as they move in a semicircle to the right. In the difficult but
entertaining sword dance a male dancer masters the handling of
the sword, swishing it back and forth, depicting a one-man duel.
And all the while the aroma of barbecued mutton lingers in the
air as the food stands prepare to close—for a few hours' rest before another day at the *mahrajan*.

In Syria fat-tailed sheep provide food for the winter months.
The flesh, mutton, is preserved by salting and rolling in its own
fat. A Syrian woman shopping for mutton today looks for fresh,
red, fine-grained flesh and snow-white fat. Mutton is less expensive than lamb; it can be used for stuffing vegetables and is
a very tasty meat when barbecued. The most popular cut of
meat is the leg of lamb, which offers tender meat for making
Kibby and *Shish kebab*. The bones are cracked and used in preparing some of the recipes. Placed on the bottom of the pan
when cooking Stuffed Cabbage Leaves, they add a great deal
to the flavor. Meat from the shoulder or breast of the lamb, a
less expensive cut, is used to stuff grape and cabbage leaves,
squash and eggplant. Although lamb is preferred, beef may be
substituted in these recipes.

ROAST LEG OF LAMB   *Faketh lahum ghanum*

    5-pound leg of lamb
    1 teaspoon salt
    2 cloves garlic, minced
    ¼ teaspoon pepper
    ¼ bay leaf, crushed
    ¼ teaspoon marjoram
    ¼ teaspoon sage
    ¼ teaspoon ginger
    ¼ teaspoon thyme
    1 tablespoon olive oil

Wipe lamb with damp cloth. Cut small gashes ¼-inch long on
top surface of lamb. Combine remaining ingredients except olive
oil. Rub well into meat so that all gashes are completely filled.
Give roast a final coating with oil. Sear in preheated oven (500°)

for 15 minutes. Reduce temperature to 350° and roast about 1½ hours. (If desired, add par-boiled potatoes and onions to roasting pan when meat is half cooked.) *Serves 6–8.*

LAMB BURGERS   *Mow-a-seer*

1 pound lamb, ground twice
½ bunch parsley, chopped
1 onion, chopped fine
Thyme, salt, pepper

Combine all ingredients. Form on a skewer or make rolls about 6 inches long. Place in dry baking pan and bake in moderate oven (350°) approximately 20 minutes. *Serves 4.*

LAMB BURGERS WITH PINE NUTS   *Kafta snoober*

1 pound ground lamb
4 tablespoons chopped parsley
1 onion, minced
1 teaspoon dried mint
Salt and pepper to taste
¼ cup pine nuts
Butter
1 12-ounce can tomato purée

Mix together lamb, parsley, onion, mint, salt, and pepper. Shape into rolls, filling each with 1 teaspoon pine nuts, which have been browned in butter. Place in baking pan and pour tomato purée over rolls. Bake for 30 minutes in moderate oven (350°). *Serves 4.*

LAMB BREAST   *Ghanum mihshee*

5 pounds lamb breast
Salt
Butter
Rice-Nut Mixture

Soak lamb in water with 1 tablespoon salt about half an hour. Drain dry and salt inside of cavity. Stuff pockets with Rice-Nut Mixture. Sew cavity and brush outside of lamb with melted butter. Roast in moderate oven (350°) approximately 2 hours. *Serves 6–8.*

RICE-NUT MIXTURE   *Hashwa roz wa jowz*

⅓ cup pine nuts
3 tablespoons butter
2 cups rice
4 cups boiling water
Cinnamon, salt, pepper
2 tablespoons minced parsley (optional)

Brown pine nuts lightly in butter. Add rice and stir 2 minutes over low flame. Add water. Cook 10 minutes. Add cinnamon, salt, pepper, and parsley and mix. Stuff lamb breast pockets.

LAMB CHILI   *Ghanum ma'a lubee*

1 pound ground lamb or beef
½ teaspoon garlic salt
¼ teaspoon pepper
Butter
1 onion, chopped
1 green pepper, chopped
1 8-ounce can tomato sauce
2 cans red kidney beans
2 teaspoons chili powder
½ teaspoon salt

Combine lamb, garlic salt, and pepper and mix well. Shape into 1-inch balls. Cook in butter over low heat until browned. Add onion and green pepper and cook 5 minutes. Add tomato sauce, beans, chili powder, and salt. Mix well. Cover and cook 45 minutes, stirring occasionally. *Serves 6–8.*

LAMB DUMPLINGS WITH YOGURT SAUCE
Sheesh barak

3 cups flour
1 pound lamb, coarsely ground
1 onion, chopped fine
Salt, pepper, allspice
Coriander (optional)

Knead flour well with a pinch of salt and about ¾ cup water. Roll dough and cut into 2-inch rounds. Combine meat, onion, salt, pepper, allspice, and coriander. Place on rounds of dough. Fold each in half and close edges. Twist around your finger into the shape of a hat.

SAUCE

- 3 quarts yogurt
- 1 tablespoon flour
- 1 egg white
- 2 cloves garlic
- ½ teaspoon salt
- 1 tablespoon dried mint
- ¼ cup butter

Combine yogurt, flour, and egg white. Beat mixture thoroughly with egg beater. Place pan on fire and stir constantly until yogurt comes to a boil. Immerse dumplings and let cook in yogurt about 20 minutes on a low fire. Pound garlic with ½ teaspoon salt and 1 tablespoon dried mint. Sauté garlic mixture in melted butter for a few seconds, then pour over the dumplings. *Serves 6.*

LAMB LIVER   *Kasabee imhamatha*

- 1 pound lamb liver
- 1 onion
- 3 tablespoons butter
- 1 cup tomato purée
- ½ cup water
- 2 cloves garlic, crushed
- Salt and pepper to taste

Rinse liver thoroughly in cold water. Boil approximately 15 minutes. Rinse again. Chop into small pieces. Brown onion in butter. Add liver and simmer. Add tomato purée and ½ cup water. Add crushed garlic, salt, and pepper. Cook approximately 15 minutes longer. *Serves 4–5.*

LAMB BAKED WITH POTATOES   *Lahmee bil saneeyee*

- 1 pound lamb, cubed
- ¼ pound butter
- 3 large potatoes, sliced
- 2 onions, sliced

1 12-ounce can tomato purée
Salt and pepper to taste

Alternate layers of lamb, potatoes, and onions in well-buttered baking pan and dot with butter. Pour tomato purée over top and add seasoning. Bake in slow oven (250°) for approximately 30 minutes. *Serves 5–6.*

LAMB AND MUSHROOMS   *Ghanum ma'a fotir*

1 pound lamb, cubed
4 onions, minced
2 tablespoons butter
1 pound mushrooms, skinned and cut in half (or 1-pound can mushrooms)
½ cup hot water
Salt and pepper to taste
Pinch of rosemary

Brown lamb and onions in butter. Sauté mushrooms in butter. Add to lamb and onions. Add hot water, cover, and simmer 10 to 15 minutes. Add salt, pepper, and rosemary. Cook over low fire for about 10 minutes. If liquid texture is desired, add more water. *Serves 5.*

LAMB STEW   *Yukhnee*

2 pounds lamb, cubed
½ cup butter
2 onions, chopped
1 clove garlic
Salt and pepper to taste
½ cup tomato purée
3 large potatoes, cubed

Sauté meat until brown in melted butter. Remove meat from skillet and brown onions and garlic in remaining fat. Add seasoning and tomato purée and cook together for a few minutes. Return meat to skillet. Add enough water to cover and cook over medium heat for about 1 hour or until meat is almost done. Add potatoes. Boil until potatoes are cooked. *Serves 6–8.*

LAMB TRIPE *Gumee*

    1 tripe
    ½ cup vinegar
    1 cup chopped lamb
    ½ cup shelled chick-peas
    1 cup rice
    4 tablespoons melted butter
    Salt and pepper to taste
    Dash of cloves
    Dash of cinnamon
    2 bay leaves

Soak tripe in salt water with ½ cup vinegar for several hours. Drain and clean thoroughly. Soak rice in water for 15 minutes. Combine lamb, chick-peas, rice, butter, salt, pepper, and cinnamon. Make pocket out of 2 or 3 pieces of the tripe. Stuff with lamb-rice mixture and sew together. Place in boiling water and add bay leaves. Cook about 40 minutes. Remove bay leaves. Serve liquor as soup garnished with dried mint. *Serves 6–8.*

LAMB CHOPS IN WINE SAUCE *Ghanum ma'a nbeeth*

    6 lamb chops
    Flour
    Butter
    Salt and pepper to taste
    ¼ cup catsup
    ½ cup white wine
    ½ cup mushrooms
    1 teaspoon A-1 sauce

Flour chops well and season. Heat butter in skillet, add chops, and brown well. Make sauce of remaining ingredients and pour over chops. Simmer about 1 hour or until chops are done. *Serves 6.*

LAMB ON SKEWERS *Shish kebab* or *Lahum mishwee*

    3 pounds boned lean leg of lamb or round steak
    3 large onions, quartered
    1 cup wine
    2 tablespoons oil

1 tablespoon dried mint
Salt and pepper to taste
4 green peppers, sliced
5–6 medium tomatoes

Cut lamb or steak into 1½-inch squares. Make a marinade of onions, wine, oil, and mint in a deep dish and marinate meat for at least 2 hours, preferably overnight. Season when ready to broil. Arrange lamb squares on skewers, alternating with onion, pepper slices, and tomato slices. Broil slowly over hot charcoals or in broiler of kitchen range, about 10 minutes. *Serves 8–10.*

MEAT-EGG ROLL   *Znood il banát*

2 pounds mutton or lamb, ground twice
1 onion, chopped
Salt and pepper to taste
5 hard-cooked eggs
Butter

Mix together mutton, onion, and seasoning. Pat out meat mixture in a rectangle. Place hard-cooked eggs on meat mixture. Roll meat around eggs. Close at edges. Place in buttered pan. Brush top with melted butter and bake in moderate oven (350°) until brown, about 20 minutes. *Serves 5.*

LAMB WITH YOGURT   *Shik-ree-yee* or *Laban immoo*

½ pound lamb chunks
1 onion, chopped
Butter
1 quart yogurt
1 tablespoon flour
1 clove garlic, crushed
1 tablespoon dried mint
Salt to taste

Boil lamb chunks in water about 30 minutes, drain, and reserve broth. Brown onion in butter and add lamb chunks. Stir yogurt in a pan until smooth. Add a little water to the flour to make a paste and add to yogurt. Cook over low fire, stirring constantly to keep from burning. When it begins to thicken, add lamb and onions. Add garlic, mint, and salt. If yogurt gets too thick, thin with lamb broth. *Serves 4.*

Shish Kebab (Lamb on Skewers) being charcoaled over hot hickory coals. Author's brother "Bob" serving *Shish kebab* at his Flaming Pit Bar-b-q Steak House Restaurant where many of these recipes were tested for serving in large quantities.

VEAL BREAST *Thillah*

1 tablespoon salt
½ cup vinegar
5-pound breast of veal
2 cups rice
4 tablespoons Rendered Butter
1 cup chick-peas
Salt and pepper to taste
Pinch of cloves
Pinch of allspice

Soak veal in water with salt and vinegar about 1½ hours. Drain and dry. Cut pocket in breast. Soak rice in water for 20 minutes. Drain, then simmer rice in butter 5 minutes, stirring constantly. Mix rice with chick-peas, salt, pepper, and spices. Stuff into veal breast. Sew opening. Place in roaster and bake in moderate oven (350°), allowing 35 minutes per pound. *Serves 6–8.*

SHEEP'S KIDNEYS *Kilwat ghanum mishwee*

½ pound kidneys
Butter
½ teaspoon salt
½ teaspoon garlic powder

Cut kidneys in half but do not separate completely. Remove skin. Brush with melted butter, salt, and garlic powder. Grill over a very hot fire 5–7 minutes. They should be underdone. Serve with water cress. *Serves 2.*

BEEF WITH ONIONS *Lahum bukkar mi bussel*

2 pounds boneless chuck
½ cup olive oil
4 pounds pearl onions
1 teaspoon whole pickling spices
½ cup vinegar
1 8-ounce can tomatoes
5 cloves garlic
Salt and pepper to taste

Cut meat in small pieces; sauté in oil. Peel onions and leave whole. Add to meat, together with spices (tied in cheesecloth), vinegar, tomatoes, garlic, and seasoning. Add a little water, cover tightly, and cook until meat and onions are tender and liquid is reduced to gravy, about 20 minutes. Remove spice bag and serve. *Serves 4–6.*

BOILED BEEF TONGUE   *Sane il bukkar*

3–4-pound fresh beef tongue
1 clove garlic
1 bay leaf
1 tablespoon cloves
1 teaspoon allspice
Salt and pepper to taste

Cover tongue with cold water and cook until water boils. Discard water, cover with fresh water, add remaining ingredients, and cook for 3 hours. Skin and slice tongue. Serve with *Taratoor. Serves 5.*

BRAINS PREPARED FOR COOKING   *Inkha matbookh*

Prepare brains for cooking by covering with cold water and soaking for 1 hour. Remove membranes and parboil for 20 minutes in salted water to which 1 tablespoon vinegar has been added. Drain. When cool, place in cold water and separate into small pieces.

SCRAMBLED BRAINS AND EGGS   *Inkha mi bythot*

Fry 1 cup Brains Prepared for Cooking in butter or margarine until brown. Add 3 whole eggs, sprinkle lightly with salt, and scramble mixture by stirring with fork. Garnish with *kamoun* (powdered cuminseed). *Serves 4.*

FRIED BRAINS   *Inkha miklee*

1 pound Brains Prepared for Cooking
1 egg
¼ pound butter

Dip brains in bread crumbs, then in slightly beaten egg, and then in crumbs again. Fry until golden brown on all sides. *Serves 4.*

BAKED BRAINS WITH SAUCE
Inkha mishwee mi marqeh

1½ pounds Brains Prepared for Cooking
2 tablespoons butter
2 tablespoons chopped onion
2 tablespoons flour
Salt and pepper to taste
½ cup water or stock
1 cup cooked tomatoes
2 tablespoons chopped celery
2 tablespoons chopped green pepper
1 bay leaf
1 sprig thyme

Brown onion in butter. Sift together flour, salt, and pepper and add to onion. Cook, stirring constantly, until thickened. Add water or stock and tomatoes. Stir until blended. Lower heat and add celery, green pepper, bay leaf, and thyme. Cook for 10 minutes, stirring occasionally. If necessary, add more water. Remove bay leaf and thyme and add brains. Bake in moderate oven (350°) for 15 minutes. *Serves 4–6.*

WHEAT AND KIBBY

Burghol wa Kibby

Beside the roads, *fallaheen* (farmers) sweat in the sun to harvest wheat. After the harvest, baskets of the freshly cut grain are taken to rivers and washed. Then the wheat is boiled in pots for hours; later it is spread in the sun to dry and harden. While it is drying, women sort the grain from the chaff. The wheat is ground in a stone mill and the grain kernels are sorted again.

While the men tend to the harvest, women cook in iron cauldrons and make bread flaps from wheat ground by hand between flat stones and baked on iron skillets.

This nutty-flavored cracked wheat is sold precooked and packaged in the United States in three forms: fine, medium, and coarse. The Arabic name for this wheat is *burghol*. The U. S. Department of Agriculture in conjunction with flour-milling companies in the United States has established a more scientific process of manufacturing *burghol* (known in some areas as *bulgur*), but almost the same steps—washing, dehydrating, cooking, drying, and cracking the wheat—are used in the United States as in the Middle East.

Kibby, the national dish of Syria and Lebanon, is made from *burghol*. Sunday dinner in a Syrian home is incomplete without *Kibby neeyee*.

RAW KIBBY *Kibby neeyee*

> 2 pounds lean ground lamb or beef
> 1½ cups cracked wheat, fine (*burghol*)
> 1 large onion, ground
> Salt and pepper to taste
> ½ cup cold water

Rinse wheat in pan of water. Drain water from wheat by cupping hands and squeezing out all moisture. Add to the wheat the

ground meat, onions, salt, and pepper. Grind all ingredients together twice. (If a grinder is not available, knead all ingredients
together well.) After grinding or kneading, add ½ cup cold
water to soften, and knead again. Melted butter, spooned over
kibby when ready to serve, is a tasty addition. *Serves 6–8.*

Kibby neeyee (Raw Kibby).

FRIED KIBBY *Kras mihshee*

Raw Kibby
¼ cup pine nuts
½ pound lamb, ground
3 tablespoons butter
½ teaspoon salt
¼ teaspoon pepper
½ teaspoon cinnamon
Bowl of ice water
Oil

Sauté pine nuts and ground lamb in butter. Season with salt,
pepper, and cinnamon. Shape *kibby* like footballs by rolling in

palms of hands into 5-inch-long balls. Press finger in opening at one end to make inside hollow. Keep pressing inside walls toward palms with finger. Place a spoonful of nut-lamb mixture in opening and close end. Dip hand in bowl of ice water while shaping these miniature footballs. Fry in hot oil until golden brown. *Serves 8.*

Kras mihshee (Fried Kibby). 1. Rubbing together spices, wheat, meat, and onions. 2. Kneading together all ingredients. 3. Perforating end of football-shaped *kibby*. 4. Placing filling in perforated end of *kibby*.

KIBBY PATTIES *Kras miklee*

In palm of hand flatten balls of Raw Kibby until about ½-inch thick, like hamburgers. Fry in hot oil until brown on both sides. Serve with *Salata kuthra*. Serves 8.

BAKED KIBBY   *Kibby bil sin-ee-yah*

Raw Kibby
Rendered Butter
1 pound ground lamb
1 tablespoon butter
¼ cup pine nuts
Cinnamon, salt, and pepper to taste

Grease a 10 by 14-inch baking pan with Rendered Butter. Dip hand in water and spread half of Raw Kibby smoothly over bottom of pan.

Simmer lamb in butter. Add cinnamon, salt, and pepper and mix. Brown pine nuts in butter and add to meat. Spread this filling evenly over the layer of *kibby* in the pan. Cover filling with remaining *kibby* and smooth surface well. Score in triangles with a knife. Loosen edges from tray with spatula. Pour 1 cup Rendered Butter over top. Bake in moderate oven (350°) until bottom is golden brown (approximately 25 minutes) and then place under broiler until top is golden brown. *Serves 8–10.*

BAKED KIBBY, FOOTBALL SHAPE   *Kras mish-wee-yee*

Raw Kibby
½ pound ground lamb
1 cup English walnuts
½ teaspoon cinnamon
½ teaspoon salt
¼ teaspoon pepper
3 tablespoons butter

Brown lamb in butter. Add walnuts, cinnamon, salt, and pepper. Shape *kibby* like footballs by rolling in palms of hands into 5-inch-long *kibby* balls. Make opening at one end by pressing with finger to make inside hollow. Keep pressing inside walls toward palms with finger. Place a spoonful of lamb-walnut mixture in opening and close end. Dip hand in bowl of ice water while shaping these miniature footballs. Place *kibby* side by side in tray that has been brushed with melted butter. Brush tops of *kibby* with melted butter. Bake in moderate over (350°) until golden brown, approximately 25 minutes. *Serves 8.*

KIBBY WITH YOGURT-RICE SAUCE *Kibby laban-ee-yee*

Kibby kishik (with exception of sauce)
5 cups water from cooked *kibby*
½ cup rice
2 quarts yogurt
1 tablespoon flour or cornstarch

Cook rice in water from cooked *kibby*. In another saucepan cook and stir yogurt until it comes to a boil. Mix flour or cornstarch with water to make a paste. Add to yogurt and cook on low fire. Stir constantly until mixture boils. Add cooked rice and cook another 5 minutes. Place *kibby* in sauce and serve hot. *Serves 6.*

KIBBY WITH KISHIK SAUCE *Kibby kishik*

Raw Kibby
½ pound ground lamb
Butter
Salt and pepper to taste

Sauté lamb in butter. Add a little salt and pepper. Make 12 football-shaped *kibby*. Perforate end of *kibby* with finger, pressing down toward palm of hand to make *kibby* hollow. Put 1 teaspoon browned lamb in each *kibby* and close end. Cook in boiling water to which ½ teaspoon salt has been added. Cook for 3 minutes. Reserve water for Kishik Sauce. Remove *kibby* from water and set aside.

KISHIK SAUCE
1 onion, diced
¼ cup chopped lamb
1 tablespoon butter
1½ cups *kishik*
5 cups water from cooked *kibby*

Brown onion and lamb in butter. Add *kishik* and mix. Cook on low fire about 1 minute. Add water to mixture and stir. As soon as mixture comes to a boil, add *kibby* and cook 2 more minutes. *Serves 6.*

NOTE: *Kishik* can be purchased from Middle Eastern food stores listed in the Shoppers' Guide.

KIBBY WITH LABAN AND WALNUTS   *Kras taweelee*

Raw Kibby
½ cup Yogurt Cheese
⅓ cup pomegranate seeds
⅓ cup English walnuts, chopped

Mix together Yogurt Cheese, pomegranate seeds, and walnuts. Shape *kibby* like footballs by rolling in palms of hands into 5-inch-long *kibby* balls. Make opening at one end by pressing with finger to make inside hollow. Keep pressing inside walls toward palms with finger. Place a spoonful of stuffing in opening and close end. Dip hand in bowl of ice water while shaping. Place *kibby* side by side in a tray brushed with melted butter. Brush tops of *kibby* with melted butter. Bake in moderate oven (350°) until golden brown, approximately 25 minutes. *Serves 8.*

PANCAKES AND OMELETS

Qatayef wa Ijee

Pancakes take a front seat at breakfast, along with eggs, cheeses, olives, and fruit. The size of a silver dollar, pancakes are stuffed with the Syrian Cottage Cheese called *Kareeshee*.

A popular lunch for busy housewives is *Ijee* (Egg Omelet), which takes only a few minutes to prepare. This tasty omelet is similar to the United States' Western sandwich. *Ijee* is served with *Talamee* (Syrian Bread).

STUFFED PANCAKES *Qatayef*

1 cup milk
1 egg
1 tablespoon butter
1½ cups pancake flour
3 tablespoons oil
½ pound Cottage Cheese (*Kareeshee*)
Honey or pancake syrup

Place milk, egg, butter, and pancake flour in mixing bowl. Stir lightly. Pour batter by teaspoonfuls into silver-dollar-size pancakes. Fry on one side only in oil. Remove from skillet. Place 1 teaspoonful cheese in the center of each disk on the cooked side. Fold disk in half and press edges together. Return pancakes to skillet and cook until brown on both sides. Remove and arrange on platter. Pour honey or syrup over all and serve. *Serves 6.*

YOGURT PANCAKES *Laza-keeyat laban*

    4 egg yolks, well beaten
    ¼ cup sugar
    2 cups yogurt
    ¼ cup melted butter
    1½ cups sifted all-purpose flour
    1 teaspoon baking soda
    2 teaspoons baking powder
    1 teaspoon salt
    3 egg whites, beaten stiff
    Honey

Combine egg yolks, sugar, yogurt, and butter. Sift together dry ingredients and add, mixing well. Fold in beaten egg whites. Drop from a spoon onto a lightly greased griddle. Brown on both sides. Serve with honey. *Serves 6.*

EGG OMELET *Ijee*

    6 eggs
    2 tablespoons parsley, chopped fine
    2 tablespoons mint leaves, chopped fine
    4 green onions, minced
    2 tablespoons flour
    4 tablespoons oil

Mix eggs with parsley, mint leaves, and onions. Add flour and mix. Fry in hot oil. *Serves 8.*

KISHIK WITH EGGS *Kishik mi bythot*

    2 eggs
    1 tablespoon butter
    ¼ cup milk
    3 tablespoons *kishik,* fine grain
    1½ cups water
    Salt and pepper to taste

Scramble eggs in butter. Add milk to lighten mixture. Add *kishik* and mix well with eggs. Add water. Boil over low fire for 15 minutes. Season with salt and pepper to taste. *Serves 3.*

NOTE: *Kishik* can be purchased from Middle Eastern food stores listed in the Shoppers' Guide.

SQUASH OMELET   *Imfarakat koosa*

3 tender squash
1 onion
½ stick butter
4 eggs
Salt and pepper to taste

Wash squash and dry thoroughly. Cut in small pieces. Sauté onion in butter. Add squash. Cook on low fire until tender. Add eggs, salt, and pepper and mix well. Cook 2 minutes. *Serves 4–6.*

EGGS AND YOGURT   *Shamameet laban*

2 cups Yogurt Sauce
3 eggs
Salt and pepper to taste

Boil Yogurt Sauce. Break eggs into a bowl. Drop eggs in Yogurt Sauce and mix with a wooden spoon. Boil 2 more minutes. Add salt and pepper to taste. *Serves 3.*

VEGETABLES

Kuthra

Every Middle Eastern housewife likes to have her own vegetable garden. From the garden come *koosa* (squash), *miktha* (cucumbers), *fool* (fava beans), and *lūbee* (green beans). The beans are eaten in the pod and also dried and stored for winter use. Turnips, okra, and eggplant are produced in abundance. A favorite nourishing food of the hard-working man is *addis* (lentils). These are cooked in soups or whole with *burghol* (wheat). The garden is usually filled with patches of onions and garlic—so necessary in the preparation of Syrian foods.

Near Maheeba's garden—with the fruits, herbs, and vegetables —there is a *bite il inib* (house of the grapes) where she enter-

Author's mother Maheeba entertaining at a *Tabooley* party under the "house of grapes and grape leaves" at her home.

tains at *Tabooley* parties. Several fence posts have been set at each end of a picnic table. A roof for the table is overgrown with winding vines, and the grapes are within reach of the guests. These vines bear the small, tender leaves Maheeba uses for making *Warak inib mihshee* (Grape Leaf Rolls). The leaves are stuffed with *hashwa* (a mixture of chopped lamb, rice, and spices) and rolled, placed in a pan over a few chicken wings or lamb bones, and mellowed with lemon juice in the last few minutes of cooking. They are also tasty as scoops for eating *Tabooley*, the favorite Syrian Wheat Garden Salad.

Vegetables stuffed with rice and meat are served as principal dishes. Several entrees are prepared; usually the table is filled with platters of Cabbage Rolls, Stuffed Squash, and Stuffed and Baked Eggplant.

FAVA BEANS WITH LAMB   *Fooleeyee*

½ pound lamb, cubed
Butter
1 onion, diced
1 clove garlic, chopped
1 pound fava beans
1 cup water
Salt and pepper to taste

Brown meat in butter. Add onion and garlic and simmer. Add beans and water. Season to taste. Cover and cook about 20 minutes. *Serves 4.*

BROCCOLI   *Lah-youn*

1 pound broccoli
6 tablespoons oil
3 cloves garlic, chopped
Salt and pepper to taste

Cook the broccoli in boiling salted water and, when tender, remove and drain thoroughly. Chop coarsely. Put the oil in a frying pan. When hot, add the cloves of garlic. When these begin to brown, add the broccoli and season with salt and pepper. Cook 20 to 30 minutes, stirring occasionally. *Serves 4.*

CABBAGE ROLLS   *Mul-foof mihshee* or *Yubrak*

2 heads cabbage
Lamb bones (optional)
1 cup canned tomatoes
1 teaspoon salt
2 cloves garlic, cut in half
Juice of 2 lemons

Carve out thick core from center of cabbage. Drop cabbage into salted boiling water, cored end down. Boil a few minutes until leaves are softened. While boiling, loosen each leaf with a long fork, remove and place in a dish to cool. Remove heavy center stems from the leaves. If the leaves are extremely large, cut in half. Fill each leaf with 1 teaspoon stuffing and roll in the shape of a cigar. Place lamb bones or cabbage stems on the bottom of kettle. Arrange cabbage rolls on top of bones or stems, alternating in opposite directions. Add tomatoes, salt, and garlic. Press down with inverted dish. Add water to reach dish. Cover kettle and cook on medium fire 25 minutes. Add lemon juice and cook 10 minutes more.

STUFFING

1 cup rice, rinsed in water
1 pound lamb or beef, fat and lean, chopped fine
½ cup canned tomatoes (optional)
½ teaspoon allspice
Salt and pepper to taste

Combine all ingredients and mix well. *Yield: about 50.*

FRIED CAULIFLOWER   *Zahra qar-na-beet*

1 egg, well beaten
Salt to taste
1 medium cauliflower
Juice of 1 lemon (optional)

Steam cauliflower with ¼ cup water. When tender, remove from water and break off flowerets. Dip into the well-beaten and salted egg. Fry until golden brown in deep oil. Sprinkle with lemon juice, or serve with *Taratoor* sauce. *Serves 4.*

STEWED CAULIFLOWER   *Qar-na-beet ib lahum*

1 large cauliflower
1 pound diced lamb
1 medium onion, minced
2 tablespoons butter
Salt and pepper to taste
2 cups boiling water

Separate cauliflower into flowerets, wash, and drain. Brown lamb and onion lightly in butter. Season with salt and pepper. Add cauliflower to boiling water. Cook until tender. Remove from water and combine with meat and onion. Simmer for 20 minutes on low fire. *Serves 4–6.*

CAULIFLOWER WITH TOMATOES AND LAMB
Qar-na-beet wa banadoora

1 cauliflower
½ pound lamb, cubed
Butter
1 cup tomato purée
1 cup water
Salt and pepper to taste

Parboil cauliflower. Brown lamb in butter. Add tomato purée and water to lamb and stir. Add parboiled cauliflower and cook until done. Season to taste. Excellent side dish with rice. *Serves 4.*

COOKED EGGPLANT   *Batinjan matbookh*

6 small eggplants
½ cup rice, soaked in water 15 minutes
½ pound diced lamb
Salt and pepper to taste
2 large ripe tomatoes, diced

Scoop out centers of unpeeled eggplants. Soak for 10 minutes with 1 tablespoon salt in pan of water. Combine rice, meat, and seasoning. Stuff eggplants about three quarters full. Place eggplants around pan (tops up). Pour 2 cups water around them. Cover and cook on low fire 25 minutes. Add tomatoes and simmer 10 minutes longer. *Serves 6.*

STUFFED BAKED EGGPLANT
Batinjan bil saneeyee or *Sheik il mihshee*

3 eggplants
1 12-ounce can tomato purée

Skin eggplant. Cut in quarters lengthwise. Sauté in butter. Place side by side in baking tray. Slit pieces in center and stuff each piece with 1 tablespoon stuffing. Pour tomato purée (thinned with a little water) over the eggplant. Bake in moderately hot oven (350°) for 20 minutes. *Serves 6.*

STUFFING *Hashwa*

1 pound ground lamb
½ pound butter
1 onion, chopped
½ cup pine nuts
Dash of allspice, nutmeg, and cinnamon
Salt and pepper to taste

Batinjan bil saneeyee (Stuffed Baked Eggplant).

Sauté lamb and onion in butter. Remove from skillet and brown pine nuts in butter. Remove from butter and mix together all ingredients.

NOTE: If you are in a hurry and do not have time to sauté in butter, place quartered eggplant in hot oven (400°) for 10 minutes. Remove from oven and follow procedure above.

EGGPLANT STEW   *Yukh-net batinjan*

    1 pound lamb, cubed
    5 medium eggplants
    1 large onion, chopped
    3 tablespoons butter
    1 No. 2 can tomatoes
    Salt and pepper to taste

Boil meat in water for 30 minutes. Peel eggplants and cut into cubes. Fry onion in butter, then add to meat. Add eggplant, tomatoes, and seasoning and cook on medium heat for 30 minutes. *Serves 6–8.*

EGGPLANT AND CHEESE   *Batinjan wa joban*

    1 medium eggplant
    1 egg, beaten
    1 teaspoon salt
    ¼ cup oil
    ¼ pound New York sharp cheese
    1 8-ounce can tomato paste
    4 tablespoons minced onion

Cut eggplant into slices ¼-inch thick. Dip slices in egg beaten with ½ teaspoon salt. Sauté in hot oil until brown on both sides. Arrange these slices in shallow baking dish. Place slice of cheese between layers of eggplant and top each stack with a slice of cheese. Pour the tomato paste around the stacks. Spread the onion over all and add ½ teaspoon salt. Bake in moderately hot oven (350°) for 25 minutes or until cheese is melted. *Serves 6.*

GARLIC EGGPLANT   *Batinjan makdoos*

12 small eggplants
2 pounds English walnuts, ground
2 tablespoons salt
12 cloves garlic
Olive oil

Remove stems from eggplants. Wash eggplants. Place in pan filled with water. Press eggplants with an inverted dish until water reaches dish. Cook on medium heat for 30 minutes. Eggplants will soften slightly. Remove eggplants and place under cold running water. When cool, dry thoroughly. Slit each eggplant on one side. Squeeze until all water is removed. Set aside for 30 minutes.

Mix together ground walnuts and salt. In slit end of each eggplant place 1 teaspoon of the walnuts and 1 clove garlic. Press opening closed. Place tightly in jar, cover, and leave until following day. Turn jar upside down on following day. If any water appears in jar, drain. Fill jar to halfway mark with olive oil. You will notice that oil will rise in jar for 3 to 4 days. Keep an eye on the jar occasionally to see that oil does not spill over. When oil decreases, add more oil to keep eggplants soaked. Keep jar covered. Eggplants will be ready to eat in about a week.

GRAPE LEAF ROLLS   *Warak inib mihshee*

Grape leaves prepared in brine can be purchased at Middle Eastern food stores listed in Shoppers' Guide. Just rinse the leaves thoroughly in cold water, squeeze out moisture, and stuff. Fresh grape leaves can be found on your neighbor's grapevine or in your own back yard.

50 grape leaves
1 teaspoon salt
Juice of 2 lemons
4 lamb bones or 6 chicken wings or necks

Soak fresh grape leaves in hot water for 15 minutes to soften. Remove from water, squeeze out moisture, and stem each. Place 1 tablespoon stuffing across each leaf, fold end of leaf like an envelope, and roll away from you. Place lamb bones or chicken wings on bottom of pan. Arrange stuffed leaves in rows in pan, alternating direction of each row. Sprinkle salt over stuffed leaves. Press leaves down with inverted dish. Add water to reach dish. Cover pan and cook on low fire for 35 minutes until tender. During last 10 minutes of cooking, add lemon juice. If rhubarb is available, try a few stalks on bottom of pan for a delicious variation.

STUFFING
    1 cup rice, rinsed in water
    1 pound lamb or beef, fat and lean, chopped fine
    Salt and pepper to taste

Combine all ingredients, mix well, and set aside. *Serves 6.*

Warak inib mihshee (Grape Leaf Rolls).

STUFFED PEPPERS   *Fly-flee mihshee*

    2 cups lamb or beef, chopped fine
    1 tablespoon butter
    2 medium onions, sliced
    ½ cup pine nuts
    Salt and pepper to taste
    ¼ teaspoon cinnamon
    3 tablespoons chopped parsley
    12 green peppers
    4 ripe tomatoes
    1 teaspoon dried mint
    2 cups water

Sauté meat in butter until browned. Remove from pan. Fry onions and pine nuts in butter until browned. Mix with meat, salt, pepper, and cinnamon. Add parsley. Cut stems off large green peppers. Dip in boiling water for 5 minutes, then remove all seeds. Drain and fill with fried meat mixture. Replace stems, securing with toothpicks, and set in a pan side by side, stems upward. Peel tomatoes and cut in small pieces. Cover peppers with tomatoes, adding mint and pinch of salt. Add water around peppers and cook until tender. *Yield: 12 peppers.*

NAVY BEANS   *Fajoom*

    1 pound navy beans
    1 onion, chopped
    1 clove garlic, minced
    1 stick butter
    1 pound beef or lamb, cubed
    1 10-ounce can tomato purée
    Salt and pepper to taste

Soak beans overnight. Following day drain and cook in fresh water about 1 hour until tender. Sauté chopped onion and garlic in butter. Add chunks of meat, salt, and pepper, and brown. Add tomato purée and simmer about ½ hour, then add beans and continue to simmer until heated through. *Serves 4–6.*

GREEN BEANS   *Lū-bee*

1 pound green beans
1½ pounds lamb chunks
Butter
1 onion, diced
1 clove garlic, chopped
1 tablespoon salt
1 12-ounce can tomatoes
2 cups water
½ teaspoon pepper

Stem beans. Cut in half and rinse in cold water. Sauté lamb chunks in butter. Add diced onion and garlic and brown. Add beans and salt. Cover and steam on low fire approximately 45 minutes. Stir occasionally to keep from sticking. Add tomatoes and water even with beans. Correct seasoning. Cook 15 minutes until tender. *Serves 4.*

OKRA   *Bay-mee*

1 pound okra
Butter
1½ pounds lamb chunks
1 cup water
1 tablespoon salt
2 cloves garlic
1 tablespoon coriander (optional)
1 12-ounce can tomato sauce
Juice of 2 lemons

Wash okra and cut off stems. Brown lightly in butter. In separate pan brown meat lightly in butter. Add water and salt. Cover pan and cook on slow fire until tender. Add crushed garlic and coriander to meat and mix. Add okra. Add water even with okra, the tomato sauce, lemon juice. Boil about 5 minutes. *Serves 4–6.*

BOILED SPINACH   *Sabanigh mus-louk*

2 pounds spinach
Juice of 2 lemons
Salt to taste

Choose new spinach. Clean and remove stalks. Cook the leaves in boiling salted water. Do not cover while cooking. Cook 7 or 8 minutes. Drain, cool, and press with hands. Shake well. Add lemon juice and salt and mix well. *Serves 4.*

SPINACH AND MEAT   *Sabanigh wa lahum*

1 medium onion
1 clove garlic, chopped
Butter
2 cups diced lamb
½ teaspoon allspice
1 teaspoon salt
2 cups water
1 pound spinach
Lemon slices

Sauté onion and garlic in small amount of butter. Add meat, all-spice, salt, and water. Simmer until tender. Add spinach and cook about 15 to 20 minutes. Garnish with lemon slices. *Serves 4.*

BAKED SQUASH   *Koosa bil saneeyee*

1 dozen green squash
Butter
1 large onion, chopped
1 pound lamb chunks
1 12-ounce can tomato purée
Salt and pepper to taste

Cut squash lengthwise in quarters. Sauté in butter until tender. Remove squash and brown onion in same skillet. Remove onion and brown lamb in skillet. Place squash on bottom of baking dish, cover with onion and meat. Add tomato purée and sprinkle salt and pepper over squash. Bake 20–25 minutes in hot oven (400°). *Serves 6.*

SQUASH WITH YOGURT SAUCE *Koosa ab-la-ma*

2 dozen small green squash
1 teaspoon salt
4 tablespoons butter

Rinse squash in water with 1 teaspoon salt. Stuff squash with lamb mixture and close end of each squash with toothpicks. Fry in butter until slightly tender. Remove from skillet and drain off all excess butter. Place in pan and set aside.

STUFFING

1 pound lamb, chopped fine
¼ pound butter
1 onion, chopped
Dash of allspice, cinnamon, and nutmeg
Salt and pepper to taste
½ cup pine nuts

Sauté meat in butter. Add onion and stir until brown. Add spices and salt and pepper. Remove from skillet. Sauté pine nuts in butter until lightly browned. Mix all ingredients together. Set aside to cool.

SAUCE

2 quarts yogurt
1 tablespoon flour or cornstarch
1 clove garlic
1 teaspoon salt
1 tablespoon dried mint, crushed

Stir yogurt. Mix flour or cornstarch with water to make paste. (An egg may be used in place of flour or cornstarch.) Add to yogurt and cook on low fire, stirring until it boils. Crush garlic with salt. Add garlic and dried mint to sauce. Pour over squash and cook 40 minutes in a covered pan. *Serves 6.*

Koosa mihshee (Stuffed Squash) 1. Coring squash. 2. Stuffing squash. 3. Cooked and ready for eating.

STUFFED SQUASH *Koosa mihshee*

Squash can be purchased prepared in brine at Middle Eastern food stores listed in Shoppers' Guide. The squash are already cored. Just rinse the squash in cold water, squeeze out moisture, stuff, and cook. City markets handle fresh green squash.

    1 dozen green squash
    1 can tomato purée
    2 cups water
    1 clove garlic, chopped
    Dried mint

Core squash. Rinse with cold salted water. Stuff, leaving approximately ¾-inch opening unfilled to allow rice to expand. Place in pan, add tomato purée and water. Add garlic and sprinkle dried mint on top of sauce. Cover and cook on low fire about 35 minutes until tender.

STUFFING

    1 cup rice, rinsed in cold water
    1½ pounds lamb or beef, fat and lean (chopped fine)
    ¼ stick melted butter
    ½ cup canned tomatoes (optional)
    Salt and pepper to taste

Combine ingredients and mix well. *Serves 6.*

SQUASH-LAMB BALLS   *Smyrna kef-ta*

1½ cups green squash, cubed
4 large onions, chopped
½ pound lamb, minced
2 eggs
Salt and pepper to taste
Flour

Simmer squash and onions together. Add lamb and simmer a few more minutes. Meanwhile beat eggs. Remove lamb from fire and add eggs, salt, and pepper. Roll into small round balls. Dip in flour and fry in deep fat. Excellent hot or eaten cold with salad. Take along for picnics. *Serves 4–6.*

SQUASH TOPS   *Kir'at koosa*

Tops of 12 green squash, peeled
Butter
1 pound lamb chunks
1 onion, chopped
1 12-ounce can tomato purée
Salt and pepper to taste

Wash tops in cold salted water. Fry in butter in covered skillet on slow fire until tender. Remove from skillet and sauté lamb in butter. Remove lamb and sauté onion until brown. In baking pan, place onion on bottom layer, add squash tops, and then layer of meat. Add purée, salt, and pepper. Let boil about 10 minutes. *Serves 4–6.*

VEGETABLE DISH   *Masbeht el darweesh*

    2 pounds ground lean lamb
    1 cup finely chopped onion
    ½ cup butter or oil
    1 cup tomato juice
    1 cup broth
    Salt and pepper to taste
    1 cup sliced carrots
    1 cup sliced squash
    1 cup peas
    1 cup string beans
    1 cup sliced potatoes

Brown meat and onion in butter or oil. Add tomato juice, broth, and seasoning. In large casserole dish, arrange each vegetable in separate layer, spreading the top of each layer with meat mixture. Cover casserole, place in moderate oven, and cook until vegetables are tender. Check liquid occasionally; add more broth if mixture appears dry. *Serves 8.*

WHEAT AND CHICK-PEAS   *Burghol bi dfeen*

    2 cups chick-peas
    ½ pound lamb, cubed
    1 cup cracked wheat
    2 tablespoons butter
    2 cups lamb broth

Soak chick-peas overnight. Boil meat in water. Add chick-peas and cook approximately 40 minutes. Reserve broth. Brown cracked wheat in butter, stirring well. Add chick-peas, meat, and 2 cups broth to wheat. Cook until done, about 20 minutes. Serve with yogurt. *Serves 4–6.*

PICKLED MIXED VEGETABLES   *Kuthra makboos*

1 cauliflower
6 small green tomatoes
1 cup cocktail onions
1 quart vinegar
1 cup water
1 tablespoon salt
1 tablespoon mixed pickling spices
3 pint jars

Trim cauliflower and separate into flowerets. Cook in boiling salted water 5 minutes. Drain and pat dry with paper towels. Cut tomatoes in quarters, add cauliflower and cocktail onions, and put into sterilized jars. Boil together vinegar, water, salt, and pickling spices. Cool and pour over ingredients in jar. Seal and store 5 days before using.

PICKLED CAULIFLOWER   *Zahra makboos*

2-pound cauliflower
½ teaspoon black pepper
1½ tablespoons marjoram
¼ teaspoon garlic powder
2 sweet red peppers
¼ cup white vinegar
1 pint salad oil
3 pint jars

Trim cauliflower and separate into flowerets. Cook in boiling salted water 5 minutes. Drain and pat dry with paper towels. Pack cauliflower into sterilized jars. Sprinkle with pepper, marjoram, garlic powder, and shreds of red pepper. Shake vinegar and oil together vigorously and pour over cauliflower. Seal and store 4 days before using.

PICKLED EGGPLANT   *Batinjan makboos*

    3 medium eggplants
    2 pounds sugar
    3 pints vinegar
    1 teaspoon paprika
    2 tablespoons peppercorns
    4 tablespoons cloves
    6 tablespoons poppy seeds
    4 tablespoons cinnamon
    4 tablespoons ginger
    ¼ pound mustard seeds
    6 tablespoons fennel seeds
    7 pint jars

Wash eggplant (don't peel); trim off stems and cube. Cook in boiling, lightly salted water for several minutes. Drain thoroughly. Meanwhile, cook sugar, vinegar, and paprika together until mixture boils. Add eggplant cubes and all remaining ingredients. Bring to a boil and boil 3 minutes. Eggplant should hold cube shape. Put eggplant into sterilized jars and cover with pickling liquid. Seal and store 2 weeks before using.

PICKLED MUSHROOMS   *Fotir makboos*

    4 pounds small mushrooms
    1 tablespoon salt
    1 tablespoon peppercorns
    1 cup salad oil
    1 quart white vinegar
    4 blades mace
    ½ teaspoon thyme
    4 pint jars

Rinse mushrooms in cold water. Trim if necessary. Put mushrooms in large saucepan; add cold water to cover and mix in salt. Cover and cook to boiling point; reduce heat and cook slowly for 5 minutes. Drain and pat dry with paper towels. When cold, pack into sterilized jars and sprinkle with cracked peppercorns. Combine oil, vinegar, mace, and thyme, heat to boiling point, and pour over mushrooms. Seal and store 1 week before using.

PICKLED ONIONS   *Bus-il makboos*

> 4 pounds small pickling onions
> 1 gallon water
> 1 pound salt
> 6 medium green peppers
> 1 4-ounce can pimentos
> 1 tablespoon dried mint
> 2 quarts white vinegar
> ½ teaspoon celery seeds
> 1½ teaspoons dried parsley
> 3 tablespoons peppercorns
> 7 cloves garlic
> 1 teaspoon caraway seeds
> 5 pint jars

Peel onions and put in water and salt. Let stand overnight. Next day rinse onions several times in cold water; drain and cut a slash halfway down from top of each onion. Pack into sterilized jars and over the tops sprinkle chopped green peppers, chopped pimentos, and dried mint.

Mix remaining ingredients in pan and bring to a boil, then reduce heat and cook slowly 30 minutes. Pour over onions. Seal and store 8 days before using. Give jars a good shake every day before using.

PICKLED TURNIPS   *Lift makboos*

> 5 pounds turnips
> 1 cup salt
> 1 clove garlic
> 1 large beet
> 1 tablespoon vinegar
> 1 gallon jar

Wash turnips. Trim off stems. If turnips are large, cut in quarter sections. If small, leave whole and cut a slash on one side. Put turnips in salt and leave for 3 days. After third day drain all liquid.

Put 1 tablespoon salt and clove garlic in large jar. Cook beet and cool. Cut beet in half and add to jar along with turnips. Fill jar with cold water. Add vinegar and cover jar loosely. Let stand 1 week before using.

SPICED GRAPES *Inib im-khullal*

3 cups sugar
1 cup white vinegar
½ teaspoon cardamon seeds
¾ teaspoon nutmeg
½ teaspoon ginger
½ teaspoon cinnamon
¼ teaspoon sweet basil
4 pounds seedless white grapes
6 pint jars

Put sugar, vinegar, spices, and basil in a saucepan. Bring to boiling point, then boil 6 minutes. Remove from heat and let cool until grapes are prepared. Syrup will be very thick at this point. Wash grapes, pat dry, and remove stems. Cut grapes in half lengthwise.

Reheat syrup until small bubbles appear on surface. Add grapes and cook several minutes. Grapes should be tender but not soft. Put into sterilized jars and seal. Let stand 2 days before using. (A tasty relish with meat or fish.)

FROZEN SQUASH *Koosa imfarez*

Method 1. Wash and dry 2 dozen green squash. Core squash. Boil 1 gallon water. Add 1 teaspoon salt and squash. Cook on medium heat until water starts to boil. Remove squash immediately and set aside until cool. Wrap by half dozens in plastic bags and freeze. When ready to use, remove squash from freezer, stuff, and cook as in recipe for Stuffed Squash.

Method 2. Prepare squash as in Stuffed Squash recipe. Fill with rice-meat mixture. Cook for 15 minutes. Remove from pan and cool. Freeze. When ready to use, follow recipe for cooking Stuffed Squash, minus fifteen minutes' cooking time.

CANNED SQUASH *Koosa makboos*

Core green squash. Place ½ teaspoon salt in opening of each squash. Store in covered jar. When ready to use, rinse thoroughly with cold water. Follow recipe for Stuffed Squash.

CANNED GRAPE LEAVES *Warak inib makboos*

Method 1. Grape leaves should be gathered when they are young and tender. Wash the leaves thoroughly, remove stems, and arrange in stacks of 10 or 15 leaves, each face up. Roll up into rolls, tie with string, and set aside. In a kettle bring to a boil 2 quarts water and ½ cup of salt. Drop bundles into this boiling water; remove one at a time after a few minutes. Cool slightly and pack tightly in sterilized pint jars. Pour the boiling water to the top and seal immediately.

Method 2. Place fresh dry grape leaves one at a time in crock, sprinkling salt on each leaf. Cover crock and store. When ready to use, rinse each leaf thoroughly with cold water to remove salt.

OLIVES

Zitoon

Green and black and light brown, olives are the native fruit of the Middle East. The olive tree grows abundantly in the arid climate and sandy soil. Sacred to the people, the olive tree is a source of wealth and food. The fruit, eaten with Syrian Bread, is a staple to both rich and poor. Long thin poles are used by men and women to beat the fruit from the tree, while children climb the trees, shaking the boughs. To keep the trees from being damaged by the beating and shaking, a full crop is picked only every other year.

Olive oil, delicately flavored at the first pressing of ripe olives, is used in Syria and Lebanon for cooking and for making soap. Some of the larger olive trees yield as much as 12 gallons of oil. Olive oil of various qualities is exported all over the world.

Sold as souvenirs in Jerusalem, Palestine, and Damascus are many articles carved from olive-wood.

CARE OF BLACK OLIVES *Zitoon aswad*

Middle Eastern food stores feature olives in huge earthen barrels topped with wooden covers. The olives are preserved in salt and water. They can be purchased by the pound from stores listed in Shoppers' Guide. Olives will keep for many days. Just rinse with cold water and fill a ½-gallon jar with the olives. Pour cold water over the olives. Add ¼ cup olive oil and 3 tablespoons vinegar. To serve, place olives in bowl and add a little olive oil and lemon juice.

FRESH GREEN OLIVES　*Zitoon akthar*

Slash each olive on one side. Place in crock. Sprinkle salt over olives. Mix every day for 8 days. After 8 days salt will draw. Empty liquid from crock. Cover crock with platter. Olives are ripe when color turns dark. When ripe, add olive oil and lemon juice. If you have dried thyme available, try mixing it with the olives.

BREAD AND PIES

Khobaz wa Fatayer

Two staples of Syria and Lebanon are wheat and barley. Long ago the villagers kept stocks of grain on the roofs of their houses.

First the grain was cleaned. Men put a small quantity of grain in a stone mortar and pounded it with heavy wooden pestles. When the grain was crushed, women sifted it and put the bran aside for the animals; the remainder was milled. The apparatus for milling was a hollow container with two compartments. The grain was placed in the upper compartment and then forced into the lower compartment. The wheat was sieved and ground until it was fine.

The women arranged *mowkadis* (molds) over a hearth so the flames would reach the insides of the molds. Once hot, the molds were placed on a plank with round holes and filled with dough, freshly kneaded and mixed with leaven. The molds were then covered and baked until the bread was ready to be removed.

The Syrian's daily conversation and habits being essentially biblical, they find the blessing of peace and security in "breaking bread" together. Bread is often referred to in the Bible: "bread and salt" . . . "bread and wine" . . . "Christ the bread of life."

SYRIAN BREAD (round thin loaves)   *Khobaz arabee*

    1 cake yeast
    5 pounds flour
    2 tablespoons salt
    1 tablespoon oil
    About 6 cups lukewarm water
    1 cup fine yellow corn meal
    1 cup flour

Dissolve yeast in 1 cup warm water. Put 5 pounds flour, salt, and oil in large pan. Add dissolved yeast and lukewarm water.

Mix well and knead, turning over many times until smooth. Cover with dry cloth and set in warm place about 1½ to 2 hours until dough rises. Cut in sections the size of an orange and roll between cupped hands. Cover and allow to rise for 30 minutes. Preheat oven to 450°.

Mix corn meal with 1 cup flour. Dip each piece of dough in corn-meal-flour mixture. Flatten dough and spread with palm of hand to size of pancake (make 12 at a time). Set aside and keep covered with plastic and dry cloth. Then, taking one at a time, spread each piece until you can flap it from one hand to another and then roll it from one arm to another until it becomes as thin as wrapping paper.

Place dough on lightly floured wooden board. Dough will slide easily from board onto floor of oven. Cook in hot oven (450°) approximately 15 seconds until lightly browned, then place under broiler for a few seconds.

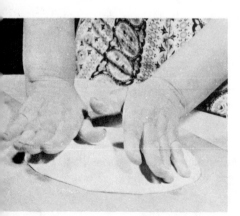
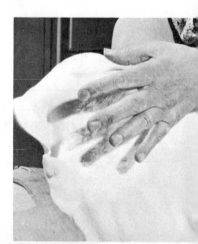

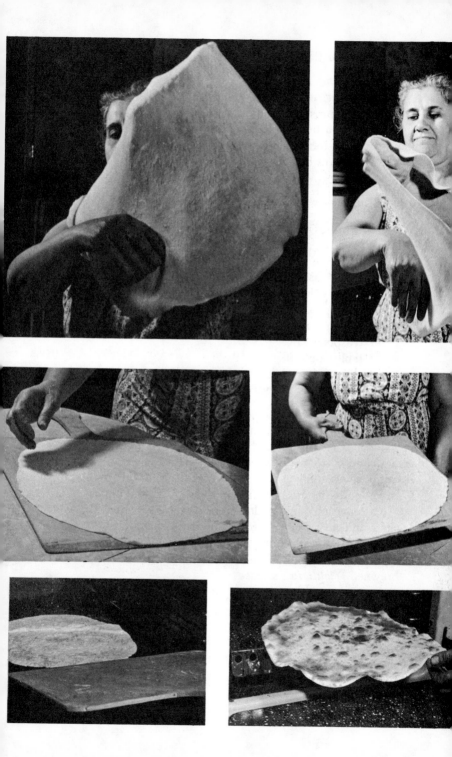

As each loaf is baked, pile one on top of another on table. When baking is completely finished, sprinkle each loaf with water and spread out on table until soft enough to fold (approximately 6 hours). Fold into triangles. Place in plastic bags and store in refrigerator. Syrian bread can be frozen in plastic bags (12 loaves to a bag). *Yield: 2 dozen loaves.*

NOTE: Boards can be purchased at Middle Eastern food stores listed in Shoppers' Guide.

SYRIAN BREAD (round bun type)　*Talamee*

1 cake yeast
5 pounds flour
1 tablespoon crushed *mahleb* (optional)
1 tablespoon sugar
1 teaspoon salt
1 tablespoon oil
¼ stick butter
About 6 cups lukewarm water

Dissolve yeast in 1 cup lukewarm water. Put flour, *mahleb*, sugar, salt, oil, and butter in pan. Add dissolved yeast and lukewarm water. Mix well and knead, turning over until smooth. Cover with cloth and set in warm place about 1½ to 2 hours until dough rises. Cut in sections about the size of grapefruit. Roll between cupped hands until smooth. Cover and allow to rise about 30 minutes.

Flatten each ball of dough to ¼-inch thickness. Cover with cloth and allow to rise for 1 hour. Preheat oven to 450°. Oil baking pan and place dough on pan. Bake until bottoms become light brown, then place under broiler until top of bread is lightly browned. *Yield: 12 Talamee.*

NOTE: *Mahleb* (kernels of black cherries) can be purchased at Middle Eastern food stores listed in Shoppers' Guide.

Cathy Jo Malooley, niece of the author, carrying round Syrian bread called *Talamee*. Cathy is wearing the traditional Arabic garments of *akal* (head coil), *hatta* (head scarf), and *abeyah* (cloak).

ANISE BREAD   *Ka'ick*

A tourist need not search for refreshments and snacks in the bazaars of Damascus. Peddlers with little carts full of glowing charcoal stand on street corners and roast corn on the cob and chestnuts. One favorite between-meal snack is *Ka'ick*, a round-shaped bread containing anise seed; the bread is sweetened with a syrup made from butter, milk, sugar, and rose water.

With boards full of *Ka'ick* balanced on their heads, peddlers gather at the school gates in the afternoon to greet hungry students on the way home.

8 cups flour
1 cup sugar
1 teaspoon anise seed
½ teaspoon crushed *mahleb* (optional)
1 teaspoon salt
½ pound butter
About 1½ cups milk
1 cake yeast
2 eggs

Mix flour, sugar, anise seed, *mahleb,* and salt. Heat butter with milk to lukewarm. Dissolve yeast in milk and add to flour mixture. Add eggs and knead well. Cover and set about 2 hours until dough rises. Then cut in small pieces 3 inches in diameter. Cover with damp cloth and allow to rise for 30 minutes. Flatten each piece to ½-inch thickness and place in dry pan in slow oven (250°). Bake until bottoms are golden brown, then place under broiler until tops are light brown. Dip in Syrup for Anise Bread. *Yield: approximately 50 Ka'ick.*

SYRUP FOR ANISE BREAD   *Qatir lil ka'ick*

¼ stick butter
¼ cup milk
½ cup sugar
1 teaspoon rose water

Combine all ingredients and boil 2 minutes. Place in a bowl and dip each *Ka'ick* in this syrup.

Ka'ick (Anise Bread) being dipped in syrup.

BASIC PIE DOUGH   *Ahjeen il fatayer*

2 pounds flour
½ cup oil or
½ cup Rendered Butter
1 cake yeast
1 tablespoon salt
About 3 cups lukewarm water

Combine ingredients, mix well, and knead until smooth. Cover with cloth and let rest in warm place until dough rises, about 1½ hours. Cut into small sections 3 inches in diameter. Cover with cloth for 30 minutes. Then with your hand flatten to thinness of pie dough. Use any of the various fillings on following pages and shape either in triangles, like turnovers, or fold over on edges, leaving center open. *Yield: enough dough for 3 dozen pies.*

NOTE: If you are in a hurry, use 3 cans of the biscuits that are found in dairy cases at your grocer's. Spread filling on the biscuit dough and bake according to the instructions in the recipes that follow.

MEAT PIES *Sfeeha*

Basic Pie Dough
2 pounds lamb or beef, fat and lean, chopped fine
4 onions, chopped
½ cup yogurt (or juice of 3 lemons)
½ cup pine nuts, sautéed lightly in butter
Salt, pepper, and allspice to taste.

Combine meat, onions, yogurt, nuts, and seasoning. Place mixture on dough patties and either shape in triangles or fold over on edges, leaving center open. Arrange pies on an oiled baking tray and bake in moderate oven (350°) for 15 minutes until bottoms are lightly browned; then broil a few minutes until tops are lightly browned. Serve hot or cold. *Yield: 3 dozen pies.*

Sfeeha (Meat Pies).

POTATO PIES *Fatayer batata*

Basic Pie Dough
5 pounds potatoes
1 pound beef, ground
Butter
1 large onion
Salt and pepper to taste
Rendered Butter

Shred potatoes. Add pinch of salt to draw moisture from the potatoes. Meanwhile sauté beef in butter. Grate the onion. Squeeze all moisture from potatoes. Combine the beef, onion, and potatoes and season with salt and pepper. Place on dough patties and close into triangular shape. Fry in Rendered Butter, about 2 minutes on either side. Serve hot or cold. *Yield: 3 dozen pies.*

YOGURT PIES *Fatayer laban ma'a qawarma*

Basic Pie Dough
¼ pound ground beef
2 cups Yogurt Cheese
1 onion, chopped

Sauté beef in butter. Mix with Yogurt Cheese and onion. Place on dough patties and close into triangular shape. Arrange pies on oiled baking tray and bake in moderate oven (350°) for 15 minutes, until bottoms are lightly browned. Brown tops lightly under broiler. *Yield: 3 dozen pies.*

YOGURT-MINT PIES *Fatayer laban ma'a na'na*

Basic Pie Dough
2 eggs
2 cups Yogurt Cheese
1 teaspoon butter
1 tablespoon dried mint
1 small onion, chopped

Beat eggs lightly. Add Yogurt Cheese, butter, mint, and onion. Place on dough patties and close in triangular shape. Arrange pies on oiled baking tray and bake in moderate oven (350°) for 15 minutes until bottoms are lightly browned. Place under broiler until tops are lightly browned. *Yield: 3 dozen pies.*

BEVERAGES

Mushroob

TURKISH COFFEE *Qahwah*

Turkish coffee is served in brass pots; some pots have long handles and others have long curved spouts resembling a pelican's beak.

In Syria, coffee beans are roasted in an open iron ladle until almost burned and then pounded in a mortar to a coarse powder. This Turkish coffee can be purchased from Middle Eastern food stores listed in the Shoppers' Guide, or you can use pulverized coffee purchased from your nearest supermarket. The coffee is served in demitasses and is to be sipped slowly. Thick grounds remain in the bottom of the cup and are used to read fortunes.

A legend about the discovery of coffee is told in Abyssinia, where the berry grows wild. Noticing that his flock of sheep became unusually perky after munching on coffee shrubs, a shepherd partook of the shrubs and was so delighted that he spread word of his discovery around the country. Since then, the practice of drinking coffee has spread all over the world. It has been said that Mohammed, after prohibiting wine, named this invigorating drink *Qahwah,* an expression meaning the "wine of Araby."

- 2 cups boiling water
- 1 teaspoon sugar
- 2 tablespoons Turkish coffee (or pulverized coffee)
- 2 cardamon pods

Bring water to a boil in a brass coffeepot. Add sugar, then gradually add coffee, stirring until mixture comes to a boil and is frothy. Add cardamon. Remove pot from the fire until froth has receded, then replace pot on brisk fire. Repeat this procedure three times. Coffee will rise fast to the top of the pot. The procedure of removing the pot from the fire is repeated three times so that coffee will not boil over the side of the pot. As the froth forms, spoon a little into each cup. The froth will rise to the top when coffee is poured into the cup. *Yield: 6 demitasses.*

Qahwah (Turkish Coffee) being poured demitasse. Author's cousin Roberto Samaan in traditional Arabic garments, smoking *narghileh* (Turkish water pipe).

PUNCH *Shraab*

Almost every known variety of fruit grows in Syria and Lebanon. A mixture of fruit juices, boiled together, makes up a drink called *shraab,* a liquid form of sherbet. Orange, pomegranate, strawberry, lemon, raisin, and rose water juices are boiled together with sugar until clear, 1 cup juice to ½ cup sugar; the mixture is bottled and put away for future use. To serve, dilute *shraab* with water and ice.

Vendors with portable equipment serve this delicious drink to customers in the streets.

CINNAMON TEA *Shy*

To 1 pint boiling water, use 3 teaspoons tea. Let the tea steep in the boiling water for 2 to 5 minutes, according to your taste in strength and flavor. Strain off tea into another hot pot. Serve with lemon wedges and a stick of cinnamon. *Serves 2.*

ANISE TEA *Shy mi yansoon*

Place 1 teaspoon anise seeds in 2 cups boiling water. Let steep for 10 minutes. Strain and add the anise liquid to 2 cups tea. Garnish tea with chopped English walnuts. *Serves 4.*

SPICE DRINK *Finjan kirfee* or *Miglee*

    4 cups water
    2 cinnamon sticks
    2 whole cloves
    2 ginger roots, cracked
    1 tablespoon anise seeds
    Sugar
    Almonds or walnuts

Add spices to water and boil until water turns dark. To serve, add sugar and an almond or walnut to each cup. (This is a healthful drink and traditionally is served to visitors of a newborn baby.) *Serves 4.*

ANISE-FLAVORED LIQUEUR *Arak*

Arak, an anise liqueur with a kick like an H-bomb, is made from the residue of pressed grapes. Great quantities of grapes are consumed yearly in the distillation of this strong spirit. Flavored with anise oil and gum mastic, it looks like water or gin. When a few drops of water are added, it becomes milky like pernod.

Unlike European and American apéritifs, *arak* is not poured over ice; ice is added to the *arak*. It should not be mixed with any other beverage.

Such delicacies as *Kibby, Baba ghanouj,* and *Batinjan makdoos* may be topped off with a snifter of *arak*. One has only to ask a liquor dealer in America where he can purchase *arak*, also known as anisette.

WINE *Nbeeth*

"Drink no longer water, but use a little wine for thy stomach's sake." I Timothy 5:23.

CANDIED FRUITS AND PRESERVES

Fa-wa-kee ma'kood wa mou-rubba

In the subtropical climate of Syria and Lebanon, the land bears abundant olives, grapes, and figs. The fields are dotted with dense, shady orange groves. On the lower levels stand beautiful summer houses, verdant with gardens and mulberry trees, which belong to rich merchants from Beirut.

Near Damascus there is a picturesque spot with fruit trees and sparkling streams called the Goota. The Goota is famous for its apricots, which are sometimes pressed and dried and sold in thin cakes called *qamardeen*.

Safarjel (quince) and colorful *ramain* (pomegranate) trees are widely grown in Palestine and throughout Syria. The trees are seen wherever there are gardens by running water. The pomegranate is filled with small seeds containing a tangy juice. These are used to decorate platters filled with Syrian foods and in fish and rice dressings.

One of the popular candied fruits is the pear. It is well worth the effort to prepare *Injas ma'kood* (Candied Pears)—especially when your guests wonder what this delicious sweet morsel is and ask you for the recipe.

ALMOND CANDY *Low-zee-yee*

      2 egg whites
      2 pounds blanched almonds, ground fine
      2 tablespoons cream
      2 teaspoons almond extract
      1 pound confectioners' sugar
      2 teaspoons rose water
      Maraschino cherries
      Red and green food coloring
      Granulated sugar

Beat egg whites until stiff. Gradually blend in almonds, cream, almond extract, sugar, and rose water until mixture is stiff enough to handle. Roll into small balls. Flatten each ball and place a cherry in center. Fold mixture around cherry. Roll one side of candy in red sugar, the other half in green sugar (granulated sugar with food coloring added).

SUGARED APRICOTS *Inkoo' mish-mush*

- 1 pound dried apricots
- ½ cup water
- 1 cup granulated sugar
- ¼ cup blanched almonds

Grind dried apricots. Place in kettle and add water. Cover and simmer until apricots thicken. Add ½ cup sugar and cook 10 minutes longer. Cool. Roll into small balls and flatten to about ½ inch thick. Place blanched almond in center of each and then dip in remaining ½ cup sugar, covering both sides. Cover with wax paper until ready to serve.

CANDIED DATES *Ajwee*

- 1 package dates
- Sugar
- Almonds

Remove pits from dates. Stuff each with an almond. Press opening to close. Roll in sugar.

SYRUPED EGGPLANT *Batinjan ma'kood*

- 12 small eggplants (size of lemons)
- 2 cups water
- 3 cups sugar
- 1 tablespoon orange-blossom water
- 1 clove
- Juice of 1 lemon
- Granulated sugar

Wash eggplants. Remove stems. Boil until tender. Remove from fire. Place in cloth sack. Squeeze thoroughly until all water is removed. Remove from sack and spread out to dry.

Meanwhile combine water, 3 cups sugar, orange-blossom water, clove, and lemon juice and boil until thick. When eggplants are dry, dip in syrup, then in granulated sugar.

CANDIED FIGS   *Teen ma'kood*

    3 pounds figs
    2 cups sugar
    1 cup water
    Juice of 1 lemon
    2 pounds chopped nuts
    1 tablespoon anise seeds
    3 pint jars

Wash and dry figs. Cut in quarters. Boil the sugar, water, and lemon juice together. When syrupy, add figs. Cook on low fire until thick. Remove from fire and add chopped nuts and anise seeds. Cool and store in jars.

STUFFED FIGS   *Teen mihshee*

    1 pound dried whole figs
    1 cup orange juice
    1 tablespoon lemon juice
    1 tablespoon grated lemon peel
    3 tablespoons sugar
    1 cup almonds (or pecans)
    ½ cup sugar

Remove stems from figs. Combine orange juice, lemon juice, peel and the 3 tablespoons sugar. Add figs and heat mixture to boiling point. Simmer in covered saucepan until fruit is tender. Drain well. Cool. Insert knife in stem end of fig and stuff each fig with an almond. Close opening and roll figs in ½ cup sugar. Dry overnight before storing.

MISKEE SWEETS   *Hilwat ib miskee*

    3 pounds granulated sugar
    2 cups water
    1 egg white
    1 teaspoon lemon juice
    2 tablespoons finely ground *miskee* (gum mastic)

Stir sugar, water, and egg white by hand in heavy saucepan. Place over high heat, stirring until mixture becomes syrupy. When it reaches rolling boil and rises in saucepan, spray with ice-cold water and remove from fire. Skim, place over heat again, and repeat process. Repeat process three times. After third time, place over heat, add lemon juice, and boil again until syrup has thickened. (To test syrup, drop a little syrup in a small cup of ice water. When firm ball can be formed with fingers, syrup is ready.) Remove from heat and cover with clean cloth until slightly cooled. Then whip with heavy wooden pestle until smooth and creamy. Add *miskee* (ground with a little sugar to prevent sticking) and continue to whip until thick and very white. Refrigerate before serving.

CANDIED ORANGE, GRAPEFRUIT, OR LEMON PEEL
Kish'r bur-d-kan, trunj, ow limoon ma'kood

Cut 1 pound rind into long narrow strips. Cover with water. Boil 30 minutes. Drain thoroughly. Cover again with cold water. Heat to boiling again and then drain. Repeat this procedure three times. Drain. Add 1½ cups light corn syrup. Cook slowly until rind is translucent. Drain. Roll in granulated sugar.

CANDIED PEARS   *Injas ma'kood*

> 5 pounds pears
> 1 pound sugar
> Ginger root (whole)
> 3 cinnamon sticks
> 1 cardamon
> 3 lemon skins

Peel pears and cut in quarters. Combine pears, sugar, ginger, cinnamon sticks, and cardamon and soak overnight. Following day bring all to boil. Add skins only of lemons. Do not stir. Skim. When thick, remove from fire. Cool and store in jars. (Quinces, peaches, apricots, and plums may be candied in the same way.)

SUGARED PEARS   *Injas im sekkar*

> 5 pounds pears
> ½ pound sugar
> Ginger root (whole)
> 1 cardamon

3 cinnamon sticks
Juice of ½ lemon
Miskee (gum mastic)
1 cup sugar

Slice pears and combine with ½ pound sugar, ginger, cardamon, and cinnamon sticks. Leave overnight. Add lemon juice the following day. Boil, then remove from fire and strain through colander, to remove syrup. When cool, lay pear strips on a cloth. Allow to dry overnight. Pound *miskee* and mix with 1 cup sugar. Dip each piece of pear in sugar-*miskee* mixture and again leave overnight. Cover with wax paper until ready to serve.

WATERMELON PRESERVES   *But-teekh mou-ra-ba*

1 pound watermelon rind
1 tablespoon lime juice or salt
2 quarts water
2 cups sugar
½ lemon, sliced thin
½ stick cinnamon
3 pint jars

Pare the rind and remove pink edge. Cut into 1-inch cubes and let stand overnight in solution of lime or salt and 1 quart water. Drain and rinse with cold water. Cover with boiling water and cook 15 minutes. Drain. Combine sugar with 1 quart water and boil 5 minutes. Add rind, lemon slices, and cinnamon. Cook rapidly until rind is clear. Let stand in syrup overnight. Reheat to boiling, pour into sterile jars, and seal. *Yield: 3 pints.*

PASTRIES AND DESSERTS

Hiloo

Syrians and Lebanese like sweets of all descriptions. Try *Baklawa*, with its many buttered layers of paper-thin pastry. The fifteenth layer has a filling of sugar, pistachios or walnuts, and orange-flower water topped with more layers of pastry.

There is a great deal of patience involved in making this *Baklawa* dough. I used to help my mother stretch the dough on a table completely covered with a cloth. Starting from the center of the table, we began stretching the dough out to the edges of the table. The dough stretches easily and becomes tissue-thin. After the dough is stretched, it is left to stiffen at room temperature. When the sheets begin to feel like paper they are cut into the desired lengths to fit the pans in which they will be baked. If there are any sheets left over, they can be frozen for future use. These pastry sheets may be purchased by the pound from stores listed in the Shoppers' Guide or from Greek stores in your community.

All sorts of sweets are sold in Damascus. One such is *Knafee*, a shredded wheat filled with a nut stuffing and dipped in syrup. These pastries are not prepared for everyday meals. They are served during the holiday seasons, on special occasions, and to guests. Desserts are not necessarily a part of the Syrian menu. *Roz eb haleeb* and *Almaseeyee* (puddings) are sometimes eaten following a meal or at breakfast.

HOMEMADE PASTRY SHEETS *Ahjeen il baklawa*

    5 pounds flour
    1 egg white
    ½ cup olive oil
    2 cups lukewarm water
    1 teaspoon salt
    Cornstarch

Top Row—*Kroon* (Nut Cakes); Center Row—*Gribee, Baklawa, Gribee*;
Bottom Row—Sugared Pears, Stuffed Shredded Wheat.

Pour flour in large pan and make a well in the center. Place egg
white, oil, water, and salt in well and stir. Gradually mix in flour
and knead dough until smooth and elastic. Cover and set in
warm place for 4 hours. Cut dough in sections (size of orange)
and dip in cornstarch. Let set another 2 hours covered with cloth.
Roll dough as thinly as possible on floured board. Place a cloth

on table. Start pulling the rolled piece of dough on the cloth toward you until tissue-thin. In just a few minutes the dough will dry and begin to feel like paper. Cut in lengths to fit baking pan. Cover with heavy wax paper. Continue to roll and pull dough, covering each sheet with wax paper. *Yield: 5 pounds.*

FOR A SMALLER AMOUNT:

    2 cups flour
    1 tablespoon oil
    ⅔ cup lukewarm water
    ½ teaspoon salt

NOTE: For extra-thin pastry sheets, sprinkle the board with corn-starch when rolling dough.

Baklawa (Diamond Pastry Delights).

DIAMOND PASTRY DELIGHTS   *Baklawa*
2 pounds pastry sheets

FILLING I

2 pounds chopped walnuts or pistachios
2 teaspoons cinnamon
1 teaspoon cloves
1½ pounds Rendered Butter

Combine chopped walnuts, cinnamon, and cloves. Brush baking tray with melted butter. Place pastry sheet on bottom of pan and brush with butter. Repeat until you have piled up 15 pastry sheets, each one brushed with butter. Distribute the nut mixture (about ½-inch thick) over bed of pastry tissues. Then add 15 rows pastry sheets on top of nut mixture, brushing each sheet with butter. With sharp knife, cut in diamond shape. A clove bud may be placed in center of each diamond if desired. Place pan on second rack in oven. Bake in slow oven (250°) for 2 hours until top turns a light golden brown. While pastry is baking, prepare syrup. *Yield: 2 dozen.*

SYRUP I

2 tablespoons honey
½ teaspoon lemon extract
3 cups sugar
Juice of 1 lemon

Boil together honey, lemon extract, sugar, and lemon. Cool and, with a spoon, pour very slowly over *Baklawa.*

FILLING II

For a slightly different taste, try this filling:

4 cups ground English walnuts
½ cup sugar
1 teaspoon rose water
1 tablespoon butter

Combine all ingredients and proceed as above. When using this filling, the following syrup should be used:

SYRUP II

> 3 cups sugar
> 2 cups water
> 1 teaspoon rose water
> Juice of 1 lemon

Mix sugar, water, and rose water. Boil and then add lemon juice. When syrup is cool, pour very slowly over *Baklawa*.

NUT RINGS　*Ish-al bul-bul*

> ½ pound pastry sheets
> 1 pound chopped walnuts
> ¼ cup sugar
> ½ teaspoon cinnamon
> ½ teaspoon cloves
> 1 pound Rendered Butter

Combine walnuts, sugar, and spices. Brush one pastry sheet with melted butter and sprinkle lightly with nut mixture. Cut pastry sheet in quarters (about 6 inches in length). Roll like cigars. Arrange in baking pan tightly, cut side down. Repeat until pastry sheets are used. Bake in moderate oven (350°) for 30 minutes. Brush each roll generously with melted butter. Dip in syrup.

SYRUP

> 3 cups sugar
> 3 cups water
> ½ pound honey
> Juice of ½ lemon

Boil sugar and water together. Add honey and lemon juice. When pastry is cool, dip quickly in warm syrup. *Yield: about 40 Nut Rings*.

SESAME PASTRY DELIGHTS *Baklawa simsum*

¼ pound sesame seeds
3 tablespoons butter
1 pound blanched almonds, ground fine
¾ cup sugar
1 teaspoon cinnamon
½ teaspoon lemon rind
1 pound Rendered Butter
1 pound pastry sheets

Sauté sesame in 3 tablespoons butter until golden brown. Combine sesame, almonds, sugar, cinnamon, and lemon rind in a dish. Brush bottom of pan with melted butter and place one pastry sheet, brushed with melted butter, on bottom of pan. Repeat until you have 4 sheets on bottom of pan. Sprinkle with nut mixture, place another layer of buttered pastry sheet and nut mixture, repeating until nut mixture has been consumed. Top with 4 buttered sheets of pastry. (See *Baklawa* recipe for cutting instructions.) Bake at 370° for 30 minutes, then reduce oven to 350° and bake an additional 25 minutes or until browned to desired shade.

SYRUP

2 cups sugar
2 cups water
1 teaspoon lemon juice
¼ cup honey

Combine sugar and water and boil until thickened. Stir in honey and lemon juice. Cool and pour over warm sesame delights. *Yield: 12–16 Sesame Pastry Delights.*

ALMOND ROLLS *Lefet lowz*

6 eggs, separated
2 cups sugar
2 pounds blanched ground almonds
2 ounces whiskey
1 pound pastry sheets
1½ pounds Rendered Butter

Beat egg yolks until light and add sugar. Beat until creamy. Beat egg whites until stiff. Add almonds and egg whites alternately to egg-yolk mixture. Add whiskey. Put 3 buttered pastry sheets one on top of another, pour one fourth of mixture on one end of pastry and roll like a jelly roll, turning the ends in to retain mixture. Repeat until there are 5 almond rolls. Place side by side in pan and pour melted butter over them. Bake for 30 minutes in moderate oven (350°).

SYRUP

    5 cups sugar
    4 cups water
    1 lemon slice

Boil sugar, water, and lemon slice until thick. Cool and pour syrup over hot pastry. Slice immediately. *Yield: 5 Almond Rolls.*

BUTTER COOKIES *Gribee*

    ¾ cup Rendered Butter
    1 cup sugar
    ¼ teaspoon rose water
    3 cups flour

Mix thoroughly butter, sugar, and rose water. Add flour and knead well. Shape as desired and place in dry baking pan. Bake in slow oven (300°) about 15 minutes until bottoms are very light brown. When cool, remove from pan and sprinkle with powdered sugar. *Yield: 32 cookies.*

NUT-FILLED CAKES *Ma'mool*

    2 cups flour
    1 tablespoon sugar
    1 cup Rendered Butter
    1 tablespoon milk
    Powdered sugar

Combine flour, sugar, and butter. Add milk and knead well. Form dough into small patties. Flatten patty in palm of hand. Fill with 1 tablespoon filling and cover with another patty; close tightly around edges. Bake in moderate oven (350°) until bottoms are light brown. Then broil until tops are very light brown. When cool, sprinkle with powdered sugar.

FILLING
- 2 cups ground English walnuts
- ¼ cup sugar
- 1 teaspoon rose water
- 1 tablespoon butter

Combine all ingredients. *Yield: 25 cakes.*

STUFFED SHREDDED WHEAT   *Knafee*

- 1 box shredded wheat (9 to a box)
- 1 quart milk
- Rendered Butter

Soak shredded wheat in cold milk until softened. Make center opening from end to end of each shredded wheat and fill, using same filling as that for *Ma'mool.* Brush baking pan with butter and place shredded wheat side by side in pan. Brush tops heavily with butter. Bake in slow oven (250°) until golden brown, approximately 30 minutes. Remove from oven and cool. Pour syrup over all.

SYRUP
- 1 cup water
- 1 cup sugar
- Juice of 1 lemon
- Drop of rose water

Boil all ingredients together.

RICE CUSTARD   *Roz eb haleeb*

- 1 quart milk
- ¼ cup rice
- 3 tablespoons cornstarch
- ½ cup sugar
- ¾ teaspoon orange-blossom water

Heat milk on medium fire until crust forms, about 10 minutes. Add rice. Stir slowly until milk boils. Cook on low fire for 20 minutes. Mix cornstarch with a little water to make a paste. Add to milk-rice mixture; add sugar and stir until custard begins to get thick. Add orange-blossom water just before removing from fire. Cool and pour into custard cups. *Serves 6.*

VANILLA PUDDING   *Almaseeyee*

> 1 quart milk
> ¾ cup sugar
> 3 tablespoons cornstarch
> 1 teaspoon orange-blossom water (or vanilla flavoring)
> Blanched almonds

Bring milk to a boil on low fire, until crust forms on top. Add sugar and stir until boiling. Mix cornstarch and a little water to make a paste. Add to milk. Keep on low fire and stir constantly until pudding begins to thicken. Add orange-blossom water and cook 1 minute longer, stirring well. Pour into custard cups and garnish with almonds. *Serves 6.*

CREAM OF WHEAT   *Halawat eb joban*

> 3 cups cream of wheat
> ½ cup Rendered Butter
> 6 cups water
> 5 cups sugar
> 2 pounds *Joban* (Syrian Cheese)
> 1 tablespoon rose water

Brown cream of wheat with butter to a very light shade. Combine the water and sugar and heat until mixture comes to a boil. Gradually add cream of wheat, stirring constantly. Cook for 5 minutes. Remove from fire. Slice the cheese and add to this mixture. Mix well. Add rose water. Serve in small dessert dishes. *Serves 8.*

MILK FARINA   *Lakmet il hilwee*

> 2 quarts milk
> 2 cups farina
> ½ cup Rendered Butter

Mix farina with the milk. Place on medium fire. Stir until it comes to a boil and let cook for 5 minutes. Melt butter and use half the amount on bottom of tray. Pour the cooked farina on top. Flatten it out and smooth with your hand; pour the remainder of the butter on top. Cool, cut in squares, and bake to a light brown in moderate oven (350°). Serve warm. *Serves 8.*

HALAWA CAKE

    1 cup Rendered Butter
    ½ cup powdered sugar
    5 eggs, separated
    2 cups farina
    1 teaspoon cinnamon
    1 teaspoon baking powder
    1 teaspoon vanilla
    1 cup chopped blanched almonds

Cream butter, add sugar. Beat egg whites stiff and add yolks to whites, mixing well. Alternately, add beaten eggs, farina, and cinnamon to creamed butter mixture. Add baking powder, vanilla, and almonds. Pour in greased 12 by 15-inch baking pan and bake in moderate oven (350°) for 30 minutes.

SYRUP

    2 cups sugar
    4 cups water

Boil sugar and water for 30 minutes. Pour over cake as soon as it is removed from oven. *Serves 10.*

HALAWA DIAMONDS

    1 quart milk
    1½ cups sugar
    ¼ pound Rendered Butter
    1 cup farina
    Cinnamon
    Walnut halves

Boil milk, add sugar, and cook 10 minutes. Heat butter in heavy saucepan. Add farina to butter and stir constantly until farina is golden brown. Add milk slowly, stirring until mixture thickens. Pour mixture into 9-inch-square greased pan and sprinkle with cinnamon. Cool for 1 hour. Cut in diamond-shaped pieces, placing a walnut half in the center of each. *Serves 10.*

SYRIAN ICE CREAM   *Booza soo-ree*

> 2 quarts milk
> 1 pint coffee cream
> 2½ cups sugar
> 3 teaspoons *sahlab*
> Ice Cream salt
> ½ teaspoon *miskee* (gum mastic)

Heat milk and cream to lukewarm. Add sugar and *sahlab* and boil. Stir until thick. Remove from fire and cool. Place ice cubes in ice cream bucket. Pour salt between layers of ice cubes. Pour mixture into bucket. Churn for 8 minutes, then add *miskee*. Churn until thick. Place in plastic containers and freeze. *Yield: 1 gallon.*

NOTE: *Sahlab* powder and *miskee* (gum mastic) can be purchased from stores listed in Shoppers' Guide. There is no substitute for these items. The *sahlab* trees of the Middle East produce fruit which is ground into a powder form.

Booza soo-ree (Syrian Ice Cream).

FISH

Samek

The waters of the Mediterranean offer a wealth of sea food, including crayfish, lobsters, shrimps, crabs, scallops, clams, oysters, mussels, and anchovies. The sardine is abundant; a favorite is *barboor* (red mullet).

In some restaurants the patron may choose his fish and then watch it being cooked. *Taratoor* (a sauce of *tahini* [sesame oil], lemon juice, and garlic) is usually served with the fish course.

BAKED STUFFED FISH   *Samek mihshee*

2-pound bass
1 small bass
Oil
½ cup pine nuts or almonds
1 small onion, chopped
Butter
¼ cup rice
1 tablespoon chopped parsley
Salt and pepper to taste

Remove backbone and small bones of larger bass. Spread fish open. Wash thoroughly and wipe dry. Rub inside and out with salt. Let fish stand for 10 minutes; drain.

Cut small bass in half. Fry in hot oil. Remove meat from bones. Brown pine nuts and onion in a small amount of butter. Cook the rice in boiling water. Add to rest of ingredients with parsley, salt, and pepper. Stuff bass and hold together with toothpicks. Brush skin thoroughly with salad oil. Brush pan with oil and bake fish in very hot oven (500°) for 10 minutes, then reduce heat to 400°. Continue baking until golden brown, approximately 30 to 35 minutes. Serve with *Taratoor* dressing. Garnish with parsley and lemon slices. *Serves 4.*

NOTE: This recipe may also be used for bluefish, catfish, pike, or shad; in stuffing, use a small fish of same kind.

BAKED FISH *Samek makhbooz*
Clean one bass or blue pike thoroughly. Salt both sides and set overnight. Following day drain. Brush skin thoroughly with oil on both sides. Place in baking pan and bake in very hot oven (450°) for 30 minutes. Serve with *Taratoor* dressing and lemon slices. *Serves 2.*

COD WITH SAUCE *Samek al qud ma'a marqet*
    2 pounds cod
    Oil
    3 ripe tomatoes, quartered
    ⅛ teaspoon salt
    ⅛ teaspoon pepper
    1 clove garlic, crushed
    1 tablespoon chopped parsley

Flour pieces of cod which have been well soaked in salt water. Brown them in very hot oil in frying pan. Remove cod and keep hot. Place peeled tomatoes in frying pan. Add salt, pepper, and garlic. The tomatoes will form a sauce which is then poured over the cod. Garnish with chopped parsley. *Serves 4.*

FLOUNDER WITH MUSHROOM SAUCE
Samek ma'a fotir
    3 pounds flounder fillets
    ½ cup water
    1 tablespoon butter
    2 tablespoons flour
    ½ cup canned mushrooms (chopped)
    1 sprig sweet basil
    ½ teaspoon allspice
    1 sprig thyme
    2 sprigs parsley
    1 bay leaf
    Salt and pepper to taste

Rub fish with salt and pepper. Bake with ½ cup water at 375° for 25 minutes. Remove from oven. Melt butter, add flour, and stir until smooth. Remove from heat and add remaining ingredients and liquid from fish. Cook over low heat, stirring constantly until thickened. Score top of fish, pour sauce over fish, and bake in oven 15 minutes longer. *Serves 6.*

HOT RED MULLETS *Samek barboor*

8 mullets
Oil
1 clove garlic
1 cup tomatoes
Anchovy fillets
12 black olives
Chopped parsley
Lemon wedges

Flour the fish and fry them in very hot oil. While the fish are frying, in another pan sauté garlic in oil. Add peeled tomatoes to garlic and simmer a few minutes. Remove from fire; add anchovy fillets and olives. Arrange fish on a long dish. Cover with sauce, sprinkle parsley over sauce, and place lemon wedges around edge of platter. *Serves 4.*

OYSTERS BAKED WITH COCKTAIL SAUCE
Mahaar makhbooz ma'a marqat

24 oysters on half shell
Salt to taste
½ cup tomato catchup
½ cup chili sauce
2 teaspoons Worcestershire sauce
1 teaspoon horse-radish
Juice of 1 lemon
4 dashes Tabasco
Bacon

Sprinkle raw oysters lightly with salt. Combine tomato catchup, chili sauce, Worcestershire sauce, horse-radish, lemon juice, and Tabasco. Cover oysters with sauce. Bake for 5 minutes in moderately hot oven (375°). Slice bacon to size of oysters and place a piece on each oyster. Bake until bacon is brown. *Serves 4.*

SHRIMP COCKTAIL SAUCE
Qary dis (or *Gambaree*) *ma'a marqat*

½ teaspoon horse-radish
4 drops Tabasco
1 tablespoon chopped celery
¾ cup tomato catchup
Juice of 1 lemon
2 teaspoons Worcestershire sauce
Salt and pepper to taste

Combine all ingredients and mix thoroughly. Place in refrigerator jar and chill. Just before serving, place small green piece of lettuce leaf in cocktail glass and arrange shrimp. Pour sauce over shrimp and garnish with parsley. *Yield: sauce for 4 shrimp cups.*

LENTEN FOODS AND MENUS

Akal Syam

In Orthodox Catholic communities Lent marks the beginning of fasting and the cessation of games and dancing. In the villages the women exchange their bright colorful dresses for the somber and dark shades. The period of the Lenten fast is preceded by the *Marfeh* (Meat-fare and Cheese-fare weeks).

When the calendar shows the approach of the Easter season, women prepare for the Lenten fast. While some countries serve pancakes and rich soups and sausages prior to the Great Lent, the Syrians serve many meat dishes with stuffed cabbage and grape leaves and *Kibby*, made of crushed wheat and ground lamb mixed with spices. Cheese-fare week brings to the table all kinds of cheeses. Just as the Great Lent ends with the breaking of the Easter egg, the boiled egg is the last food eaten prior to the Lenten fasting period.

Lenten dishes are prepared without meat but with vegetables and oil; oil gives foods an entirely different flavor from those cooked in any other way. Aside from its nutritional qualities, oil is also a preservative, making it possible to keep foods fresh for many days without spoiling. This is important because most Lenten foods are eaten cold.

Orthodox Christians abstain not only from meat but also from eggs, milk, and cheese during all fasting days. Fasting is observed during the Great Lent, every Wednesday and Friday throughout the year (unless a feast takes precedence over the fast), and on all the fast days listed on the pages immediately following.

FASTS PRESCRIBED BY THE HOLY EASTERN ORTHODOX CATHOLIC CHURCH *Il syam*

The Great Fast. Beginning seven weeks before Easter, Lent is the most important period of the year for the Holy Eastern Orthodox Catholic Church. The fast is divided into two parts.

The first forty days commemorate the fast of Christ in the desert. During this fast, according to the Scriptures, Satan appeared before Christ to tempt Him.

The Passion-week fast, a separate fast, commemorates the suffering and passion of Christ. Orthodox Christians abstain from meat and dairy foods, but children and sick persons need not.

A period of self-denial, contemplation, and prayer, the Great Fast begins on the Monday after Cheese-fare Sunday—forty days before Palm Sunday—and ends on the eve of Palm Sunday.

Holy Week, from the evening of Palm Sunday to Holy Saturday, is a special fast in honor of Christ's passion.

The Weekly Fasts. Each Wednesday and Friday is observed with fasting, unless a feast takes precedence over the fast. The fast on Wednesday is in memory of the betrayal of Christ; the fast on Friday is in memory of His passion and death on the Cross.

The Fast of the Holy Apostles. Beginning on the Monday after All Saints' Sunday—the Sunday following Pentecost—and lasting until the Feast of the Holy Apostles (Peter and Paul) on June 29, this fast varies in length depending on the date of Easter.

The Fast of the Theotokos. Preceding the Feast of the Falling Asleep of the All-holy Theotokos, this fast begins on August 1 and lasts until the day of the feast, August 15.

The Fast before Christmas. Beginning on November 15, this fast lasts until the day of the Feast of the Nativity, December 25.

Special Fast Days.
August 29. The Beheading of St. John the Baptist.
September 14. The Elevation of the Holy Cross.
January 5. The Eve of the Epiphany.

When fasting is forbidden.
The Church forbids fasting during the following periods:
From December 25 to January 5.
The week after the Sunday of the Pharisee and Publican.
The week after Meat-fare Sunday requires abstinence only from flesh-meat.

The week after Easter.
The week after Pentecost.
All Saturdays, except Holy Saturday.

FASTS PRESCRIBED BY THE HOLY ROMAN CATHOLIC CHURCH*

Abstinence. All Catholics over seven years of age are bound to observe the law of abstinence. The law of abstinence obliges in two ways: partial abstinence and complete abstinence.

Partial abstinence on Ember Wednesdays and Saturdays and on the vigil of Pentecost. The law of partial abstinence means that meat, and soup or gravy made from meat, may be taken only once at the principal meal. The law obliges even those who are not bound to fast or who are excused or dispensed from the law of fasting.

Complete abstinence on Fridays except when a Holy Day of Obligation falls on a Friday, or when the law of abstinence ceases; on Ash Wednesday, vigil of Immaculate Conception (December 8) and vigil of Christmas (now observed on December 23). The law of complete abstinence prohibits the use of meat and of soup and gravy made from meat.

Fast. All Catholics over twenty-one years of age and under fifty-nine years of age (unless they are excused or have been dispensed) are bound to observe the law of fast. On days of fast, only one full meal is allowed. Two other meatless meals, sufficient to maintain strength, may be taken, but together they should not equal another full meal. The fast can be affected in three ways by the abstinence.

Fast, partial abstinence: in this case the abstinence is part of the fast, and therefore those who are not obliged to fast do not have to abstain. This is true on the weekdays of Lent, except Ash Wednesday, Fridays, and Ember Days.

Fast, partial abstinence: in this case the abstinence is to be observed by those who are not fasting. This is the rule on Ember Wednesdays and Saturdays and vigil of Pentecost.

Fast, complete abstinence: in this case the abstinence from meat must be observed by those who are not fasting. This is the rule on Ash Wednesday, the Fridays of Lent, the vigil of Immaculate Conception, and December 23.

* submitted by Monsignor Herbert Winterhalter, St. Patrick's Church, Terre Haute, Indiana.

LENTEN MENUS

Cracked wheat and tomatoes
Cauliflower stems
Chick-pea pie
Hot peppers
Pickled vegetables
Lenten cakes
Coffee

Lentils and wheat
Thyme-sumac pies
Fava bean salad
Pickled turnips
Fresh vegetables
Turkish delight
Coffee

Eggplant stew
Potato kibby
Wheat garden salad
Lettuce
Syrian bread
Stuffed dates
Coffee

Lentil-potato soup
Fried potato kibby
Lenten cabbage rolls
Spinach salad
Sesame candy
Tea

LENTEN PIES

Fatayer Syamee

LENTEN PIE DOUGH   *Ahjeen il fatayer il Syam*

- 2 pounds flour
- ½ cup oil
- 1 cake yeast
- 1 tablespoon salt
- About 3 cups lukewarm water
- ½ teaspoon *mahleb* (optional)

Mix ingredients and knead with water. Cover and let rest in warm place about 1½ hours. When dough rises, cut into small sections 3 inches in diameter. Cover with cloth and allow to rise again for 30 minutes. Then flatten with your hand to thinness of pie dough. Use various fillings on following pages and either shape in triangles or leave face of pie open as suggested in recipes. *Yield: enough dough for 3 dozen pies.*

Placing chick-peas on dough before baking *Fatayer homos* (Chick-Pea Pie).

CHICK-PEA PIE   *Fatayer homos*

> Lenten Pie Dough
> 1 pound chick-peas

Soak chick-peas overnight with 1 teaspoon baking soda in water to cover. Wash thoroughly following day and drain off water until peas are dry. Place on pieces of dough (open-face pies). Bake in moderate oven (350°) for 15 minutes, then place under broiler a few minutes. Serve hot or cold. *Yield: 3 dozen pies.*

SESAME-SEED PIE   *Fatayer simsum*

> Lenten Pie Dough
> 1 cup sesame seeds
> ½ cup sugar
> Oil

Mix sesame seeds and sugar with just enough oil to hold mix together. Place on dough (open-face pies). Bake in moderate oven (350°) for 15 minutes, then place under broiler 1 minute. *Yield: 3 dozen pies.*

SPINACH PIE   *Fatayer sabanegh*

> Lenten Pie Dough
> 2 pounds spinach
> Salt
> 3 onions, chopped fine
> Juice of 3 lemons
> 1 cup ground walnuts
> Pepper and allspice to taste
> 1 cup oil

Wash spinach thoroughly and cut into small pieces. Sprinkle with salt. Squeeze until all water is removed. Add onions, lemon juice, walnuts, and spices. Mix well. Then add oil and mix. Place spinach mixture on pieces of pie dough and close into triangular shape. Brush oil on baking tray and arrange pies in rows. Bake in moderate oven (350°) for 15 minutes until bottoms are lightly browned. Place under broiler until tops of pies are lightly browned. Serve hot or cold. *Yield: 3 dozen pies.*

THYME-SUMAC PIE   *Fatayer zahter*

> Lenten Pie Dough
> 4 tablespoons *zahter*
> Olive oil

Mix *zahter* with just enough olive oil to make paste for spreading on pieces of dough (open-face pies). Bake in moderate oven (350°) for 15 minutes, then place under broiler for 1 minute. Serve hot or cold. *Yield: 3 dozen pies.*

NOTE: *Zahter,* a blend of thyme and sumac powder, can be purchased at Middle Eastern food stores listed in Shoppers' Guide. There is no substitute for this tangy product.

LENTEN SALADS

Salata Syamee

FAVA BEAN SALAD *Fool imdamis*

- 1 teaspoon baking soda
- 2 cups dried fava beans
- 1 onion, chopped
- 1 clove garlic, chopped
- 2 tomatoes, quartered
- 1 teaspoon mint
- 2 tablespoons lemon juice

Soak beans overnight in water with baking soda. Following day rinse; cover with water and boil for 1 hour. Cool, then add onion, garlic, tomatoes, dried or fresh mint, and lemon juice. *Serves 4.*

NOTE: Dried fava beans can be purchased by the pound at Middle Eastern stores listed in Shoppers' Guide; canned fava beans are available at your supermarket.

LIMA BEAN SALAD *Salatet fasoolya*

- ½ pound lima beans
- 1 teaspoon salt
- 1 clove garlic, minced
- Juice of 1 lemon
- 2 tablespoons olive oil

Boil beans until tender and drain. Add salt, garlic, lemon juice, and oil to beans. Mix thoroughly. Serve hot or cold. *Serves 3.*

NOTE: String beans may be substituted for limas in this recipe.

SYRIAN BREAD SALAD *Fa-toosh*

- 2 loaves Syrian Bread (unsoftened)
- ½ bunch green onions
- ½ bunch parsley

1 cucumber
½ bunch fresh mint (or 2 tablespoons dried)
2 tablespoon fresh thyme (or 2 tablespoons dried)
1 teaspoon salt
¼ teaspoon pepper
Juice of 3 lemons
½ cup olive oil
Black olives

Break hard Syrian Bread into bite-size pieces. Cut all vegetables into small pieces. Mix vegetables with bread in salad bowl. Add salt, pepper, lemon juice, and oil and mix well. Garnish with black olives. *Serves 6.*

DANDELION SALAD *Salata hindbee*

1 pound dandelion leaves
Salt
Oil
1 onion, chopped
Juice of 1 lemon
1 clove garlic, chopped

Wash dandelion leaves thoroughly. Chop leaves fine. Sprinkle with salt. Rinse and squeeze out moisture. Coat with oil. Add onion, lemon juice, and garlic. *Serves 4.*

SYRIAN POTATO SALAD *Batata arabee salata*

1 pound potatoes
Olive oil
Juice of 1 lemon
1 onion, chopped
1 teaspoon cold water
Salt and pepper to taste
1 tablespoon chopped parsley
Olives
2 tomatoes, sliced
1 tablespoon dried mint

Boil potatoes, then peel and cube. Coat with olive oil. Add lemon juice, onion, water, salt, and pepper. Garnish with parsley, olives, sliced tomatoes, and dried mint. *Serves 4.*

SPINACH SALAD   *Salatet sabanegh*

> 1 pound spinach
> Salt
> Juice of one lemon
> Oil
> 1 onion, chopped
> ½ cup English walnuts, chopped

Sprinkle spinach with salt. Chop fine. Rinse thoroughly and squeeze out moisture. Add remaining ingredients, using just enough oil to coat spinach. *Serves 4.*

TOMATO-ONION SALAD   *Banadoora-bussell salata*

> 4 tomatoes, sliced
> 1 medium onion, chopped
> Olive oil
> 1 tablespoon dried mint
> ¼ teaspoon garlic powder
> Salt and pepper to taste

Place tomatoes and chopped onion in salad bowl and use just enough oil to coat salad. Sprinkle with mint. Add garlic powder, salt, and pepper. Toss and serve. *Serves 4.*

WHEAT GARDEN SALAD   *Tabooley* or *Suf*

> 1 cup cracked wheat, fine
> 1 bunch green onions
> 2 large bunches parsley
> ¼ bunch mint
> 4 large tomatoes
> Juice of 4 lemons
> ¼ cup olive oil
> Salt and pepper to taste

Soak wheat in water a few minutes. Squeeze dry by pressing between palms. Chop onions, parsley, mint leaves, and tomatoes very fine. Add wheat, lemon juice, olive oil, salt, and pepper. Mix well. Serve with fresh lettuce leaves, grape leaves, or cabbage leaves used as scoops. *Serves 6.*

Preparing the most popular of all Arabic salads, *Tabooley* (Wheat Garden Salad).

LENTEN KIBBY

Kibby syamee

FRIED POTATO KIBBY *Kras Syamee*

2 pounds potatoes
1 cup cracked wheat
Salt and pepper to taste
1 cup flour

Boil potatoes. Peel and mash. Rinse and squeeze cracked wheat between palms to drain off the water. Knead potatoes and wheat together thoroughly. Add salt and pepper. Then blend in flour. Shape into small football-shaped *kibby*. Perforate one end and fill, using 1 teaspoon filling in each *kibby*.

FILLING

1 onion, sliced
Olive oil
1 cup pine nuts
1 teaspoon lemon juice

Sauté onion in olive oil. Brown pine nuts in oil and mix with onion. Add lemon juice. Stuff *kibby*. Fry in oil until golden brown. *Serves 6.*

POTATO KIBBY *Kibbet batata Syamee*

2 pounds potatoes
1 cup cracked wheat
1 cup English walnuts, ground fine
1 onion, grated
Salt and pepper to taste
1 large onion, sliced

Boil potatoes. Peel and mash. Rinse and squeeze cracked wheat between palms to drain off the water. Mix all ingredients together. Add a little water and knead well. Place in platter and garnish with onion that has been sautéed in olive oil. *Serves 6.*

LENTIL DISHES

Aklat addis

STRAINED LENTILS *Addis imsafa*

½ pound lentils
8 cups water
¼ cup rice
1 onion, chopped

Sort and rinse lentils. Cook in water for 20 minutes. When cooked, reserve broth. Place lentils in colander and mash. Place mashed lentils in pan with broth. Add rice. Cook on low fire for 10 minutes, until all liquid is absorbed. Brown onion in olive oil. Garnish lentil platter with onions. *Serves 3.*

LENTILS AND WHEAT *Imjadara*

2 cups lentils
8 cups water
1 cup cracked wheat
Salt and pepper to taste
1 onion, diced
½ cup oil

Sort lentils and rinse with cold water. Add lentils to pan filled with approximately 8 cups water. Do not cover. Boil about 20 minutes, until lentils are soft, then add wheat. Add salt and pepper and cook another 15 minutes, stirring occasionally to prevent sticking, until all liquid is absorbed. Fry onion in oil. Add oil to pan of lentils and garnish platter of lentils with fried onions. For leftovers, fix Lentils-Wheat with *Kishik* (*Imjadara markoo'a*). *Serves 4–6.*

LENTIL-POTATO SOUP *Addis imqala*

2 cups lentils
6 cups water
Salt and pepper to taste
6 small onions
2 large potatoes
1 large onion, chopped
Olive oil
Lemon slices

Sort and rinse lentils. Cook in water for 15 minutes. Add salt
and pepper. Quarter onions and add to cooked lentils. Cut
potatoes in cubes and add to mixture. Cook 10 more minutes.
Brown chopped onion in olive oil and use with lemon slices as
a garnish. *Serves 4.*

LENTILS AND RICE *Imjadara ma'a roz*

1 cup lentils
8 cups water
1 cup rice
Salt and pepper to taste
2 large onions, chopped
4 tablespoons olive oil

Sort lentils and rinse with cold water. Cook lentils in 8 cups
water over medium fire for 20 minutes. Add rice, salt, and pepper and cook another 15 minutes. Fry onions in olive oil. Remove onions, pour oil over rice-lentil mixture, and mix. Set
until cool. Garnish with onions. *Serves 5.*

NOODLES AND LENTILS *Rishta*

1 cup lentils
8 cups water
Salt and pepper
2 cups flour
2 cups lukewarm water

Sort and rinse lentils. Cook in water for 20 minutes until tender.
While lentils are cooking, prepare noodle dough. Mix flour
with lukewarm water and ½ teaspoon salt. Knead well.

Place on floured board and roll with rolling pin. Cut in half. Sprinkle each half with flour. Roll each half as you would a jelly roll and cut in strips ½-inch wide. Add to cooked lentils and cook until done, about 30 minutes. Add salt and pepper to taste. *Serves 4.*

LENTILS WITH TOMATOES   *Addis ma'a banadoora*

    1 cup lentils
    8 cups water
    1 onion
    1 green pepper
    3 pimentos
    4 tablespoons oil
    2 cups tomatoes
    Salt and pepper to taste

Rinse lentils with cold water. Cook in boiling salted water 20 minutes. When tender, drain. Sauté onion, green pepper, and pimentos in oil. Add tomatoes, salt, and pepper. Add drained lentils and cook about 30 minutes, uncovered. Serve hot. *Serves 3–4.*

LENTEN SAUCES

Marqeh

SESAME OIL WITH LEMON *Taratoor or Tahini*

- 1 cup sesame oil
- 4 tablespoons water
- Juice of 3 lemons
- 1 clove garlic, crushed
- ½ teaspoon salt
- 2 tablespoons chopped parsley

Stir sesame oil in can. Pour 1 cup into a large bowl. Add cold water and stir. You'll notice that water thickens the paste and lemon juice thins it. Add lemon juice and stir into a smooth sauce. Mash garlic with salt and mix with sauce. Garnish with parsley. This is an excellent fish and meat dressing; use also with cauliflower, eggplant, and salads. *Serves 6.*

NOTE: Sesame oil can be purchased in various-size cans at Middle Eastern food stores listed in Shoppers' Guide.

CHICK-PEA SESAME OIL SAUCE *Homos bi tahini*

- Sesame Oil with Lemon (*Taratoor*)
- 1 cup chick-peas
- ½ teaspoon baking soda
- 1 tablespoon olive oil
- ½ teaspoon salt
- 3 tablespoons pomegranate seeds
- 3 tablespoons chopped parsley

Soak chick-peas with baking soda in water overnight. Following day drain off water. Place peas in kettle, add water to cover; cook until well done, about 1 hour. (Soaking is unnecessary if you use canned chick-peas.) Place chick-peas in large bowl, mash, add Sesame Oil with Lemon and salt. Mix well. Place in a flat dish. Make several dents in mixture and spoon olive oil into the dents. Garnish with parsley and pomegranate seeds. *Serves 4.*

Spooning olive oil over *Homos bi tahini* (Chick-Pea Sesame Oil Sauce). The picture includes a platter of *Taratoor* (Sesame Oil with Lemon), a can of *Sesame Tahini,* small dish of chick-peas, pomegranate seeds, pine nuts, and other vegetables for garnish.

EGGPLANT WITH SESAME OIL   *Baba ghanouj*

> 1 medium eggplant, dark-skinned (pierced with fork to let steam escape)
> 2 cloves garlic
> Salt to taste
> 3 tablespoons sesame oil
> Juice of 2 lemons
> 2 tablespoons water
> 2 tablespoons pine nuts
> 2 tablespoons pomegranate seeds
> 2 tablespoons chopped parsley

Broil eggplant with skin on, turning it frequently. Remove skin under cold water and mash eggplant. Pound the garlic with salt, add sesame oil, lemon juice, and water. Then mix with eggplant and salt. Spread on a platter and garnish with pine nuts, pomegranate seeds, and parsley. *Serves 4.*

Baba ghanouj (Eggplant with Sesame Oil). Picture shows broiled eggplant being mashed with a wooden masher, bowl of *Tahini,* can of olive oil, dish of chopped parsley, chick-peas, vegetables, and pomegranate seeds to be used as garnish.

SESAME OIL WITH AVOCADO   *Taratoor avocado*

   1 avocado
   3 tablespoons Sesame Oil with Lemon

Mash avocado and add to Sesame Oil with Lemon. Make mixture smooth enough to spread on chips, toasted bread, crackers. Fill celery stalks for canapés.

WHEAT AND VEGETABLE DISHES
Akal Qum-eh wa kuthra

FAVA BEANS *Fooleeyee*

    1 onion, diced
    1 clove garlic, diced
    Oil
    1 pound fava beans
    Kizbaṛa (Syrian parsley)
    Salt to taste
    1 cup water

Brown onion and garlic in oil. Add fava beans, *kizbara*, salt, and water. Cook until beans are tender, about 30 minutes. *Serves 4.*

GREEN BEAN STEW *Yukhnee lūbee akthar*

    1 onion, diced
    1 clove garlic, chopped
    ¼ cup olive oil
    1 pound green beans
    1 cup water
    1 10-ounce can tomatoes
    Salt and pepper to taste

Sauté onion and garlic in oil. Cut beans in half. Add to onion and garlic. Cover and let steam for 30 minutes, mixing frequently. Add water and tomatoes until even with beans. Add seasoning to taste. Cook 15 minutes or until tender. *Serves 4.*

LENTEN CABBAGE ROLLS   *Yubrak Syamee*

> 1 large head cabbage
> 1 teaspoon salt
> 2 cloves garlic, chopped
> Juice of 3 lemons

Carve out thick core from center of cabbage. Drop cabbage into salted boiling water, cored end down. Boil a few minutes until leaves are softened. While boiling, loosen each leaf with a long fork, remove, and place in a dish to cool. Remove heavy center stems from the leaves. If the leaves are extremely large, cut in half. Fill each leaf with 1 teaspoon stuffing and roll in the shape of a cigar. Place cabbage stems on the bottom of kettle. Arrange cabbage rolls on top, alternating in opposite directions. Add salt and garlic. Press with inverted dish and add water to reach dish. Cover kettle and cook on medium fire 45 minutes. Add lemon juice and cook 10 minutes more.

STUFFING

> ½ cup chick-peas
> 1 teaspoon oil
> 1 cup rice (or cracked wheat)
> ½ bunch minced parsley
> Salt and pepper to taste
> Pinch of cinnamon, nutmeg, allspice

Soak chick-peas overnight. Following day remove from water and rub peas with fingers to remove outer skins. Mix peas with oil, rice, parsley, seasoning, and spices. *Serves 4.*

FRIED CAULIFLOWER   *Zahra miqlee*

> 1 cauliflower
> ½ bunch parsley, chopped (optional)
> 1 onion, chopped
> 1 tablespoon flour
> Salt and pepper to taste
> Oil

Separate cauliflower into flowerets and parboil in salted water. Remove from water and dip in mixture of chopped parsley, onion, flour, salt, and pepper. Fry in hot oil. Serve with *Tahini* sauce. *Serves 3.*

CAULIFLOWER STEMS   *Qarnabeet*

1 pound tender cauliflower stems
1 onion, chopped
1 clove garlic, chopped
Oil
½ cup chick-peas
1 cup water
Salt to taste
Juice of 2 lemons

Cut stems into 1-inch pieces and wash thoroughly. Sauté onion and garlic in oil. Add chick-peas and simmer. Add water and boil until chick-peas are done, about 30 minutes. In another pan cook stems until tender, about 20 minutes. Remove from water and add to chick-peas. Cook on low fire for a few minutes. Add salt and lemon juice. Serve cold. *Serves 4.*

COOKED DANDELION GREENS   *Hindbee mut-bookh*

1 pound dandelion greens
2 medium onions, minced
2 tablespoons olive oil
Salt and pepper to taste
Lemon slices

Brown onions in oil. Mix in fresh dandelion greens. Toss until all greens are flavored with oil. Cover and steam on low fire until greens are cooked, about 15 minutes. Serve hot or cold, garnished with lemon slices. *Serves 4.*

STEWED EGGPLANT   *Imnazalee* or *Tabakh roohoo*

½ cup chick-peas
½ teaspoon baking soda
1 clove garlic, chopped
1 onion, chopped
⅓ cup olive oil
2 green squash, cubed
1 eggplant, cubed
1 large can tomatoes
Salt and pepper to taste

Soak chick-peas with baking soda in water overnight. Following day drain. Remove skins by rubbing peas between fingers. Sauté garlic and onion in olive oil. Add chick-peas, cover, and simmer about 15 minutes. Add unpeeled squash, eggplant, and tomatoes. Cover and cook on medium fire until vegetables are tender, about 30 minutes. Serve hot or cold. *Serves 6.*

LENTEN STUFFED GRAPE LEAVES *Warak inib Syamee*

> 1 cup cracked wheat
> ½ cup canned chick-peas (2-ounce can)
> ½ bunch parsley, minced
> Salt and pepper to taste

Soak grape leaves in hot water 15 minutes to soften. Remove from water and stem each. Combine wheat, chick-peas, parsley and seasoning. Put 1 teaspoon of the stuffing on each leaf and roll. Arrange in rows in pan, each row in opposite direction. Add 1 tablespoon salt. Press stuffed leaves with inverted dish. Add water to reach dish. Cover pan and cook for 35 minutes on medium fire. Add lemon juice and cook another 10 minutes. *Serves 4.*

OKRA STEW *Baymee Syamee*

> 1 pound okra
> Juice of ½ lemon
> 2 onions, chopped
> ½ cup olive oil
> 1 cup stewed tomatoes
> 1 cup water
> 2 tablespoons chopped parsley
> Salt and pepper to taste

Wash and carefully trim okra not too close to the top. Sprinkle well with lemon juice and let stand for 20 minutes. Prepare sauce by frying onions lightly in olive oil. Add tomatoes and water. Add parsley and simmer a little longer. Put half the tomato sauce on the bottom of a casserole, drain okra and put on top of sauce. Cover with remaining sauce, season, cover, and simmer gently or bake in slow oven (300°) about 30 minutes until okra is tender. *Serves 4.*

SYRIAN MASHED POTATOES   *Batata arabee mum-ou-sa*

4 medium potatoes
1 onion, diced
¼ cup oil
Salt and pepper to taste
Juice of 1 lemon
1 onion, sliced
½ cup pine nuts

Boil potatoes. Peel and mash. Add diced onion, oil, salt, pepper, and lemon juice and knead together. Fry onions and pine nuts in oil and use to garnish potatoes. *Serves 4.*

RICE AND SPINACH   *Roz eb sabanigh*

1 large onion
½ cup oil
2 pounds spinach
3 cups rice
Salt and pepper to taste
6 cups boiling water

Dice onion and brown in oil. Wash spinach and cut in small pieces. Add onion and oil to spinach and cook. Rinse rice, add to spinach, stir well with salt and pepper to taste. Then pour water over the whole. Cook on medium fire for 10 minutes, then on low fire for 15 minutes. *Serves 6.*

COOKED SPINACH   *Sabanigh imqala*

2 onions, chopped
⅓ cup olive oil
1 pound spinach, chopped
Salt and pepper to taste
¼ cup pine nuts
¼ cup pomegranate seeds (optional)
Lemon wedges

Brown onions in olive oil. Add spinach, salt, and pepper. Cook on low fire until spinach is cooked, about 20 minutes. Brown pine nuts in oil. Add with pomegranate seeds to spinach. Garnish with lemon wedges. *Serves 4.*

SQUASH BAKED WITH TOMATOES
Koosa ma'a banadoora

    2 pounds squash
    2 tablespoons oil
    3 tomatoes, sliced
    2 medium onions, sliced
    Salt and pepper to taste

Wash squash and cut into halves lengthwise. Remove seeds and place in oiled baking dish. Cover with tomato and onion slices. Sprinkle with salt and pepper. Cover and bake in moderate oven (350°) about 45 minutes. *Serves 4.*

FRIED SQUASH   *Koosa miqlee*

Wash green squash. Slice. Salt and let stand for 30 minutes. Fry in hot oil until golden brown. Drain on paper towels. Serve with Sesame Oil with Lemon.

NOTE: Eggplant and green tomatoes may be prepared the same way.

BAKED VEGETABLE DINNER   *Aklat kuthra makhbooz*

    1 pound okra
    1 pound squash
    1 pound potatoes
    1 pound tomatoes
    1 pound onions
    ¼ cup chopped parsley
    1 cup olive oil
    Salt and pepper to taste

Peel potatoes. Slice all vegetables and arrange in baking pan, sprinkling parsley, olive oil, salt, and pepper between layers. Add a little water; bake in moderately hot oven (350°) about 1 hour. *Serves 10.*

WHEAT AND CHICK-PEAS   *Burghol Syamee*

    ½ cup chick-peas
    ½ teaspoon baking soda

1 onion, chopped
Olive oil
1 cup cracked wheat
1 12-ounce can tomato purée
2 cups boiling water
Salt and pepper to taste

Soak peas with soda in water overnight. Following day drain. Remove skins by rubbing peas between fingers. Sauté onion in olive oil. Add peas, cover, and simmer about 5 minutes. Add cracked wheat and cook, stirring occasionally, for 2 minutes over medium fire. Add tomato purée and boiling water. Cook on low fire for 20 minutes or until water is absorbed. Add salt and pepper. *Serves 4.*

CRACKED WHEAT AND TOMATOES
Burghol ala banadoora

1 onion, chopped
¼ cup oil
1 cup cracked wheat
2 cups boiling water
1 10-ounce can tomato purée
Salt and pepper to taste

Sauté onion in oil. Add wheat and cook, stirring occasionally, for 2 minutes over medium fire. Add boiling water and tomato purée. Cook on slow fire until water is absorbed, about 20–25 minutes. Add salt and pepper. *Serves 4.*

LENTEN DESSERTS

Hiloo Syamee

LENTEN CAKES *Karabeej Syamee* or *Kroon*

3 cups flour
⅔ cup oil
½ cup sugar
1 teaspoon anise seeds
1 teaspoon *mahleb,* crushed
½ cup water

Combine ingredients and knead well. Cut dough into small patties. Flatten patties in palm of hand to 2½ inches in diameter. Fill with 1 tablespoon filling and bring edges together. Bake in moderate oven (350°) until bottoms are lightly browned. Place under broiler until tops are lightly browned. Let cool, then dip in syrup.

FILLING

2 cups ground English walnuts
¼ cup sugar
1 tablespoon orange-blossom water

Combine ingredients.

SYRUP

1 cup water
1 cup sugar
Juice of 1 lemon
1 drop orange-blossom water

Boil together until syrupy. *Yield: 50 cakes.*

TURKISH DELIGHT *Lakoum-Tutlee*

3 tablespoons gelatin
½ cup cold water
2 cups sugar
½ cup hot water
Grated rind and juice of 2 lemons
Grated rind and juice of 1 orange
Red or green food coloring
½ pound pistachio nuts, chopped
Confectioners' sugar

Soften gelatin in cold water. Combine sugar and hot water and heat to boiling. Add gelatin and simmer 20 minutes. Add citrus juices, rind, and coloring. Strain into loaf pan. The pan should be large enough so the mixture is ½- to 1-inch deep. Add chopped nuts. Chill until firm. When cold, cut into cubes and roll in confectioners' sugar. *Yield: 2 dozen.*

SESAME CANDY *Sikar simsum*

1 pound sugar
4 ounces honey
½ cup water
½ pound sesame seeds

Blend sugar and honey in pan. Add water and cook over low heat, stirring frequently, about 12 minutes or to soft-ball temperature on candy thermometer. Remove and add sesame seeds. Spread on buttered pan to ¾-inch thickness. When cool, cut into 2 by 1-inch pieces. *Yield: 2 dozen pieces.*

TRADITIONS AND FOODS OF THE ORTHODOX CATHOLIC CHURCH

HOLY ALTAR BREAD *Prosphoron* or *Kurban*

Holy Communion is observed every Sunday in the Eastern Orthodox Catholic Church. In this service the sacraments of the Eucharist are bread and wine. The priest commemorates the Last Supper, saying: "He took bread, and gave thanks and broke it, and gave unto them saying, Take eat, this is my body which is broken for you; this do in remembrance of me." (Luke 22:19)

The wine, having the color of blood, is from the pure juice of the vine. The bread, which must be leavened, is from clean

Kurban (Holy Altar Bread) and Holy Seal used in making Kurban.

wheat. It is baked in a flat, round loaf called *Prosphoron* (Greek) or *Kurban* (Arabic), and is stamped with a seal, as shown in Figure 1.

In the Holy Communion service, five loaves commemorate the loaves with which the Lord satisfied five thousand souls. Each loaf (called oblation) has been stamped with the seal.

In the center portion of each loaf is impressed the sign of the Cross, surrounded by the Greek letters IC (meaning Jesus), XC (meaning Christ), and the word NIKA (meaning conquer). This center portion is called the Lamb in memory of Christ.

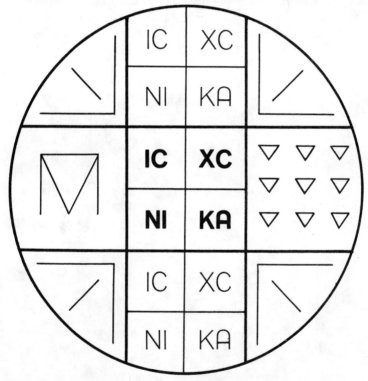

The priest removes the center portion from the first loaf and places it on the paten. From the second loaf he removes the large triangular piece in honor of the Blessed Virgin and places it on the paten. From the third loaf he removes the nine smaller triangular pieces in commemoration of the Angelic Hosts and the Saints of the Orthodox Church, and also places them on the paten. From the fourth, parts are taken for the living, and from the fifth, parts are taken for the dead.

The priest partakes of the Holy Communion (bread and wine) and these sacraments are then given to parishioners during the divine liturgy. Prior to church services, the applicant confesses his sins to the priest. During the service he walks with bowed head toward the church altar where the priest stands holding the sacred chalice. The applicant holds under his chin the silk napkin hanging from the priest's hand to make sure that no part of the sacrament falls on the floor. The priest dips a small golden spoon into the chalice containing the divine sacraments of the Last Supper and administers it to the lips of the parishioner. In the background the choir can be heard singing the communion hymn, "Receive Ye the Body of Christ."

Sunday School class partakes of Holy Communion in St. George Orthodox Church.

Following the divine liturgy, the priest distributes the remaining portions of the *Kurban* to the parishioners. The *Kurban* is prepared by Orthodox families wishing to remember a loved one; prayers are said by the priest during services for all members of the family, living and deceased.

1 cake yeast
5 pounds flour
1 teaspoon salt
1 tablespoon orange-blossom water
Lukewarm water
Holy Stamp

Dissolve yeast in 1 cup of warm water. Pour flour and salt in pan. Add dissolved yeast and orange-blossom water. Add ap-

Author's uncle, Rt. Reverend Archimandrite George Ghannam, distributing *Kurban* to parishioners at St. George Orthodox Church, Worcester, Mass.

proximately 6 cups lukewarm water over flour and knead, turning over until smooth. Cover with cloth and set in warm place
about 1½ to 2 hours, until dough rises. Cut in sections about the
size of grapefruit. Roll between cupped hands until smooth.
Cover with a plastic sheet and place a dry cloth over the plastic.
This will prevent dough from drying.

Flatten each ball of dough with hands to ¼-inch thickness. Allow to set for another hour, cover with plastic and cloth. Preheat
oven to 350°. Stamp each loaf in center with Holy Stamp. With
tip of knife pierce loaf at four corners of the Holy Stamp and
make five holes around loaf about 1 inch from edge. This will
prevent rising. Bake in oven until bottoms become light brown.
Remove from oven and brush face of *Kurban* with cold water.
Broil until loaves are light brown.

NOTE: The Holy Stamp may be purchased from stores listed in
Shoppers' Guide.

EASTER EGGS   *Bythet il eed*

Most of us take Easter eggs for granted, boiling and coloring
them, giving them to relatives and friends, hiding them for the
children to hunt down. The real meaning of the Easter egg,
however, is often overlooked.

One of the earliest religious uses of the egg was by the
Egyptians in worshiping Ra. As a symbol of fertility and of re-
newed life among the ancient Egyptians and Persians, the egg
was customarily colored during spring festivities. The Egyptians
colored the eggs red to represent the sun; the shell represented
the earth, and the white of the egg represented heaven.

The egg is also a symbol of the resurrection of Christ, since
it has a new life within its walls. Among Christians, the Easter
egg represents the sealed tomb in which the body of Christ was
placed after His crucifixion: the shell being the sealed tomb having dormant life inside.

During the early days of Christianity only red—signifying the
blood of Christ—was used to color the eggs. Other colors, however, are commonly used today, such as white, ivory, and tan
to represent the fine linen cloth in which Christ's body was
wrapped before it was placed in the sepulchre. Green represents

the vegetation of the springtime—the awakening of the earth from the deep slumber of winter. Blue represents the blue of the sky—the peace and joy of the Easter season. Yellow represents the early morning starlight of the resurrection. Purple represents the passion of the crucified Christ and the joy of the resurrected Christ. Multicolored eggs represent the time when Jesus gave up the ghost. Sweet-smelling essences, traditionally mixed with the colorings, are in remembrance of the ointment-bearing women who, early on the first Easter morning, went to anoint the body of Christ with rich spices and perfumes.*

For Easter, Syrian and Lebanese children gather vegetable roots, onion and pomegranate skins to make coloring for the eggs, which are taken to church and blessed by the priest. Then they are distributed among the parishioners after the services on the eve of Easter. Not only in Syria and Lebanon but also in America these same impressive services prevail in Orthodox Catholic churches. During the service the congregation follows the priest three times around the inside of the church; each person carries a lighted candle. Everyone leaves the church except a man, representing Satan, who stands in the dark behind the closed door to prevent the priest from entering. The priest, representing Christ, approaches the closed door and chants for the doors to be opened that the King of Glory may enter. The chanting is repeated three times, and Satan vanishes. The priest throws open the door to symbolize the victory of Christ over Satan. The church is immediately illuminated and the multitude, singing the message of resurrection, "*Al Maseeh Kam* [Christ Is Risen]," follows the priest. After the service the fast is broken with a *Bythet il eed* (Easter Egg), a bowl of *Shouraba il Roz* (Chicken-Rice Soup), and a sweet dessert of *Roz eb haleeb* (Rice Custard).

At the conclusion of the divine liturgy in the Orthodox Church the eggs are blessed and distributed among the congregation by the priest. Members of the congregation then greet each other and hit the eggs together to signify the breaking of Christ's tomb. Eating eggs at Easter is symbolic of breaking fast, since eggs are forbidden during Lent.

All eggs of the feast should be broken to show that Christ has conquered death and has risen, thereby granting new life to all who believe in Him.

After having abstained from meats and dairy products during

* adapted from writings of Reverend Elias G. Karim, St. Nicholas Orthodox Church, San Francisco, California.

the Great Lent, everyone begins the Easter dinner. Days of preparation have been spent in baking pastries and bread, rolling grape leaves, coring squash, and paring eggplant. Following the dinner, an assortment of pastries is served to the guests along with Turkish coffee and, of course, the colorful *Bythet il eed.*

BOILED WHEAT FOR REQUIEM LITURGY
Kilbee or *Ruhmee*

An old rite of the Orthodox Catholic Church is the requiem liturgy. In this service it is customary to distribute portions of *kilbee* (cooked wheat germ) in memory of the deceased on the fortieth day after a death, as well as on the first anniversary.

The boiled wheat germ symbolizes the resurrection. The Lord said: "Verily, verily, I say unto you, except a corn of wheat fall into the ground and die, it abideth alone; but if it die, it bringeth forth much fruit" (John 12:24). Sugar added to the *kilbee* indicates the sweetness of everlasting life.

Today in America, as well as in parts of Europe and the Middle East, the wheat offering in church by the family of the deceased symbolizes the act of charity.

> 5 pounds whole wheat
> 4 cups chopped walnuts
> 2½ cups granulated sugar
> 4 teaspoons cinnamon
> 3 boxes raisins
> 1 box powdered sugar
> 3 ounces silver dragees
> 1 pound candy-coated almonds

Pour wheat in large kettle and cover with water. Allow to stand overnight. In the morning, drain and cover with fresh water. Cook about 4 hours or until tender. Stir often with wooden spoon to keep from sticking. Drain and spread on a large cloth to absorb excess moisture. Mix with walnuts, sugar, cinnamon, and raisins. Mound slightly on serving trays lined with wax paper and edged with paper doilies. Sprinkle powdered sugar over top and press down with paper to make a smooth compact top. Cut out a large cardboard cross and make an impression with it in sugar. Fill space with the silver dragees: On either side of cross, form initials of the deceased with raisins. Make border with almonds. *Yield: 1 medium and 1 small serving tray.*

FEASTS

Easter. The Feast of Christ's Resurrection, Holy Easter, is the major feast of the Church.

The Twelve Great Feasts. The eight Great Feasts in honor of Christ and the four Great Feasts in honor of His Mother are called the Twelve Great Feasts.

September 8.   The Nativity of the Theotokos.
September 14.   The Elevation of the Holy Cross.
November 21.   The Presentation of the Theotokos.
December 25.   Christmas (the nativity of Christ).
January 6.   Epiphany (the baptism of Christ).
February 2.   The Presentation of the Lord.
March 25.   The Annunciation.
The Sunday before Easter—Palm Sunday.
Forty Days after Easter—The Ascension of the Lord.
Fifty Days after Easter—Pentecost.
August 6.   The Transfiguration.
August 15.   The Falling Asleep of the Theotokos.

MARCH 25 FEAST DAY

March 25 is the feast day of the Annunciation of the Virgin Mary in the Orthodox Catholic Church. Traditionally, sea foods are eaten on this day.

Shrimp cocktail
Hot red mullets
Anchovy fillets
Syrian potato salad
Spinach pies
Thyme-sumac pies
Turkish coffee
Lenten cakes

AUGUST 6 FEAST DAY

The feast day of the Transfiguration of Christ is celebrated on the sixth day of August in the Orthodox Catholic Church. Although this day falls in the fifteen-day Lenten period of August

1–15, because it is a feast day of the Church a concession is made and fish is the accepted meal of the day.

> Tomato juice
> Baked fish—Sesame oil with lemon
> Fried squash
> Fried tomatoes
> Salad
> Syrian bread, bun-type
> Turkish coffee

AUGUST 15 FEAST DAY

August 15 marks the feast of the Assumption of the Virgin Mary in the Orthodox Catholic Church. This feast day is the termination of the fifteen-day Lenten period.

> Fruit cocktail
> Baked chicken—Rice-giblet dressing
> Raw kibby
> Baked eggplant
> Meat pies
> Salad
> Coffee
> Vanilla pudding

BOILED BARLEY   *Iyouk*

Iyouk is served on the feast day of St. Barbara, which falls on December 4. The feast day of St. Barbara commemorates the third-century martyr who died by her father's hand rather than renounce her belief in Christ.

> 1 cup yellow barley
> 1 cup sugar
> 1 cup raisins (soaked ½ hour)
> 1 teaspoon anise seed
> ½ cup chopped walnuts

Boil barley in quart of water on low fire for 30 minutes, adding more water during cooking. Add sugar and stir well. Add raisins and anise seed. Simmer 10 minutes. Garnish with walnuts.

THE FEAST OF EPIPHANY *El-Gitas*

Epiphany, considered one of the oldest and most important festivals of the Christian Church, is celebrated on the twelfth day after Christmas. Families spend the morning at the many cathedrals in Damascus and Beirut. Processions of worshipers can be seen walking to the cathedrals to seek comfort and redemption on this day of Epiphany in commemoration of the baptism of Jesus in the Jordan River. The interiors of the Orthodox Catholic cathedrals show beautiful Byzantine artwork in the icons that surround the Royal Door of the church altar. The priests have long beards and wear long flowing robes. Following church services, the priests visit the homes of their parishioners and bless the corners of all the rooms of the house with holy water. Before they leave, the traditional material feast of *Zalabee* and *Awam* is served.

Frying *Zalabee* (Doughnut Cakes) for Feast of Epiphany.

My mother told me of her activities in Syria the day before Epiphany when she helped her mother prepare *Zalabee* and *Awam.* These doughnut-shaped cakes were fried in olive oil and, when cooled, they were sprinkled with sugar to signify sweet and everlasting life. Although today the method of making these cakes has been simplified, at one time the dough used for the cakes was the result of being "baptized." The ceremony for the baptizing of the dough began with tying the dough in a white cloth. It was then carried to a fountain, immersed in the name of the Holy Trinity, and the baptismal chant repeated. The dough in the white cloth hung in the tree for three days, then was taken to the house. The dough rose without yeast. This new leaven, miraculously raised, provided the yeast for the next year. From this dough, small crosses were made and placed wherever food was stored in the dwelling.

Spooning dough in oil in making *Awam* (Spoon Doughnuts) for Feast of Epiphany.

In America today, following evening Epiphany services in the Orthodox Catholic church, parishioners gather in the church hall to partake of the *Zalabee* and *Awam* prepared by members of the church. During the week of Epiphany the priest visits all the homes of parishioners to bless them with holy water.

DOUGHNUT CAKES *Zalabee*

    4 cups flour
    1 teaspoon salt
    ½ cake yeast
    1 tablespoon oil
    Lukewarm water
    Granulated sugar

Mix flour, salt, yeast, and oil with water, kneading and leaving mixture soft. Set until dough rises, about 1 hour. Cut in strips 2 inches wide and about 7 inches long and fry in skillet of hot oil until golden brown. Upon removing from skillet, sprinkle with granulated sugar. *Yield: 12 cakes.*

SPOON DOUGHNUTS *Awam*

    2 medium potatoes
    2 cups flour
    ½ cake yeast
    Lukewarm water

Peel potatoes, cube, and boil. Remove from water and mash. Add flour, yeast, and water. Knead, leaving mixture soft. Set until dough rises, about 1 hour. Pick up small portions of dough with a spoon and drop in skillet of hot oil until browned. Remove and dip in cold syrup.

SYRUP

    1 cup water
    1 cup sugar
    Juice of 1 lemon
    Drop of orange-blossom water (optional)
Boil all ingredients together and chill. *Yield: 2 dozen.*

SHOPPERS' GUIDE

Ingredients imported from Syria and Lebanon may be purchased at special food markets listed below. The chief importer and exporter is A. Sahadi & Co., Inc., 195–99 Washington St., New York 7, New York.

ALABAMA
Lignos Groceries, 160 Government St., Birmingham
ALASKA
Mama Matha's House of Shish-kebab, 421 Fourth Ave., Anchorage
ARIZONA
Aboud Brothers Market, 1045 N. 24th St., Phoenix
CALIFORNIA
J. M. Armelli Liquor Co., Los Angeles
(Specialize in *arak*)
Cano Import Co., 2771 West Pico Blvd., Los Angeles
Nassraway's Pastry Shop, 5921 Hollywood Blvd., Hollywood
(Imported groceries, nuts, olives, pastries and Syrian bread)
New Santa Clara Market, 799 Haight St., San Francisco
Greek American Grocery, 473 Tenth Ave., Oakland
G. B. Ratto & Co., International Grocers—Importers, 821 Washington St., Oakland 94607. Phone: Te-Z-6503
(European and middle eastern specialties)
Sunnyland Bulghur Co., 1435 Gerhart St., Fresno
COLORADO
Economy Grocery, 1864 Curtis St., Denver 2
CONNECTICUT
Dimyan's Market, 116 Elm St., Danbury
Betar's Market, 703 Broad St., Bridgeport
DISTRICT OF COLUMBIA
Aloupis Co., 916 Ninth St., N.W., Washington 11
FLORIDA
Joseph's Imported Food Co., 621 Fields Ave., Jacksonville
Rahal & Sons, Inc., 1615 S.W. Eighth St., Miami
(Specialize in oriental pastry, food, bread)
T.N.G. Near East Bakery, 878 S.W. Eighth St., Miami

GEORGIA
>   Roxy's Delicatessen, 1011 Peachtree St. N.E., Atlanta

HAWAII
>   Gourmet Bazaar, International Market Place, Honolulu 15

ILLINOIS
>   Columbus Food Market, 5534 W. Harrison St., Chicago 44
>   Washington Dairy Prod. Co., 625 S. Halsted St., Chicago 7

INDIANA
>   Bob Corey's Flaming Pit Bar-b-q Steak House Restaurant, 1719 S. 13th St., Terre Haute
>   Mrs. E. Freije, 2825 Central Ave., Indianapolis
>   Athens Imported Food, 103 N. Alabama St., Indianapolis
>   Mrs. Joseph Sabb, 22 Judith Lane, Terre Haute

IOWA
>   George A. Skaff & Sons, 801 Court St., Sioux City

KENTUCKY
>   A. Thomas Meat Market, 315 E. Jefferson St., Louisville

LOUISIANA
>   Central Grocery Co., 823 Decatur St., New Orleans

MAINE
>   Model Market, 89–95 Middle St., Portland

MARYLAND
>   Panos & Milionis, 204 N. Greene St., Baltimore

MASSACHUSETTS
>   Charles T. Homsey Wholesale Groc., 388 Tremont St., Boston
>   Syrian Grocery Impt. Co., 270 Shawmut Ave., Boston 18

MICHIGAN
>   Abdella Impt. Co., 2461 Russell St., Detroit
>   Mourad Grocery Co., 2410 Market St., Detroit 7
>   Oriental Pastry Shop & Grocery, 411 Monroe Ave., Detroit

MINNESOTA
>   The Pavo Co., Inc., 119 N. Fourth St., Minneapolis

MISSISSIPPI
>   George M. Nassour, 909 Cherry St., Vicksburg

MISSOURI
>   Italo American Impt. Co., 512 Franklin Ave., St. Louis 1

MONTANA
>   Hepperle's Store, Box 117, Plevna

NEBRASKA
>   Olson's Grocery, 5608 Blondo St., Omaha

NEW JERSEY
>   N. Nafash & Sons, 2717 Bergenline Ave., Union City

NEW MEXICO
    Arthur's Fine Liquors, 3407 Central Ave. N.E., Albuquerque
NEW YORK
    Malko Bros. Cassatly Co., Inc., 197 Atlantic Ave., Brooklyn
      (Oriental groceries, pastries, mosaics, and art inlaid work)
    Malko Importing Corp., 184 Atlantic Ave., Brooklyn 1
      (Wholesale dealers in oriental and domestic food products and
      pastries)
    Dilbert's, 9308 Third Ave., Brooklyn
    Sahadi Importing Co., Inc., 187 Atlantic Ave., Brooklyn
    Kassos Brothers, 570 Ninth Ave., New York City
    Dilbert's, 22 W. 34th St., New York City
    Atlas Oriental Pastry Shop, 419 Elm St., Buffalo
    Thomas Christou, 90–28 Parsons Blvd., Jamaica
    International Foods, 142 Front St., Rochester 14
    Kizmet Fancy Grocery, 240 Main St., Hempstead
NORTH CAROLINA
    James Heonis Co., 218 S. Blount St., Raleigh
OHIO
    Ellis Bakery, 577 Grant St., Akron 11
      (Specialize in Syrian bread, *baklawa*, imported groceries)
    Shiekh Grocery Co., 652 Boulevard Rd., Cleveland 15
    Metropolitan Coffee Co., 8½ N. Howard St., Akron 8
OKLAHOMA
    Royal Coffee & Tea Co., 115 S. Robinson St., Oklahoma City
OREGON
    Joe Hanna & Sons, 6418 S.E. Foster Road, Portland 6
PENNSYLVANIA
    Stamoolis Brothers, 202 Penn Ave., Pittsburgh 22
    Sherwood Grocery, 224 S. 60th St., Philadelphia 39
RHODE ISLAND
    Anthony Lozier, 182 Washington St., Central Falls
    Near East Market, 41 Cranston St., Providence
SOUTH CAROLINA
    Mitchell's Grocery, 137 N. Dargan St., Florence
    Caras Greek Prod. Co., 2002 Main St., Columbia
TENNESSEE
    Barzizza Brothers, 176 N. Main St., Memphis 3
TEXAS
    European Importing Co., 910 Preston Ave., Houston
    Purity Importing Co., 4507 Swiss Ave., Dallas
UTAH
    Lingos Grocery, 126 West 2nd South St., Salt Lake City

VIRGINIA

Galanides Inc., 902 Cooke Ave., Norfolk 4

Greek American Importing Co., 518 E. Marshall St., Richmond 19

WASHINGTON

Acropolis Food Market, 1206 Underwood St., N.W.

Angelo Merlino & Sons, 814 Sixth Ave. So., Seattle 4

WEST VIRGINIA

Haddy's Food Market, 1503 Washington, Charleston

WISCONSIN

Topping & Co., 736 N. Second St., Milwaukee 3

GLOSSARY

Qa-moos

Syrians and Lebanese speak the Arabic language. In spelling the Arabic names, I have tried to present phonetically each word in acceptable Arabic.

One of the richest languages in the world, Arabic has full vowels, pronounced as follows: the *a* in the word *bakdownas* is pronounced like the *a* in the word "daughter." Arabic-speaking people differ as to the best spelling of Arabic names in English. *Bakdownas* (parsley) may also be properly spelled *ba'downas.* Just as pronunciation differs from Boston to Birmingham in America, so Arabic dialects change from village to village. A small number of sibilants produce a hissing sound, as in *sittee* ("grandmother"). The vowel *u* is pronounced as in "bus" or *bus-il* (onions).

The *k* in *bakdownas* and *gh* in *ghanum* ("lamb") are pronounced with a guttural sound produced by a contraction of the larynx. The *r* is always rolled.

I hope you will find entertainment in adding these words to your Arabic vocabulary.

Pertaining to Food and Drink

Ad'-dis	*Lentils*
Ah-jeen'	*Dough*
Ah'-sal	*Honey*
Ah-seer il li-moon'	*Lemon juice*
Aj'-wee	*Dates*
A'-rak	*Anise-flavored liqueur*
Bak-down'-as	*Parsley*
Ba-na-doo'-ra	*Tomato*
Ba-tin-jan'	*Eggplant*
Bay'-mee	*Okra*
Bhar hub' wa na'im	*Allspice*

Boo'-za	*Ice Cream*
Bur'-ghol	*Wheat, crushed*
Bus'-il	*Onion*
By-thet il eed'	*Easter eggs*
By-thot'	*Eggs*
Dib'-s	*Molasses*
Fa-tay'-er	*Pies (turnovers)*
Fil'-ful	*Pepper*
Fis'-dok	*Pistachios*
Fool	*Beans, fava (or horse)*
Fo'-tir	*Mushroom*
Gha'-num	*Lamb*
Gri'-bee	*Cookies, butter*
Ha'-bek	*Basil, sweet*
Ha-leeb'	*Milk*
Hind'-bee	*Dandelion*
Ho'-mos	*Chick-peas*
Hub-al-hal'	*Cardamon*
Hub-et il bara'-ky	*Caraway, black*
I'-jee	*Omelet*
In'-ib	*Grapes*
In-jas'	*Pears*
Jaj	*Chicken*
Ji'-zar	*Carrot*
Jo'-ban	*Cheese*
Jun-za-beel'	*Ginger*
Ka"ick	*Anise bread*
Ka-moun'	*Cuminseed*
Ka-ree'-shee	*Cheese*
Kha-roof'	*Sheep*
Kho'-baz	*Bread*
Khŭs	*Lettuce*
Khyar	*Cucumber*
Kir'-fee	*Cinnamon*
Kiz'-ba-ra	*Coriander*
Koo'-sa	*Squash*
Kur-ban'	*Altar bread*
Kuth'-ra	*Vegetables*
La'-ban	*Yogurt*
La'-hum	*Meat*
La-hum ba'-kar	*Beef*
La-hum i'-jil	*Veal*
La-hum khun-zeer'	*Pork*

Lift	*Turnip*
Lowz	*Almonds*
Lū-bee	*Beans, green*
Mah'-leb	*Cherry kernels, black*
Mar-da-koosh'	*Marjoram*
Mar'-qeh	*Sauce*
Ma-war'-id	*Rose water*
Ma-za'-har	*Orange-blossom water*
Mi'-leh	*Salt*
Mul-foof'	*Cabbage*
My	*Water*
Na"na	*Mint*
Nbeeth	*Wine*
Qah'-wah	*Coffee*
Qa-mar-deen'	*Dried apricots*
Qa'-tar	*Syrup*
Qum'-eh	*Wheat*
Ra-main'	*Pomegranate*
Roz	*Rice*
Sa-ba'-negh	*Spinach*
Sa-far'-jel	*Quince*
Sá-la-ta	*Salad*
Sa'-mek	*Fish*
Sa'-min	*Butter*
Sfee'-ha	*Meat Pies*
Sha-hum khun-zeer'	*Bacon*
Sha-mon'-der	*Beets*
Sha-ree'-yee	*Orzo*
Shou'-ra-ba	*Soup*
Shraab	*Fruit juices*
Shy	*Tea*
Si'-kar	*Sugar*
Sim'-sum	*Sesame*
Snoo'-ber	*Pine nuts*
Ta-fah'	*Apples*
Ta-heen'	*Flour*
Teen	*Fig*
Thi'-ra	*Corn*
Thume	*Garlic*
War-ak al gar'	*Bay leaf*
War-ak in'-ib	*Grape leaf*
Yan-soon'	*Anise*
Yukh'-nee	*Stew*

Zah'-ra	*Cauliflower*
Zah'-ter	*Thyme*
Zbeeb	*Raisins*
Zite	*Oil*
Zi-toon'	*Olives*

Relating to Religion

Al'-lah	*God*
Ba-khoor'	*Incense*
Eed il fa'-seh or	
Eed il Ka-beer'	*Easter*
Eed-il Mee-lad'	*Christmas*
El Gi-tas'	*Epiphany*
Il Ab'	*The Father*
Il Ibn'	*The Son*
Il Rooh il Ko'-dos	*The Holy Ghost*
Il Tha-looth'	*The Trinity*
Il Ko-tab il Moo-kad'-as	*The Holy Scriptures*
Il Ma-za-meer'	*The Psalms*
Il Ra-say'-il	*The Epistles*
Il sa-boo il a-lam'	*Passion week*
Il Sa-lot il Rub-anee'-yet	*Lord's Prayer*
Il Syam'	*Lent*
Il Too-rot'	*The Bible*
Il Un-jeel'	*The Gospel*
Ka-dees'	*Saint*
Kas	*Chalice*
Knee'-set	*Church*
Mab'-kha-rut	*Censer*
Ma-lake'	*Angel*
Mariam il Ath'-ra	*The Virgin Mary*
Moo-kha'-lis	*Saviour*
Mus'-be-hut	*Rosary*
Na'-bee	*Prophet*
Ra-sool'	*Apostle*
Sa-leeb'	*Cross*
Tir-tee'-let	*Hymn*
Ya-soo' il Ma-seeh'	*Jesus Christ*

RECIPE INDEX

ARABIC RECIPE INDEX

MEDITERRANEAN

SEA

CYPRUS

Lands of the—
Eastern Mediterranean

EGYPT

• Cairo

NILE R.